THE YEAR IN
BLOOM

GARDENING for all SEASONS
In the PACIFIC NORTHWEST

▪ ANN LOVEJOY ▪

Sasquatch Books

ISBN 0-912365-11-0
Library of Congress Catalog Card Number 87-0604 780

Design by Elizabeth Watson
Illustrations by Patrick O. Chapin

Typeset in Cheltenham
by Weekly Typography & Graphic Design, Seattle, Washington

Sasquatch Books
1008 Western Avenue
Seattle, Washington 98104
(206) 467-4300

Other gardening titles from Sasquatch Books:
  Growing Vegetables West of the Cascades
  Winter Gardening in the Maritime Northwest
  Gardening Under Cover
  Three Years in Bloom
  The Border in Bloom
  Winter Ornamentals
  North Coast Roses
  Water-wise Vegetables
  Growing Herbs

 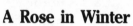

JULY 125

AUGUST   147

SEPTEMBER 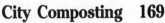 167

OCTOBER 189

INTRODUCTION

My association with Ann Lovejoy began on a sunny June day in 1985. It's my habit, weather permitting, to walk from my downtown office home to Madison Park. I was puffing my way up Capitol Hill. Christopher Lloyd (or some Brit) had been in town that week, raised an eyebrow, hunched up his shoulders, and muttered, "We all know what the English garden is, but just what *is* the American garden?" I was thinking about that when I looked to my left and saw an obstreperous assortment of perennials (some rare, some common as dandelions) spilling down a bank to the sidewalk. Plunked in the middle of the bed was a sign: "Please leave the flowers for all of us to enjoy!" The house above the garden was modest, but sturdy and orderly. Vines scrambled up the porch pillars, and chipped terra-cotta pots erupted in bloom. There it was, a perfect example of the American garden: youthful, all embracing, naive, and eager. It was a treat to behold and, on that hot south-facing bank, a bit of a miracle.

I went to the door and knocked, just to tell the gardener how wonderful I thought the garden was. Toddlers scampered to the front door, a voice from somewhere in the middle of the house said, "Tell the man to come in," then hollered out to me, "I'll be there in a minute." That was Ann.

Before I left we'd planned lunch together and I'd promised to give her a *Gardenia jasminoides* 'August Beauty'. I still haven't forked over the gardenia, but we did lunch. I learned as much about gardening in that hour and a half as I've learned in *any* hour and a half. I scribbled notes, Ann chatted on. Then she said, "I really want to write about gardening," her eyes as bright as a bed of zinnias. And I said, "Write something, anything, and send it to *The Weekly*. If it's as good as you talk, it will get published." She wrote it and it got published and for this Ann credits me with getting her going in her career. I feel like the witless Jack. I came upon this bean, planted it, and up shoots an incredible stalk.

Well the vine grew: one column after another to make me, and the lucky readers of Greater Puget Sound, laugh, identify, try harder, be daring, race out into the garden and do it! Because Ann said to, in the dead of winter we mixed up a hole of muck for roses, then went inside to pollinate cut alstroemeria with a Q-tip, and wait for seeds to form. Her ideas shoot out like big glossy leaves and clusters of scarlet blossoms. The vine keeps growing. You're here with yet another example of its vigor in your hands. And high up as I look and hard as I squint, I see no end in sight. But I do have one strong hunch about it—that up there, at the top, there's going to be a giant.

Steven R. Lorton
January 1987

FROM THE AUTHOR

Wherever you live, however grand or small your plot, gardening can be wonderful fun. No matter how much you know, there are always new plants to learn about, to try, to enjoy; the plant kingdom is endlessly fascinating. West of the Cascades, the Pacific Northwest provides one of the most benign and encouraging climates on earth for gardeners; plants from all over the temperate world flourish here as in few other spots. Only England's celebrated climate can match or rival our own. Nowhere is there a better place to experiment with and sample the incredible variety of plants available to modern gardeners than right here in our own back yards.

This being the case, it seems odd that so few of our yards could reasonably be called showcases for such possible floral or herbaceous wealth. Most of them seem rather to be showcases for the most ordinary of plants: privet or box, conifers of various sorts, a rose or two, perhaps a sagging old hydrangea, and, of course, a lilac. Now, all these plants are perfectly nice plants, and there is no need to uproot them simply because the combination is repeated endlessly up and down the street. What could happen, though, if we varied the routine? Let's try a climbing rose here, a trailing vine there, a splash of silver foliage in this dark corner, the glow of brilliant red and purple leaves and fruit back there. . . . Even tiny yards can be living, breathing gardens, full of change, ebbing and flowing with the season, yet always full of interest and life.

My own Seattle garden is on a plot thirty-five feet wide and sixty feet deep. Not a bad size, you will say, and indeed it could be a fine garden, if there weren't also a house, a large sandbox, and a full-sized swing set sharing the same space. We all have design problems to cope with. Even so, there is something in bloom in our garden every day of the year, if only a primrose or a lowly periwinkle. From February through November, there is a good deal in bloom, and even as this book was going to press (in January), we gathered over a dozen kinds of flowers from our yard. With a bigger site, so much more is possible.

"Isn't it a lot of trouble to garden like that?" is a question I am often asked. If it were, I wouldn't do it. Much as I love my garden, I can't afford to spend much time on yard work. One of the purposes of this book is to introduce to the busy gardener's notice a number of choice plants that require very little fussing, yet perform with style for long periods of time. They are not exactly low-maintenance plants; any living thing in an artificial setting requires some sort of help. These plants respond well to the simple care routines outlined in the text, and most need attention only once or twice a year. All, however, deserve more than that; if your garden plants aren't getting looked at, admired, even savored, root them out and replace them, choosing plants you love, plants that you will want to visit often. I dislike the phrase "low maintenance" because it sounds so final; a garden that is being "maintained" is static. A living garden is always in flux, changing to reflect the gardener's taste and interests. New plants are tried, old ones pruned or divided, moved to new spots or given away, according to performance. You, the gardener, are the creative genius of the place, and the garden, the landscape, on however modest a scale, is a unique expression of your relationship to your plants, to your home, to your neighborhood.

To most gardeners, the work of tending one's plants is pleasurable in itself. The smallness of many urban gardens allows us the luxury of hand weeding. As you work in companionable closeness with your plants, you can evaluate their needs quickly. An anonymous hoe can't select promising seedlings for the nursery bed, or transplant thick clumps of self-sown alyssum and forget-me-nots into well-spaced sweeps or even edgings. As you weed, you absorb, almost subliminally, invaluable information about your plants, what they like and need, how to make them thrive. Along the way, you can give overwhelmed plants more space, and control takeover bids from the overly vigorous.

Control is often a big issue with American gardeners, giving rise to the common criticism that our plantings look regimented. English visitors often say that plants "don't look comfortable" in our scrupulously tidy, repetitious gardens. The better we know our plants—their habits of growth, eventual sizes, propensities to sprawl or spread—the better we can place them where they can be "comfortable," letting them grow as they like without the need for constant pruning and restraint. Low, mounded edging plants should spill over the border edge onto the grass; grass is not holy, and the plant will look far prettier than when shorn back. In a well-

iv

grown cottage garden, not one bit of earth will show between the plants. In some of our gardens, it almost looks as if clean, swept dirt and crew-cut grass are dearer to the caretaker's heart than the poor plants, strictly lined out in ribbons and rows. I don't think such gardeners really hate plants, but I do think that as we take the time to really look at our plants, we quickly discover more felicitous ways to place them, to give them complementary companions, and to enjoy them for what they are. The gardener's relationship with his plants ought not to be combative, yet control, with the lightest of hands, is part of the art of gardening. The greatest control comes from the most intimate knowledge; when you know your plants, you don't ask them to do what they can't, and you place them where they can readily do what they should do to best advantage. Result: a burgeoning, living garden, and a delighted and enthusiastic gardener.

Among the pages of this book you will find a number of thumbnail sketches, portraits of plants which can play strong roles in Northwest gardens with only minimal support from the gardener. In most cases, appropriate and attractive partners or neighbors are suggested, and the kind of care required is indicated. Gardening is essentially a soft science, and is not best performed "by the book." You may find recommendations here that contradict those in your standard reference books. This is not unusual; many excellent and reputable garden writers contradict each other on any number of points, technical and otherwise. All of the information found here is based on local experience, but that does not mean that you have to agree with it. If your experience leads you to prune, or feed, or plant, at times or in ways that I don't, stick with what works for you. On the other hand, if standard advice has failed you in the past, some of these suggestions may bring you success.

There is very little mention of pesticides in these pages; the urban environment is already so battered, it does not seem like a good idea to add poison to the burden. We don't use them in any case, having so few pests to contend with that it would hardly be worth the trouble. As our soil improves, plant pests are correspondingly reduced; healthy plants are less prone to insect attack or diseases. Over the years, our stolid Seattle clay has turned into rich and crumbling loam, thanks to annual "feeding" and mulching. When the soil is in good heart, properly placed plants grow well, needing little or no fertilizers.

Coastal Northwest autumns are mild and protracted, giving gardeners

V

the seldom-exercised opportunity to indulge in fall pyrotechnics. There are hundreds of plants—annuals, perennials, shrubs, and trees—that we can add to our gardens for autumn and winter blossoms, bright fruit, or splendid foliage effects. Many of these plants are lovely the whole year through, some almost unchanging, others altering with each season. In England, fall, and even early winter, is considered prime work time in the garden. Almost any plant that performs in spring or summer is best planted, divided, or moved in the fall. Many trees and shrubs can be planted then, and any number of seeds can be sown from September on. Hardy fall-sown annuals will germinate early and build into blooming plants while their spring-sown cousins are straggling along, weeks behind them. We can plant bulbs here till the ground freezes over—if it ever does—resuming our efforts as soon as a thaw opens things up again.

Some readers have written to say that nurseries don't carry much of a selection in the fall; this is a two-way street. Nursery people won't stock extra plants, which need a fair amount of winter care when in pots, unless we gardeners prove that we will buy them. As demand picks up, the supply is never far behind. At this point, the only people I see in local nurseries after Labor Day are professional gardeners and landscapers. They know the benefits of fall planting, and are taking advantage of them for their own customers. Even if you aren't ready to plant, it is great fun to cruise nurseries in fall, on the lookout for plants that color especially nicely or have an attractive shape even when bare. Few people seem to know that many azaleas have splendid autumn tints; why not get two or three seasons of interest and color from one plant?

It isn't necessary to make radical, sweeping reforms in your yard right away. Experiment; plant lilies between those old shrubs, and see how the tall spires of nodding trumpets glow when backlit by streaming summer sunshine. Train a clematis or two to scramble into a tree, especially if you have one of those spring-bloomers that look so dull except during those brief, transforming weeks of blossom. A tumble of starry flowers could brighten the yard for months without harm to the tree. Spangle that boundary hedge with vines that have scented flowers, or dangling lantern-blossoms. Weave in a few strands of gold-splashed ivy to add luster in winter. Visit some unfamiliar nurseries, try a few unfamiliar plants. Staff people at the better nurseries will be pleased to help you choose plants that will perform well in your yard.

Most gardens, by accident or by design, have their peak display in spring and early summer. With very little trouble, the average range of plants is easily extended to include some that reliably produce a second crop of flowers in late summer or autumn, others that bloom steadily through a mild winter, still more that begin their season as commoner plants are closing up shop. Conduct a bit of research, both in local nurseries, and through the perusal of mail-order nursery catalogs. An hour or two spent in this way brings you to a delightful conclusion: in much of the Northwest, it really is possible to have something, whether shrub, perennial, or tree, at its best on any day of the year. As you experiment to find the right plants and the happiest combinations for your particular conditions, I hope you will find, as I do, that the work involved is renewing rather than tiring, thrilling rather than tedious.

All gardeners have a perfect garden of the inner eye. While we may know in our hearts that such visions are rarely achievable, the pursuit of our vision provides satisfactions that the strictly pragmatic can't imagine. To make a garden, on any scale at all, is to create an environment, a world of one's own. To be in the garden, absorbed in such creative efforts, is to be deeply content. The garden may not ever be finished, and will certainly never be perfect. That is as it should be; the point is not mastery, but cooperation. When gardeners give plants their intelligent attention, the results are bound to be wonderful. Could there be any better reward for our thought, our planning, our experiments, and our labors, than an entire year in bloom?

Ann Lovejoy
Seattle, February 1987

Note: The bold plant names found in the margins throughout the book are a scanning aid and not intended as a definitive index of all plant names. These plant references appear as they do in the text, and may include a plant's latin name, its common family name, and/or a hybrid name (often shown with single quotes— i.e., 'Hollandia'). Common family names such as "Tulip" or "Daffodil" are listed only once on each page, following its first latin reference. All subsequent plant listings fall under this common family name until a new family is listed. In chapters focusing on a single plant family (for example, roses), no common family is mentioned in the margins.

JANUARY

A Rose in Winter

Mud, muck, and careful planning make for finer roses

Cold Weather Characters

Shrubs with style add zest to the winter garden

Winter Jasmine

Scentless but bright as sunshine, winter jasmine
is a winner

Territorial Seed Company

This Northwest catalog could change
your eating habits for life

A ROSE IN WINTER
Mud, muck, and careful planning
make for finer roses

One of the things I like best about roses is the excuse they give me to play in the mud. A fine day during a January thaw is the best of all possible times to go out and fork up another patch of the iris bed, root out all (hah!) the witch grass, and dig a nice big hole. Make it at least two feet deep, and about the same around or more if you're really tired of the iris. When your hole is worth looking at, stand back, appreciate your good work, then start mixing in the rose vitamins.

Amendments are the stuff dreamy roses are made of. Manure from chicken, cow, or goat; straw bedding from farm or stable; compost, sawdust, soy meal or bone meal, kelp meal, and lots of peat moss all squished together make a nice, mushy mess. Fork it around well, adding judicious helpings of the lowly dirt you displaced, till all is one. You end up with a mounded heap which will settle as it melds, so don't be concerned if it looks too big. At planting time, any extra earth can be strewn about the border or tipped onto the compost heap. This mixture may well be redolent of its rude origins; think of it as essence of future roses. Rose plants are what is known as gross feeders, thriving on an ample diet of rich and wonderful muck.

There are as many theories about rose culture as about raising children, and most of them have their points. The literature bristles with studies proving one or another of these points and flatly contradicting the others, much like those ubiquitous studies on the effects of vitamin C, coffee, or cholesterol. I do not say that my technique is the best or only way to grow roses, but I will say that it has yielded excellent and consistent results over many years, and for a wide range of conditions. Roses do not need handling with kid gloves, but they do respond to careful soil preparation with vigorous

1

bloom, good health, and disease resistance. Isn't that what it's all about?

By April, when it's time to plant, our mixture will be mellowed and ready for our roses. The usual approach, digging the hole(s) after the plant(s) arrive, is far less satisfactory, as the manure may be too fresh, the surrounding plants will be advanced in their new growth, and quarters will be far more cramped. No, it's better to do it now, especially since there is little else that needs doing in the garden just now except coping with the ever-present weeds.

When cold rain chases you out of the muddy garden, take an hour to curl up with a specialty catalog or two and dream about summer. Mull over just what you hope for from your roses. It's a great mistake to zip out to a garden center and pick out something with a pretty picture on the tag, especially when the something is as long-lived as a rosebush. Consider many attributes: fragrance, color, hardiness, resistance to pests and to disease. Do you want a bush or a shrub, a climber or a miniature, or perhaps a standard, formed like a little tree? Do you prefer delicate sprays of tiny roses or great fat ones like cabbages? Long, elegantly tapered buds or plump, rounded ones, dainty silk-petaled single flowers or opulent, ruffled doubles? Are we shooting for late spring bloom, or summer, or fall? Do you prefer one enormous burst of blossom, or a steady but lesser display over many months?

A really good catalog will assist the decision-making process with solid advice and practical information, far more helpful than those with luscious but misleading pictures accompanied by gushing blurbs insisting that each pictured rose is the best ever. One of the most useful catalogs for Northwest gardeners is *Roses of Yesterday & Today*, from the California nursery (see Appendix A for address) dedicated to the preservation of old, rare, and unusual roses. This catalog lists both species and hybrids, some of great antiquity, others brand-new. The selection varies, but is always chosen for horticultural or garden-variety excellence, robust health and, of course, beauty. Most of these roses are exceedingly fragrant, illustrating vividly a founding principle of this nursery: roses ought to smell as wonderful as they look.

A number of climbing and shrub roses long lost to cultivation have been rescued by past owners of RY&T, and the present owner, Patricia Wiley, continues that tradition. These old war-horses have the distinct advantage of rude health, a delightful surprise for those used to the simpering, sickly ways of modern roses. Each year's catalog discusses a couple of hundred plants in terms which give even the most non–rose-minded gardeners the urge to bulldoze the house to make yard space for all of them—just one of each.

Consider the claims of 'Climbing Shot Silk', a strong and stately plant bearing large blossoms of raspberry pink shot with gold, the colors blending over distance to a sumptuous shade of coral. Fulsomely fragrant, the flowers open from chubby, pointed buds to wide blossoms of outstanding form and distinction. The heavy canes carry fewer thorns than many of its relatives, and its long, strong stems make for excellent cut flowers. It also has an exuberant habit of blooming abundantly and repeatedly throughout the summer. Other than that, it's nothing special. Trained around a window, this plant will definitely improve a not-so-great view.

'Old Blush' is a small Chinese shrub rose, airily constructed and about four feet in diameter when mature. The clustered blossoms are a clear, robust pink without strident overtones. Each flower is loosely doubled, each tight bud as finely chiseled as an enameled bit of jewelry. They have a fresh, light scent, smelling exactly as a pink rose should. This is the traditional "monthly rose", so called for its habit of producing a bloom or two in every month of the year (as well as all summer). In England (and New England), 'Old Blush' was often the dooryard rose for both manor and farm. Unappreciative of the fat life in the border, it does best in ordinary garden soil.

'Gruss an Aachen' is delicious, perfectly formed, and of the palest apricot or perhaps peach (Mrs. Wiley says shell pink, but in my yard it's a stronger color). In habit,

'Climbing Shot Silk'

'Old Blush'

'Gruss an Aachen'

3

it is an ideal urban garden rose, growing only about three feet tall, yet very sturdy and healthy. An eager bloomer, it repeats joyfully throughout the season. Long, slender buds open into potently scented double blossoms, flat as a plate. These make good cut flowers, delightful when crammed into tight little Victorian nosegays. The foliage is especially healthy looking; it simply laughs at both black spot and powdery mildew, twin banes of rosarians.

This kind of disease resistance is especially important to me since I don't spray any of my roses. It's far too time consuming and difficult, and I prefer not to use or handle poisons in any case. 'Our neighborhood is overrun with small children and pets, neither of which are improved by contact with deadly toxins. It's a shame that so many of us eschew roses, believing the myths of their tyrannical and endless needs. In fact, roses in mixed company are generally freer of disease than those sequestered in roseries; en masse, they are compellingly attractive to their special pests. The traditional rose garden was designed for convenience of culture, not for beauty (few roses make attractive plants). Since few modern gardens have room for separate rose gardens, it's fortunate that roses can be perfectly satisfactory border or shrubbery ingredients.

Much of the mystery about roses is nonsense, but a few things do matter. Planting where roses get plenty of light and free air circulation will reduce or eliminate molds and fungal problems, even in the Pacific Northwest. Powdery mildew is most common on plants with dry roots; watch for this where roses are planted by walls, and combat it with extra water. Our careful soil preparation well in advance of planting time will pay off for years in plant health. In the fall, a deep and generous mulch of muck (manure, compost, and peat) will give these heavy feeders something to chew on over the winter, when root growth is the order of the day. In spring, an extra handful of bone meal with another serving of compost and manure will get the blossom season off to a good start. Manure tea (a dilute solution

'Reine des Violettes'

'White Pet'

'Just Joey'

'Kathleen Mills'

of manure and water) makes a noticeable difference in a hot spell; roses will perk right up and bloom will improve markedly. To prepare this rather high tea for your roses, use a good scoop of manure, at least one cup per gallon of water. Put the manure into a bucket, add the water and let the mixture steep for a few hours (overnight is fine). Give a generous serving to any bloom that looks droopy; all will appreciate this kind attention visibly.

These hardy roses are the ones to plant if you haven't any roses yet, or even if you have; many yards have a hoary bush or two which take up a lot of space for a negligible return. If you've tried mulching and heavy, restorative pruning without results, get out the garden fork, root the things out and start over. Don't make the mistake of planting your new roses where others have grown, however, as the soil will not support another rose in that place (due to the mysterious "rose sickness"). Just shuffle things around a bit, and replace the dud with something spectacular; perhaps the violet-colored 'Reine des Violettes', the bluest rose around. 'White Pet', with sprays of diminutive roses on low, graceful plants of the sturdiest good health. 'Just Joey', all the rage in England, its flowers the irresistible creamy color of tangerine sherbet and hauntingly fragrant. 'Kathleen Mills', a silvery pink single that looks as fragile as glass, its luminous, lightly ruffled petals centered with exquisite garnet red stamens tipped in gold. . . .

Daphne odora

Raphiolepis umbellata
R. ovata

R. indica
Indian hawthorn

COLD WEATHER CHARACTERS
Shrubs with style add zest
to the winter garden

A rare fall of snow lies on the ground and the early morning garden is hushed and still. This is the time to go exploring, when cat and bird trails are the only markings on the fresh white carpet. Some poor frozen plants look as miserable as cats in the snow; the gold-edged *Daphne odora* is blackened and burnt where shoots project beyond the snowy blanket, but all below is fresh and lively green, the flower buds still plump. Creamy as ivory, flushed with rose, they are ready to open as soon as the weather relents. The rhododendrons are curling their leaves with distaste for the chilly air, refusing to take on the white plant's burden and shrugging it off as fast as they can.

Certain plants are splendidly ornamental; the raphiolepis bends with Japanese grace under its load, the rounded leaves drooping elegantly, each topped with a puff of snow. This one is *Raphiolepis umbellata* (also sold as *R. ovata*), its leaves oval as teardrops, poised to splash on the emerging daffodils below. The leaves are a deep and lustrous green with a lighter central rib, arranged in pairs and punctuated here and there with open clusters of round berries. Bitter blue-black, hard and dull, when caught by a stray gleam of sun they shimmer with reflected light.

There are a number of named varieties of this attractive small shrub, seen more often in California, where it is quite popular, than in the Northwest. Most of the hybrids are of *R. indica*, differing chiefly in the size and color of the small flowers which bloom variously from fall through earliest spring in the Northwest. The indicas (Indian hawthorns) are considered a little tender for this area, and indeed the past few years have been on the harsh side, but in a sheltered spot they have survived as far north as Bellingham and the B.C. border. All raphiolepis are evergreen, leaves long and tapered (as

6

Raphiolepis umbellata

Prunus lusitanicus
Portuguese laurel

Clematis montana

Sarcococca humilis
Sweet box

in the indicas) or oval, all leathery as a handbag, close grained and with a good substance. These shrubs have an open, branching habit and are perhaps four or five feet tall at maturity, though capable of greater heights when well pleased. In full sun, the branching is dense and compact, while in semishade it will be looser and less structured, requiring pruning to keep it neat.

R. umbellata begins to open its tight fuzzy buds in February or March. Up they spring in little spurts, the small, starry blossoms the same satiny flesh pink as ballet shoes. They have a simple fragrance, much like that of the ordinary hawthorn, very pleasant in late winter. Mine was planted in its youth very close to a sapling Portuguese laurel (*Prunus lusitanicus*). The combination is architecturally pleasing, the raphiolepis rounded and smooth as a stone at the laurel's feet, the multiple trunks and rippled, light-catching leaves of the laurel leading the eye upward. Later in spring, the last flowers of the raphiolepis mingle with those of the vigorous *Clematis montana*, followed by long and fragrant spikes of laurel blossoms. With all this contrast of leaf and form, this abundance of flowers, buds, and berries, the evergreen pair maintain a strong and handsome partnership throughout the year. Placing very young plants like this, in close proximity with a partner, allows them to grow together in interesting entwining ways without impairing the growth of either. They may never achieve their full size, but in a small garden this is not a drawback.

The frosty air carries a haunting fragrance, honey with hints of vanilla and cardamom. Nature's version of a Swedish bakery comes from the sweet box (*Sarcococca humilis*), an evergreen shrublet of surpassing elegance. Though small, it is so precisely formed, each neat leaf set with such distinction, that the plant as a whole has real presence in the garden. The white flowers are insignificant; tiny knobbed stubs surrounded with a greenish bract. If they didn't give off this disproportionately potent fragrance, they would hardly be noticed. A branch or two brought into the house will scent the kitchen and make people think that you are

7

Sarcococca hookerana humilis

S. humilis

one hell of a fine cook.

There seems to be a fair amount of confusion in the classification of sarcococcas since while there are two or three distinct types, within each type there are several species. It is not uncommon to be sold the same thing under two or three different names or to find different plants sharing a common, often incorrect, name. Since all are lovely plants with numerous graces it would matter little except that only one sort, *S. hookerana humilis*, is a subshrub, while the others range from three or four up to as much as six feet in height. In gardens where space is at a premium, that ranks as a large plant. It is certainly possible to incorporate such a finely constructed mid-sized shrub even into quite small gardens, but much heartache and bewilderment are avoided when the ultimate size is a known factor at planting time.

The one we want is usually labeled *S. humilis*. It has tapered, sharply tipped leaves arranged alternately along the twiggy branches. Burnished to a high gloss, the leaves are of a particularly rich green which looks buoyantly healthy in winter. The tiny flowers open from late December through February and lure reluctant gardeners out to soak their feet in the dripping shrubbery, blessing the mildness of the Northwest winter which allows such treats, even as they curse the endless rain. In the fall, the lustrous leaves are enlivened by clustered berries which ripen from green through red into purple and black, an attractive feature for several months. This sarcococca rarely exceeds two feet in height, yet in time forms glossy, spreading mats, an unusual ground cover which always looks well groomed and presentable with very little help from the gardener.

WINTER JASMINE

Scentless but bright as sunshine, winter jasmine is a winner

Jasminum nudiflorum
Winter jasmine

'Buttercup' ivy

Gloriously naked and not shivering a bit, winter jasmine (*Jasminum nudiflorum*) is spangled with brilliant yellow flowers off and on throughout our mild winters. The leafless branches are of a glossy, rich green that sings of spring in the quiescent winter garden. Fat with red-flushed buds, the arching wands make a wonderful tracery of color against the pale house walls. Each stem carries many flowers in succession; about an inch long, they flare from short necks into five-lobed stars. Unlike their summer cousins, they don't have that ravishing family perfume, making do with a mild, wild scent that is elusive and far from spectacular. Scent or no, for sheer cheerfulness winter jasmine can't be beat.

Once commonly planted, it is still to be found in older gardens and apartment courtyards all over town. Look around and you may find some; at first glance, it looks a bit like forsythia, but its season begins far sooner. As early as October, the chubby buds begin to open, and they continue opening in happy bursts through March. Frost will slow them down, but each period of clement weather brings a new flush of flowers, making its own sunshine. We should take a lesson from those gardeners of the past and get some winter brightness of our own.

Few gardens wouldn't have a place for this attractive shrub. Depending on your treatment, at maturity this jasmine will make a small bush perhaps four feet in height and girth. Trained against a wall (fastened with hooks and twine every few feet) it can achieve far greater spread. Not a true climber, it enjoys the company and support of other plants and can be woven through an ampelopsis or a climbing hydrangea to good effect. Twined through a gold-splashed variegated ivy like 'Buttercup', it is very pleasing indeed. Easily kept

9

Senecio greyi

to whatever size you like by pruning, this shrub is not troubled at all if such pruning is done during blossom time. Sunlight seems to come in with the cuttings, so forthrightly bright are they. Arranged with restraint, the distinctive form is properly appreciated. Since the heaviest bloom is on first-year wood, you can cut to your heart's content. Native to China, this sturdy plant likes to rough it, wanting only an occasional summer watering and an annual mulch of compost and manure to give of its best. Commercial shrub fertilizer is acceptable as well, at something less than full strength.

Winter jasmine takes very well to container culture, even thriving in large window boxes. It is not at all fussy as to aspect, making it a great choice for brightening up a north wall. It tolerates clay or sand, lime or acid soil, sun or shade, doing well in almost any position. Summer watering in dry years will repay you with a good flower crop, though established plants are quite drought-tolerant. If you can give them some water for their first year or two, these shrubs make a wonderful slope or hillside planting. The spreading roots limit erosion and with their willing habit of rooting the tip of any branch that touches the ground, they colonize very satisfactorily. Planted generously among mat-forming junipers and the silvery elegance of the evergrey shrub, *Senecio greyi*, these jasmines can transform such a problem area into a showpiece all year round.

Left unpruned, winter jasmine is an open, lax shrub, delightful when cascading over a rock, pouring down a slope, or tumbling over the edge of a large container. For a compact, bushier shrublet, prune hard after the flowers are finished (midspring) and pinch out the tip of each new stem at two or three feet. This promotes branch production and gives satisfying fullness, so you can cut flowers generously for the house without appreciably depleting the show. A ring of stout stakes and twine, discreetly introduced, can give definition to a shapeless bush, and if you use green garden twine, it will hardly be noticeable even in winter. In summer, the trifoliate leaves (in threesomes) will cover your handi-

Crocus ancyrensis
Golden bunch crocus

C. susianus
Cloth of gold crocus

work, but it doesn't rate a close examination at that season in any case. Wall-trained specimens need trimming to a general outline but if you want coverage, you can't just whack the thing back to the ground each year. Keep a framework of branches and simply cut off all the side shoots.

Several regional nurseries carry these charming shrubs in pots, and they are always available at Seattle's Arboretum plant sales in May. If you know anyone who grows this jasmine, ask if you can try to root a new plant for yourself. Take a branch long enough to reach the ground easily and gently bend it down. It helps to rough up the dirt in that immediate area a bit, making it easier for the new roots to get in there. Force the tip to stay put by pushing a half-hoop of wire into the ground (the bottom of a clothes hanger, bent, works fine) to pin the shoot in place. Most of them will root within a few weeks, but wait until new growth is obvious before cutting the little plant from the mother bush. Check around older plants for volunteers; these can be gently detached and potted up or put right into the ground where you want them to grow.

Tuck corms of golden bunch, the early bunch-flowering crocus (*C. ancyrensis*), and the cloth of gold crocus (*C. susianus*) under the skirts of your jasmine for a golden, starry carpet in earliest spring. These vigorous bulbs will spread into lakes of color, mirroring the jasmine's golden blooms. Winter jasmine is an easy-going shrub, especially rewarding for those unsure of their horticultural skills. The least bit of attention repays more than it deserves and even new plants will bloom generously in their first season, bringing sunny warmth to the dullest months of the year.

TERRITORIAL SEED COMPANY
This Northwest catalog could change your eating habits for life

The climate of the maritime Pacific Northwest is best described as quixotic, but then so are the gardeners. Thousands of plants from all over the world will grow, even thrive, here, yet one of the most frequently attempted is among the least likely to succeed. I refer here to the supreme tomato, planted across America in unmatched quantities. In the coastal Northwest, tomatoes are the Waterloo of many an otherwise excellent gardener. The tepid and uncertain sunshine, mercurial temperatures, and first endless then abruptly non-existent rain all work together to create a climate with many merits, yet one distinctly non-optimal for the culture of tomatoes.

That is why the catalog from Oregon's Territorial Seed Company (see Appendix B) is received with glad cries all over the maritime Northwest. It is a perfectly fascinating booklet in its own right, full of cultural tips, recipes for balanced organic fertilizer and/or soup, and a good deal of accurate and specific advice for our area. This emphasis on local conditions is what really makes it outstanding. The workers at this research station-cum-seed company are dedicated to maintaining a wide and area-appropriate selection of vegetables. In an age when most seed companies are owned by petrochemical firms that constantly whittle down their offerings in the interest of streamlining production, packaging, and distribution, such a goal is admirable indeed. The owner, Steve Solomon, and his family eat from their garden every day of the year. You may not even wish to do that, but wouldn't you like to grow tomatoes that actually ripen and taste great as well, to succeed with sweet peppers, hot peppers, even eggplants? Every variety of every vegetable offered from this remarkable firm has been extensively tested and even specifically developed to do well in this area. In fact, they won't even ship seed east of the mountains.

Here, as nowhere else, you will find about twenty varieties of tomatoes which will yield a satisfying harvest in your backyard, not just in Ohio or in catalog-picture land. Several kinds have been bred at OSU, and what works in the Willamette Valley generally works in Western Washington as well. If, however, a variety is unsatisfactory in Seattle, the catalog will mention that and probably explain why. If 'Big Boy' has let you down, try 'Oregon Eleven', small but dripping with tasty juice and beginning to ripen by the end of June (it's true, folks). A new variety we tried last year, 'Oregon Spring' had larger fruit with a fresh, sprightly flavor much appreciated by our informal taste-tester panel. A long-time family favorite, 'Sweet 100' was finally toppled from its pillar by a little runt called 'Sweetie'; earlier, even sweeter, and just as perfect for salads and skewers. One of the weirdest tomatoes going is Burpee's 'Long Keeper', a kind we tried and got to like very well when it was in the testing stage. The skin is pale red and looks somewhat anemic though it tastes fine. This variety has the most bizarre keeping quality of any tomato anywhere. You can pick the fruits half-ripe at first frost and bring them indoors where they actually continue to ripen with almost undiminished flavor for several months. Even after many long weeks on the shelf, it beats anything the supermarket has to offer all hollow. Territorial carries all of these and more.

The first time we ordered from these folks the catalog was pretty small and on the informal side, chatty appraisals appearing beside the descriptions of each variety. We were so taken by the account of a broccoli called 'Waltham 29' that we ordered several packets and gave some to our friends. That year, we all enjoyed a tremendous and ongoing harvest, and at our house, we were still eating broccoli-ettes, the plentiful side shoots, the following March. The plants are not as uniform in size and shape as the fancier hybrids, but they are flavorful, crisp, and not stringy. To encourage the production of side shoots, you harvest the main head when it

'Oregon Eleven'
Tomato

'Oregon Spring'

'Sweetie'

'Long Keeper'

'Waltham 29'
Broccoli

13

'Joi Choi'
Green

'Tokyo Beau'

'Merveille des quatre
saisons'
Lettuce

looks pretty good, cutting rather high on the stem and leaving the lower, undeveloped leaves and shoots intact. As they mature and are cut, more are produced continually. Six plants gave enough for several people to eat broccoli frequently for months on end.

Territorial has a lovely selection of salad makings. There are better than a dozen sorts of mustard and mixed greens, many of which have an enchanting delicacy of texture and taste unmatched by standard grocery fare. 'Joi Choi' is an outstanding example, as is 'Tokyo Beau'. Among the lettuces, a packet called 'Super Gourmet Salad Bowl' contains six kinds of looseleafs, each easily distinguishable even as seedlings; a rare example of a usable, effective, and intelligent mixture of seeds. Anyone with any gourmet pretensions whatsoever is probably already growing 'Merveille des quatre saisons' lettuce, gorgeous and totally delicious. French sorrel will please many a palate as well, and is a far cry from the weedier types; this is the stuff that omelets are made of—heavenly.

If January seems early for such musings, think again. Many a vegetable garden is doomed to failure precisely because it was the hasty product of the first warm weekend in May. Such installations are seldom thought out ahead, and usually show it sooner or later. It's so much more fun to enjoy the bounty of a thoughtfully planned garden than to struggle grimly with a haphazard one. This is an excellent time to be mulling over the possibilities, estimating your wants and needs, planning the location of each sort according to its particular demands. It isn't too early to renew your stock of fertilizers, check the hoses, sharpen the blades of your shovels, or oil the handles of all your tools, either, but that requires more effort. We'll do that stuff in February. For now, let's content ourselves with making some sketches of the proposed pea patch, noting the locations of the trellising poles, the paths of the sun and the sprinkler. Think it all through on paper. That way, when May rolls around, you probably won't run long rows of sweet corn in front of lower-growing bush beans, blocking whatever light there is, and you certainly won't plant the onions near the sprinkler head (they need to dry out as they ripen). Such planning can be a very pleasant exercise, one which may spare you a good deal of heartache and waste, and one which will increase your respect for garden notes. This last is a discipline that all of us reach sooner or later; it might as well be now. It is surprisingly helpful and less arduous than popularly supposed.

You will find this theme of discipline and planning echoed throughout the Territorial seed catalog, for it is the product of some mighty serious gardeners. The catalog is unpretentious in tone and appearance—in fact, you could easily mistake it for a newspaper insert and throw it away—but that really would be a mistake. Take the time to read the excellent advice; it is refreshing to find such a reliable and honest resource. If it states that a certain tomato will crack, well, some of them will, but if it also assures you that the flavor is fine, it is sure to be delectable. Many of the hybrid types listed are not available commercially, due to some flaw that makes them unmarketable, unshippable, or inconvenient to raise on a large scale.

There is a lot to browse through, not just suitable varieties of vegetables, but charts and tables, pest control advice, suggestions for proper fertilization, watering techniques, ways to get the jump on the season, and always a few lengthy asides which touch upon the philosophical, the moral, the environmental, and occasionally even the spiritual side of gardening. A few years ago, Steve Solomon wrote *Growing Organic Vegetables West of the Cascades*, far and away the best vegetable book for the Northwest. Getting the catalog is like getting a new chapter every year, and would be worth paying for. Even the first one's free, but beware; this catalog is addictive and could change your eating habits for life.

FEBRUARY

17

THE WAVE
February's bulb blitz begins

ebruary sees the beginning of the annual bulb
blitz. The earliest daffodils are out in full force,
having begun in late January with such delights
as the tiny *Narcissus minimus*, followed by the hoop
petticoats, *N. bulbocodium* varieties, of which there are
many. Another early bloomer is 'Tete-a-tete', a mini
cyclamineus hybrid with nodding twin trumpets, ears
laid back like a nervous horse. Soon the tough little
'February Gold' arrives. Wind resistant and lovely, these
shapely golden trumpets make pools of sunny color
which last for weeks. Six or eight bulbs planted together
will provide a good show and combine cheerfully with
primroses, forget-me-nots, or velvety pansies. If you plant
these in quantity, the garden will be swimming in sunlight.

The inevitable wind and rain of coastal springs can
wreak havoc with the taller daffodils and tulips. Spreading a mulch will reduce mud splashing, and planting
shorter, more windproof varieties is equally good strat-
egy. To avoid starting a slug farm, use rough shredded
bark rather than leaves for your mulch. When the first
shoots are well up, scatter the bark with a lavish hand.
This is a pleasant task; each tender leaf is an intimation
of delights to come, and protecting future flowers makes
us feel virtuous and clever at the same time. Sprinkle
a good handful of bone meal around the emerging
greenery, and add a healthy dusting of diatomaceous
earth or slug death (Corry's is a good choice for the
balancing of both environmental and practical concerns).
If you think bark looks lowly and vulgar, you may carpet
your beds with cut straw, peanut hulls, or well-ground
leaves. Tidy up a bit as well, pulling away the more obviously draggled remains of autumn. Mulching and grooming will improve the look of your beds enormously, and
this is appropriate, since last year's leftovers don't make

Narcissus minimus
Daffodil

N. bulbocodium
Hoop petticoats

'Tete-a-tete'

'February Gold'

19

Anemone blanda
Windflower

Greigii hybrids
Tulip

Stachys lanata
'Silver Carpet'

Tulipa tarda
Tarda tulip

the best frame for the fast approaching spring beauties.

Anemone blanda, the windflower of ancient Greece, emerges from the ground like a little clenched fist, purple-red with cold. The knobbly buds are glossy and surprisingly hard to the touch. Slowly the lacy leaves unfurl, frizzy as new parsley, a dark spruce green deckled with bronze. These leafy ruffs surround long-lasting starry flowers in soft shades of white or pink or a good clear blue. Ten corms will encircle a cluster of five or six species tulip bulbs nicely. These are the earliest tulips, shorter and smaller than their tall hybrid cousins. Called "species" to distinguish them from garden hybrids, they have been considerably hybridized themselves, but the label remains, a handy if slightly inaccurate way of differentiating these more compact and early tulips from the more common kinds.

Species tulips bloom in luminous shades of pink or cream, or in brighter yellows and oranges. None are strident, but some of the reds are quite vivid and far-carrying, and all have greater garden impact than you might expect from such small things. One group, the greigii hybrids, has broad leaves that are marbled like Persian endpapers in old books, intricately patterned in grey, sea green, chestnut, and burgundy. Named after an eminent Russian horticulturist who discovered the original species in the wilds of Turkestan, these hybrids have romantic associations which enhance their understated charms. As a group, these tulips are as lovely in leaf as in bud and blossom, and planted with the non-flowering clone of lamb's ears (*Stachys lanata*) called 'Silver Carpet', they fill a garden corner with supreme elegance.

These and other species tulips have the advantage of reappearing for many years, many increasing readily. Those planted in full sun with good drainage will often multiply, and any seed pods which develop can be gathered when ripe (usually June) and sown into flats if you want still more. The fresh and brilliant blossoms of the Tarda tulip (*Tulipa tarda*) come in robust sprays, four or five buds to a stalk, each clear yellow petal deeply feathered with white. The more delicate *T. turkestanica* is an ivory-pale wildling with a greenish-yellow throat, something out of a Turkish miniature. There are several forms of the delicious *T. saxatilis*, all pink with throats of yellow, black, or red, and all about six inches tall.

These little tulips and daffodils have surprisingly blatant flowers and make a brave show despite their lesser stature. Dwarf forms of both are even better than the big ones for interplanting with the so-called "minor" bulbs (a wide and eclectic group of small bulbs ranging from grape hyacinths to anemones). Short and sturdy, they weather well, giving wonderful garden value for long weeks. There are many varieties available, generally quite cheap (often costing less than a quarter per bulb) and the whole group is decidedly worth investigating.

Lots of people plant grape hyacinth (*Muscari armeniacum*); its portly six-inch spikes of cobalt blue bells appear in most gardens sooner or later, invited or not. It could charitably be described as a generous self-seeder. Plant ten bulbs this fall and in three or four years you will be pelting squirrels with the extras. Perhaps this is as good a time as any to explain a certain phrase; if a catalog says, "increases rapidly," read "spreads like wildfire" and be warned. With grape hyacinth, every bell sets seed, every seed sprouts, and soon your garden is a mass of seedlings like plump and satisfied grass. The foliage expands greatly as it matures, smothering everything in its path. I still grow this bulb, because it is so beautiful and so generous in its bloom, but now it is strictly confined to beds where it can't cause trouble. Even at that, I dig out huge clumps for anyone who asks and sometimes resort to hacking the floppy ripening foliage to the ground when it encroaches. This deters the bulb very little, though it relieves the neighboring plants a good deal.

Fortunately, grape hyacinth has a number of equally attractive cousins with less promiscuous habits, plants more lastingly welcome in the border. *Muscari comosum* 'Plumosum' looks just as feathery as it sounds, a hazy plume of blue that increases slowly. These tufted, fluffy

Tulipa turkestanica

T. saxatilis

**Muscari armeniacum
Grape hyacinth**

**Muscari comosum
'Plumosum'**

21

Muscari
'Blue Spike'

M. alba

'Baby Moon'

Pushkinia libanotica
Striped squill

Scilla siberica
Siberian squill

Chionodoxa
Glory-of-the-snow

Narcissus triandrus albus
Angel's tears

flowers are well set off by miniature daffodils. Several hybrids have garden value; 'Blue Spike' carries royal blue, fully double flowers with an intense fragrance, and a white form, usually called *M. alba*, is also perfumed. Both look very pretty with little flat-cup daffodils like the primrose-yellow 'Baby Moon', pink anemones, and the pale blue striped squill, *Pushkinia libanotica*.

Siberian squill (*Scilla siberica*) blooms in a sparkling mountain lake blue and has the fey appeal of many wild things, very different from the more formal looking muscaris. This increases slowly, appreciating dappled shade better than glaring sun. It multiplies best in woodsy wildflower gardens, a good companion for the several forms of *Chionodoxa* or glory-of-the-snow. The most common chionodoxa has flowers like azure stars, touched with white at the heart. A pale pink form turns up in the catalogs from time to time, but it is usually quite expensive, and valuable more because it is a relative rarity than for any particular distinction of form or color. All of these are good companions for an enchanting little heartbreaker, angel's tears (*Narcissus triandrus albus*). Four inches tall, with drooping white flowers of exceptional finish and the texture of raw silk, this is the unrivaled gem of the early garden. It has brought many a visitor to his knees, eliciting undignified cries like "Oh WOW" and "Good God!" All these diminutive flowers are appropriate to this subtle season; not quite winter, not quite spring, theirs is the new leaf at the turning of the year.

THE SCENT OF VIOLETS
Rewards for garden cleanup
in early spring

I t's hard to stay out of the garden, even in winter. One chilly day in late winter I was out prowling around, cutting back the fall-blooming clematis, clearing out withered leaves and stalks, seeing what was poking up and what wasn't looking too thrifty after those hard November frosts. The sun was shining in a feeble sort of way and as I worked I kept getting drifts of an enticing smell. It wasn't from the primroses, though quite a few of the polyanthus hybrids (the ones from Ernst or the grocery store) have a sweet and cheerful fragrance. It wasn't the *Sarcococca humilis* or sweet box, which smells of wild honey; this was more like real perfume. It made me think of my grandmother, and it wasn't till I scooped up an armload of rotting leaves that a handful of tiny purple violets was revealed, barely open but pouring out that evocative odor.

Violets! They were so unexpected that I didn't even recognize that sweet-old-lady scent. Looking closer, I found other clumps, fat with swelling buds. Purple, white, pink, soft yellow, all had been planted under the lilac bush in the side yard last fall and hidden under the leaves ever since. We had trimmed off the lower lilac branches and made a new bed under its skirts. This snug and sheltered place is thickly planted with small plants too easily overlooked in the bigger beds: tiny bulbs, dwarf hostas, delicate ferns, and these violets. They had been forgotten until the winter sun enticed the purple ones out of dormancy.

Most of these violets were ordered last year from the catalog of Lamb Nursery (see Appendix A). The nursery is an astonishing place, tucked in among the Burger Kings and Tire Marts of Spokane's Division Street. A couple of blocks back from all the neon, you run into parking strips planted solid with oriental poppies, pure blocks of bright color: orange, rose, soft pink, flame,

23

**Viola odorata
'Semperflorens'**

V. odorata 'Alba'

V. vilmoriniana

cream, and scarlet. Behind that are neat rows of iris, banks of chrysanthemums, ranks of roses. A whole city block is full of amazing plants, yet there is no sign, no sales office, no attempt to draw in customers. Lamb is mainly a mail-order nursery, though visitors are welcome and can browse all they like while the proprietor goes about her business. It has quite recently changed hands, but the present owner is just as dedicated and capable as the past one, and has the designer's flair for choosing the right plant for the right place as well. I always come away with a boxcar-load of stuff, because the offerings are choice, the price is right, and the plants are well rooted and vigorous. This year's catalog lists fifteen kinds of violets and it's hard to choose a dud.

Those purple ones that bloomed so early are listed as *Viola odorata* 'Semperflorens', and they really are nearly ever-blooming. Mine came from Lamb via my mother's garden years ago. She brought them to me in a little basket, in full and fragrant bloom at Christmas time. You can easily duplicate this feat by digging clumps and bringing them indoors in November. Even a moderately sunny (Northwest-style) window is enough to encourage the eager blossoms. A low dish filled with these velvety, fragrant flowers nestled among the dark, heart-shaped leaves makes an unusual centerpiece for the Christmas breakfast table or a very welcome gift for the hard-to-please.

The white variety is *V. odorata* 'Alba', equally scented and so bountiful in bloom that you can hardly see the leaves. Less showy, though still very abundant, the delicate 'Rosina' sports properly rosy-faced flowers over a long season. My favorite violet has velveteen petals of apricot overlaid with gold: *V. vilmoriniana*. Although it has but a slight, evanescent fragrance, this bit of sheer gorgeousness is worthy of a place in any garden. Any or all of these violets make attractive ground covers for window boxes or tubs full of lilies, agapanthus, or what have you.

Violets multiply well, and the purple flowers and dusky leaves, dark green suffused with purple-black, of

V. labradorica, the Labrador violet, quickly form an uncommon carpet for small spring bulbs. Clumps of white windflowers, *Anemone blanda*, glimmer attractively in this subfusc setting. For a richer, sumptuous effect, combine these black Labs with delicate species tulips. *Tulipa linifolia*, lipstick red and elegant to the sharp little tips of its precisely formed petals, is outstanding in such a position. Red or yellow greigii tulips make an impressive splash as well, their sea green leaves streaked and marbled with burgundy.

An old favorite from across the water is *Viola* 'Maggie Mott'. Lovers of English gardens (and English novels, where the characters are always out deadheading the Maggie Motts) will instantly recognize this one. It is a pansy, not a violet, but they are very closely related and share the ever-blooming tendencies. Maggie does indeed need to be deadheaded, as do all pansies, in order to produce her endless stream of light blue flowers. Each has a creamy eye, like clouds in soft summer skies, and the steady removal of those past their prime ensures their rapid replacement. For pink or white roses, Maggie is the requisite ground cover, to be planted in broad swathes beneath the shrubs.

Lamb has a lot more to offer than violets, so if you visit Spokane, make a point of finding this nursery; it's worth the trip in itself. It has enjoyed an excellent reputation for many years; Katherine White (*Onward and Upward in the Garden*) was well pleased by Lamb's offerings and Allen Lacy (garden writer for the Wall Street Journal) gets his hardy fuchsias from Lamb. You'll be in good company if you, too, fall for the charms of this understated catalog.

Viola labradorica
Labrador violet

Anemone blanda
Windflower

Tulipa linifolia
Tulip

Viola 'Maggie Mott'
Pansy

ONGOING AMARYLLIS

Grow these big bulbs on for future horticultural fireworks

N ow that the Christmas bulbs are fading, let's consider a few ways to deal with them. The traditional approach, tested by time, is to throw them out. This has the merit of simplicity, and is certainly the easiest to carry out. Another common technique is to grow them on haphazardly, watering as the spirit moves, forcing dormancy as summer begins. In fall, we slosh on the water again; at this rude awakening, the plant puts out a sullen leaf or two, but no flower—and why should it bloom for such treatment? Out it goes.

There is another way. It requires slightly more effort, but gives gratifying results and leads to a spectacular finale if all goes well. Let's take things from flower fade point, which is right about now if you got the bulb for Christmas. Snip off any spent blossoms as they fade, but leave the stalk to wither a bit and when it does, trim it off a few inches from the base of the bulb. An exception to this rule would arise in cases where the willing worker threw another bud scape. When this occurs, go ahead and trim the first stalk before it withers, since it will detract seriously from the attractions of the second. Once back on schedule, all stalks properly wizened, begin a regular feeding program using half-strength fertilizer several times a month. Provide all the light you can, natural or artificial. Dust off those strap-like leaves now and then to keep them glossy. Coddle the plant along, treating it like a house plant, until the time is ripe for an outdoor debut.

When the weather is fairly settled and frost is a thing of the past, you can begin the transition to the big world. Take the potted bulbs outside, but keep them on the back porch, or somewhere out of direct sun, to get used to the stronger light outside. The next weekend, move them to a half-sun position, and the week after that they can go to their summer home. The ideal place is in full sun, on a south- or west-facing slope. Less than ideal conditions can still give good results, so settle for the sunniest, driest spot you have, whether window box, patio, or driveway side. If you do have a sunny hillside for them, the bulbs can be planted right in the ground. Anywhere that the slugs roam free, it is better to keep the bulbs elevated and in pots. If you have several bulbs, they can be grouped in a large container, a sort of nursing home for tired amaryllis. A fluffy bed of rich, peaty soil is in order, and a handful of steamed bone meal, worked into the dirt before placing the bulb, will be beneficial as well.

If the bulbs are to be planted right into the ground, prepare the soil deeply, forking in some peat moss, compost, and bone meal, and stirring it all in so that there are no streaks or lumps. Set the bulbs in at a bit of an angle, out-facing like a gargoyle, to prevent water collecting in the necks and causing crown rot. The current leaves may scorch, turning dark mottled red, but that's O.K. Soon there will be lots of new ones, and the more the better, because the leaves are the key to more flowers. Since the bud stalks are produced with every fifth leaf, you want as many leaves as you can get.

Sunshine and fast drainage are crucial to the success of this project, but a further warning may be needed: it is easy to forget that full summer brings middle-aged spread to the garden. Wherever you park your amaryllis, look ahead and don't leave them where they will later be swamped by large-leafed neighbors. On decks or patios, it is easy enough to shift containers (except big, heavy ones), and as the broad, glossy leaves are perfectly presentable, the amaryllis can hog the sunny spots with your roses and whatnot without causing you shame.

Water enough to encourage growth without encouraging mold (this will depend on the weather, won't it). Continue frequent feeding, several times a month, and use a variety of fertilizers just for balance: all have good points, but different blends of trace minerals, and variety makes for healthier plants. Never fertilize a plant in dry

27

soil, however; this can shock and burn any plant, but is especially harmful to the young and recently transplanted. Wet the soil thoroughly first, let the water percolate down to the roots, and then apply the dilute fertilizer. Peat-based potting soil dries out fast and is difficult to rewet without unpotting the plant, which is rather disruptive and a pain in the neck. This is where larger pots or containers have the advantage; the soil is deeper and less prone to evaporation than in small pots, where the surface exposed to the sun is proportionately greater. Small containers can literally bake their contents in the August sun. This is not what is meant when garden books say a plant (usually a South African bulb) "likes a good baking." In the ground, where roots can range far, finding cool runs beneath shrubs or rocks, that is fine. In a container, such a baking is lethal.

By September, you can stop watering. As growth slows down, the leaves begin to ripen off, soft and yellow as banana peels. In a wet year, dig the bulbs up a little early rather than risk having them rot in the cool, moist weather. Otherwise, dig at the first light frost, usually late October to mid-November. Usually the bulbs will be dormant, but it doesn't matter if they aren't. Toss any dead or limp leaves on the compost heap and bring your bounty inside. Check carefully for soft spots or signs of rot. Small areas can be cut out with a sharp knife (dip it in a strong bleach solution between cuts to avoid spreading possible disease or virus). Even if all bulbs are hard and smooth, a mild bleach bath can't hurt; there is no point in bringing more life indoors than you intend to. Find a bucket, and pour in a gallon of water and ¼ cup bleach. Drop in the bulbs and get a plate or pie pan which fits inside the bucket yet is large enough to cover the bulbs. Weighted with a rock, the plate will keep the bulbs pushed under the bleach solution, so any wildlife which may be aboard has no last haven of refuge. You would be surprised at the fleas, beetles, bugs, slugs, and other faunal detritis which you can unwittingly bring indoors without this precaution. A few hours submergence is plenty, and the bulbs can be air dried overnight on some newspapers.

Repot in rich soil; try commercial potting soil mixed half and half with peat moss, with 1 cup of steamed bone meal added per dry gallon of soil, unless you have your own pet recipe. If your amaryllis were happy outside, they are likely to have offsets, chubby bulblets attached to the older bulbs. There are several good ways to treat these. Detached from the mother bulb and potted up in individual four-inch pots, the bulblets can be grown on to blooming size in a few years. Potted in terra cotta, they make impressive holiday gifts, as you casually mention that you raised them yourself. A whole group of offsets may be potted up in a larger container to grow on together with luxuriant effect. When one big bulb has numerous babies, pot up mother bulb and all into an oversized container where they can remain and mature over the years. If the bulblets are grouped unevenly, gently detach them, rearrange them attractively, and in a few years you will have something special to show off. This is how amaryllis are grown in France and Italy; they gain character and dignity with the years, becoming a distinctive showpiece in any setting. Of course you can always cheat and cram several brand-new bulbs together, but the varying sizes and shapes of the children clustering around the grande dame have particular charm.

In a wet or busy year you may lose a bulb or two, but with luck your bulb collection will increase, yielding lots to enjoy and plenty to give away. This year, think twice before you toss those bulbs away. Before long, you could have horticultural fireworks without spending a penny for them.

SLUG BOOTS
The Northwest's answer to pesticides

I recently read a delightful account of gardening in the Deep South in which the wise gardener never set foot into the garden patch without the protection of a sturdy pair of snake boots. Where snakes are plentiful, irritable and poisonous, it clearly pays to have half an inch of shoe leather between you and those curving fangs. Not only is your calf covered, you have a fairly deadly weapon of your own, right at foot. When deadly snakes rear their ugly little heads, you simply stomp them to belt material. Now, here in the Northwest, venomous snakes are not everyday fare, but another sinister and slimy character lurks beneath every leaf, waiting to attack the unsuspecting gardener. Anybody who has ever stepped barefoot on a large and squashy slug will immediately see both the charm and the application of this concept. Slug Boots. I like it.

Northwesterners would do well to emulate this custom, modified to the peculiar rigors and pests of our climate. To be really practical, slug boots must not be made of leather, which is unimproved by constant immersion in water, but of sleek, shining, supple, and sensuous plastic. The pair I finally settled on are fire engine red, with a determined little heel and a nicely patterned tread—not too deep, or it would defeat the whole purpose. Those slithery little buggers would curl up and hide in a deep tread. They are very sneaky, and very determined. Many people don't know just how serious a pest they can be. The day we found one exploring the depths of our Melitta coffeepot was the day I realized the extent of the problem. We all read the newspaper article about the electrical blackout up in Lakewood. A whole community lost its power thanks to the slime-trail of an errant slug making its leisurely way across a circuit board. We read it and chuckled; electricity, big deal. But nobody messes with my coffeepot. I got out those slug boots, tromped on that slug, and a few more I found lying around, and I was sold. You do need that tread, though, since the little suckers are slippery. I soon got into the rhythm, something like clog dancing, and have been practicing assiduously ever since.

Now, we don't stoop to using much poison around here, since that would be politically and environmentally incorrect, but any of the widely available baits based on metaldehyde are acceptable, especially for those who simply can't dance. It attracts with the powerful allure of a blend of bran (which slugs find irresistible) and an alcohol analog that is fatally intoxicating. It is well known that slugs love to party; just leave a beer bottle in the garden overnight if you want proof. Set it on its side near the infant lettuce, with a tablespoon or so of beer left in it (any more would be a waste of B-vitamin complex). You are sure to find half a dozen crocked and reeling gastropods whooping it up in there in the morning. In my book, slugs are born to die anyway; surely this is an essentially thoughtful and gracious way to usher them out of this world?

If all this grisly death talk is too painful, you can simply speed slugs on their merry way, getting them out of your garden, but not necessarily all the way into slug heaven in one swoop. Just scoop one up, loosen up the old throwing arm and let fly. Slugs are great travelers, and any sensible one would quickly decide to skip the return trip to your yard, given such treatment. If you can't bear the idea of handling slugs, take advantage of a natural and symbiotic partnership; pick them up with a mollusk. It is not widely known that snails and slugs are mutually adhesive, but such is the case. Many squeamish souls who would sooner lose their lettuce than touch a slime creature can toss a snail over the fence without much trouble. Next time you do this, look around for a baby slug, moosh it with the sticky part of your snail, and wish them bon voyage.

Since slugs are migratory, it isn't enough to empty the yard once a year. More will creep over the border at night, eluding the most vigilant patrols, to sup well at your salad bar before moving on. Snails have a less restless spirit. They are little homebodies; when they find a cozy place to sleep, in the crown of your favorite daylily, nestled among the agapanthus, or snuggled deep into the heart of a bulb, they develop a fondness for it and are very apt to return there day after day. You can take advantage of this habit by leaving a few bricks or boards around on the garden paths. Before too long, such spots become social centers, and you in your slug boots are the star turn.

There are a number of patented little fences and barriers which purport to be slug-proof, but nothing is really proof against the depredations of this slippery little character except the full weight of your disapproval. Actually, there are a few good tricks to try, other than the above-mentioned commercial bait, the most environmentally acceptable one around. Diatomaceous earth, generously sprinkled around the plants you want to keep, can keep those howling and snapping slugs at bay. It is particularly useful if pets or kids seem interested in the metaldehyde bait. (Both are fascinated by those little green plastic huts in which the bait is supposed to be protected from rain, which makes them more dangerous than useful.) The diatomaceous earth is made of the crushed exoskeletons of diatoms, tiny fossilized critters that are as brittle and sharp-edged as glass when pulverized. Harmless to humans and pets, the stuff punctures slugs and snails with hundreds of pinpricks as they crawl through it. That causes them to leak out all their innards, which is fairly final. It is, however, expensive.

An acquaintance of the family has earned his doctorate studying the ecology of banana slugs, and he has shown us a series of pictures which are really quite endearing. In them, a saucer of milk is set down, and one by one, the slugs approach, bending their little horns curiously, tasting the milk, at first cautiously, then avidly dipping in to the dish. The final shot of a whole tiny herd of slugs slurping is absolutely cute. A gardening friend recounts a fascinating tale of the courtship and mating ritual of slugs, as she observed it one fine day.

Apparently as slugs merge, a clear and crystalline droplet forms, dangling on a long thread and spreading slowly into a scalloped, pulsating sac. As the embrace is completed, the bag of living water is drawn up and reabsorbed. The process is lengthy, and as our friend describes it, lovely and moving, almost lyrical. Perhaps we ought to reconsider, make room in our hearts for these little creatures, defenseless and guileless.

Well, maybe. But when I see another crop of promising seedlings mown down wholesale, a brand-new and long-awaited plant gnawed to the bare and quivering roots, the glossy new leaves of my miniature hostas tattered and ragged, I give no quarter. Let them eat metaldehyde! After all, it's not as if slugs are an endangered species. I do make a few concessions; I don't bait routinely, just when seedlings are rowed out, when seeds are sown, or when fragile treasures are transplanted. However, when I uncover a nest of gastropod eggs, round and shimmering like tiny pearls, those future sluglets and snailings go straight under the fierce little heels of my slug boots.

MARCH

35

AN ARMLOAD OF LILACS

Pruning tips and choice varieties of an old-fashioned favorite

B y early March it was perfectly clear that this was not going to be a banner year for my lilacs. This wasn't really surprising, since old-fashioned lilacs tend to be biennial in their blooming habits. They will flower weakly or not at all the year following a strong show, and last year we enjoyed a total all-out explosion of blossoms on both of the old shrubs. This year, both would normally be duds. Thanks to a pruning technique I've been practicing for a couple of years, both are flowering more heavily than they ever have before on an off year.

If you have been disappointed in the performance of an older lilac shrub, think back and see if yours, too, might be pulling this biennial stunt. I used to ascribe such failures to my pruning habits, pollution, disease, the weather, all sorts of things. I never knew what the problem really was until I found references in several gardening books to a pruning trick that certain avant English gardeners (Christopher Lloyd and others) were using to modify the biennial blooming habit of older strains of lilac and other shrubs. That clicked: biennial! Of course! Furthermore, the method sounded simple and was definitely worth a try. After several seasons of trial, we too are enjoying some pretty good results.

In order to best understand the following description, take this book in hand and go stand in front of your lilac; all will be clear to you when you actually look at the shrub. This is how the pruning method works; in early spring (now, for instance) it is possible to tell which of the lilac's swelling buds will bear flowers if you examine them closely. The flower buds are fatter, rounder, and shorter than those which will become leaves. The leaf buds become flatter and longer until they unfurl. If you aren't too sure about your identification, try cutting a bud in half; the immature flowers look like a tiny cluster of green grapes in the bud. Lots of fat flower buds mean a good bloom year, and that's the best time to try this technique. Each branch has a number of shoots at the end. What you want to do is trim about a third of them by cutting out the tip and the following pair or two of shoots, leaving a Y-shaped pair or two of stout twigs with leafy buds. Those will now bear flowers next season, in the normally poor year. After a couple of seasons of this, the bloom pattern gets evened out and every year is a good one.

Since you are already thrashing around in the heart of your lilac with the pruners, you might as well have a go at a general pruning while you are at it. Take out any branches that look weak, spindly, or less than vigorous. When that's done, remove the wimpier or less graceful of any branches that are crossed or rubbing against each other. This is a good way to tackle a suckering shrub like lilac, which tends to fill up with far too many hopeful shoots. Pruning is often neglected; it is thought to be difficult, an esoteric skill that requires specialized knowledge. Lilac is a great shrub for uncertain pruners; it's hard to kill a lilac, and the bush will bloom all the better for a thorough and vigorous thinning.

Start with the obvious; remove anything dead or breathing its last, and continue as above. Soon the basic framework of the plant emerges and you begin shaping it artistically. Look at pruning in practical terms first; the point is to remove trash wood, to open up the interior of the plant to air and light, all of which will improve the plant's health as well as looks. It is better to attempt and fall a tad short in the art department than not to attempt at all, so next time you feel that sting of irritation at your plant's unrewarding behavior, grab those pruners and have at it. The season in which you prune lilac is relatively unimportant, so have a stab at it whenever you feel the urge (or get up your nerve). Deadheading, cutting off the faded flower trusses, does not affect floral display in subsequent years, whatever you may read to the contrary. If the faded flowers offend

'Sensation'

'Excel'

'Congo'

you, however, you may pluck them out. Left on the shrub, the seedheads attract many birds in winter, a bright ornament to any garden. If you feel lazy, you may explain to those who chivvy you about the un-trimmed lilac that you are inspired by ecological con-cern and love of your fellow creatures to leave those seedheads in place.

Our bushes have been in the yard for at least fifty years, according to an elderly neighbor. By the time we got here, they had degenerated into scantily bloom-ing thickets of scraggly suckers surrounding enormous gnarled trunks. The most restorative thing you can do to a plant like this is to cut the biggest trunks to the ground. Clear all the old wood from the center, even if it means taking out most of the bush. It will respond by throwing up suckers, new shoots from the ground. Choose half a dozen of the strongest ones to fill in the gaps left by your surgery, removing the others. This will usually result in a burst of blossom the following year, but older plants may disappoint you by failing to repeat the performance the year after that. If you notice alter-nate good and poor bloom years on your lilac, the English method of selective pruning can make a big difference in just a couple of seasons.

If you haven't any lilac yet, you could choose from numerous modern varieties which bloom well every year. A particularly handsome one is called 'Sensation', with very fragrant flowers of rich purple, each with a crisp white picotee edge. 'Excel', a raspberry pink lilac, is resistant to an ugly leaf blight caused by pollution and quite common in cities. One of my lilacs gets this problem—leaf roll necrosis—nearly every year. The dis-ease is well named, since it causes rolled-up, blackened leaves; it looks dreadful but doesn't really harm the plant. An occasional washing with mild soap (not detergent) solution helps; try to remember to give the lilac a bath when you wash the car.

Newer varieties of lilac come in stronger, clearer colors than the old-fashioned ones; the sumptuous 'Con-go', for example, is almost burgundy colored, wine red

'Primrose'

'Firmament'

Clematis macropetala

'Madame LeMoine'

'Vestale'

with purple highlights. Even more unusual is 'Primrose', with delicate, pastel yellow flowers. 'Firmament', the bluest of lilacs, is gently tinted, almost sky blue. Either of those two make a perfect host for spring-blooming pink *Clematis macropetala*. The eminent 'Madame Le-Moine' is still the queen of the whites, her fragrant creamy trusses of double flowers opening like mounds of driven snow. This one really does need to be dead-headed, however, as the flower heads look dreadful in decay. A more modern white, 'Vestale', has large, dense clusters of single flowers, very showy and less obtrusive in death. Local nurseries carry many good choices and you can't go wrong unless you forget to ask about fragrance, as some very lovely kinds are scentless. Think of an armload of odorless lilac! It seems a horti-cultural horror to rob this unassuming shrub of half of its off-and-on glory.

CLEMATIS MONTANA

Happy trails and fragrant flowers on superb spring-blooming vines

T he clematis (KLEM-a-tis is preferred) family album is a fat one with over 200 species and many hybrids represented in dazzling array, dominated by the florid summer-blooming beauties with enormous blossoms and a relatively short but spectacular season. They are all lovely, if perhaps a bit obvious, but I have a preference for some of the less insistent members of the clan. One of the really rewarding ones is *Clematis montana*, a strong and splendid deciduous vine that deserves a place of prominence. Nursery people tell me that it is not a good seller because gardeners want the larger-flowered kinds. I feel sure that once seen, this early bloomer would be in demand. It is perfectly true that the flowers are not showboats, but *C. montana* and several other seldom-seen species clematis have charms and strengths which make them as good or better choices for most gardens than the big, flashy hybrids that hog the limelight.

My vine of *C. montana* is now in full bloom, a great glory of pale blossoms. It has built up to this performance over the past month and will continue well into May with a light spangling of flowers all summer and a lesser, farewell display in the fall. Just now one can hardly see the leaves for the closely packed flowers. These look a bit like dogwood with their four rounded petals. They open white but with age turn ivory pink and become flushed with lavender along the slightly ruffled edges. Like anemones, they have a thick, fluffy central puff of stamens, here in palest yellow, and the whole blossom is faintly tinged with green. This is a flower to savor and appreciate at close hand, a few floating in a flat bowl or tucked with a sprig of leaves into a desk-top bud vase for inspiration.

The leaves are a definite point in its favor, a good strong green with a matte finish, rippled and veined in

41

'Sugarbush'
Daffodil

'Ice Follies'

'Spellbinder'

Clematis montana
'Rubens'

an interesting light-catching texture, faintly hairy, which gives a silvery glimmer to the edges and undersides as they move in the wind. They grow in divisions of three, rather long and tapered with a roughly scalloped or toothed edge. Having mobile stems, they twist and flutter easily. The new growth has a coppery cast, greeny gold and attractive as a background behind spring bulbs, especially daffodils with a bit of green in their make-up: perhaps 'Sugarbush', 'Ice Follies', or 'Spellbinder'.

A pinker-flowered sister is *C. montana* 'Rubens', vigorous and lovely, with round red balloon-buds which open a warm rosy color and fade to old blush. This one has deeper green leaves edged faintly with reddish bronze, and the new foliage in spring is distinctly red-tinted. She too is great with bloom just now, fat swags of flowers hanging off the house in cheerful greeting.

The first blossoms of both varieties lack the size and perfume that later flowers will achieve. Their honey-vanilla fragrance fills the air as you pass the vines in April, but one sniffs earlier flowers in vain. Scent in certain flowers is often like that, a bit fickle, appearing most strongly when the plant is at its fullest flush of strength, when the sun is warmest, or when no one else is around.

Another beauty of these vines is that of the seed-heads left by the passing flowers. As petals fall, long strands of silky floss emerge, furry beards which function like dandelion fuzz, parachutes to transport the tiny seeds. These persist a long time and can make a striking winter feature on vines grown in a sheltered corner out of the wind. The seeds may be gathered easily but with caution, since on a breezy day the tiny seeds may be inhaled. Unfortunately, they cling with little barbed fingers to the gardener's throat, uncomfortable at best, dangerous at worst. This issue can be avoided by ignoring the usual advice and NOT stripping off the tails when cleaning the seeds. Simply tuck some barely moistened peat moss into a ziplock bag and gently stir in a few seeds. Stored in the refrigerator, they will germinate at their leisure, often quite erratically. Check every month or so for sprouts, which can easily be grown on to blooming size.

If you do find seedlings, take them by the ears (the leaves) rather than the stem and transplant to small (two-inch) pots filled with damp potting soil. Stick the entire business into a plastic bag and close loosely. This prevents the little things from drying out or developing water-stress. In a few days, you can open the bag, and as growth continues, remove the bag entirely. The seedlings develop quite fast, requiring only routine care, but develop best in strong filtered sun. While potted, they need protection from drought and severe frosts, but once they are planted in their permanent place (in their second year), cold will not harm them.

These Chinese natives are very strong growers and will throw their arms in happy flowering trails over an arbor, a fence, a net, or a trellis. They would be equally pleased to rush over a steep bank, clamber through shrubs, and dangle from treetops. Since they flower on old wood, any pruning or shaping should be done just after the spring show is past. They will stand being cut back quite heavily but like to have a full summer to recover in. All clematis like to have a cool root-run but want to grow into the sun; this is accomplished by planting them in the shade of taller perennials or behind shrubs—or, traditionally, by covering the root zone with flat rocks, though that has always seemed odd to me. Who wants a bunch of flat rocks in the garden beds?

Give new clematis a deeply dug bed, adding compost, lots of peat moss, and some sand or gravel to the soil to make a rich but fast-draining medium for the roots. Where the soil is acid, as it generally is throughout the maritime Northwest, add a good handful of lime, incorporating it well so it can be taken up by the roots. Bone meal is also useful, and can be added as a top dressing annually (unlike the lime, which doesn't get absorbed unless mixed into soil or compost). Plant deeply, so the roots are several inches below the surface, but not so deeply that you bury the crown. It is a good idea to cut the top growth back when setting in new

43

plants, removing the upper several pairs of leaves. Clematis dislike being handled, so be gentle. Tenderly encourage what's left of the top growth to find its way up, over, around, or through whatever you have chosen for it to decorate. Water well, and keep it adequately supplied with water for its first season, and you will probably not have to think much about this particular plant again, except to admire its billowing blossoms each spring.

Above all, these species clematis are healthy, sturdy, and easy to please. They seem resistant to the dreaded clematis wilt that loves to cut the lusher beauties down overnight. Pests simply ignore them; this is a real plus for the busy gardener. Both varieties of *Clematis montana* will quickly produce large vines and put on big, long-lasting floral displays. There are clematis for practically every season, all delightful plants, but for sheer ease, abundance, and beauty, nothing can top the spring duets of the Montana sisters.

THE GRASS IS GREENER
Velvety turf can be yours, if you are willing to stoop for it

One February day we strolled past a man who appeared to be attacking his parking strip with an electric drill. Curious, we stopped to ask about it and learned that tired, neglected lawns (this one qualified handily) can be quickly restored to good health by aeration, drainage, and feeding. None of these things work as well alone as in combination, our informant continued, brandishing his drill for emphasis. Golf courses keep their immaculate, seamless good looks through just such a process, the man explained. Lawn care professionals use a large machine to punch and fill holes in the tight turf rather than a hand drill, but the technique can be applied on a smaller scale to the home lawn.

Our tutor then demonstrated his adaptation of the idea for us. The implement of choice was an ordinary ½-inch electric drill with a large auger bit which chewed out holes about five inches deep and spaced about three or four inches apart. Sand mixed with commercial grass fertilizer was dribbled into the holes, topped off, and watered in well. For larger areas, he likes to use a long-tined garden fork, jumping heavily to produce the deep holes, something like a pogo stick without bounce, I would guess. Hmm, we thought, and went on our way.

Happening to return to the area three weeks later, we just had to check out the results. I am pleased to announce that the turf was terrific. The grass was thick and deep green, in visible contrast to the ratty stuff on either side. Our instructor had done his job nicely, working right up to the property line but not an inch over, so his handiwork was now flanked by strips of patchy, bare-looking non-lawn.

If your lawn needs rejuvenation you could certainly do worse than to try this method. If you think you might feel a little silly drilling the lawn, clog dancing in golf

45

**Veronica filiformis
Speedwell**

shoes might do the trick as well, a fine group activity. Worried about what the neighbors might say? When last we passed that fine-looking patch of grass, our friend was back by request, working on the rest of the strip. Obviously, the neighbors loved it.

For the true velvet look, the weeds must go. Deep-rooted perennials, especially those which make large, flat rosettes that escape the lawnmower, need to be cut, not pulled, out of the ground. I use an old kitchen knife, a boning model with a long, thin blade. It's great for getting dandelions out of the cracks between pavers or bricks as well. Tap-rooted weeds can be very hard to get rid of, as the least scrap left behind will send up new growth aggressively. You can win at last by capitalizing on this; cut them, then feed the spot generously with fertilizer. This forces new shoots to develop fast, lusher than the root scraps can really support. Continue to cut and feed, and the toughest plant will be overcome by sheer exhaustion.

Lots of people are driven mad by invasions of the tender-looking lace and tiny bright blue flowers of speedwell (*Veronica filiformis*), and I am often asked how to get rid of it. This little creeper has highly invasive roots which quickly penetrate the sod, making the dainty little flower impossible to root out by ordinary means. It thrives in moist shade and poor soil, so the best way to get it out of your lawn is to cut down all your trees and raze the neighbor's house; this lets in more light, which will certainly slow its progress down. Ed Hume* has been heard to say that he thinks it's kind of pretty, really, and the English are famous for letting their lawns fill up with little daisies, clovers, and just such bright-eyed plants as speedwell. Any other questions?

An actively growing, properly cut lawn is the best defense of all. Few weeds can compete with well-established turf, and by practicing good lawn-care techniques you can avoid most of the weed and disease problems in the first place. Probably the most important things are feeding annually, setting the lawnmower cutter blades high (two inches) to avoid mutilating the crowns of the grass plants, and mowing on the right schedule for the grass rather than for the help (you or your lawn service). This can mean every five to six days when growth is strong, tapering to every other week or so as the summer heats up and grass starts to go dormant. The other biggy is water; a growing lawn needs about an inch a week. Given all this, and it isn't really so much to do over the course of a year, your lawn can be more than just presentable, it can be the thick green carpet of our innermost eye, the refuge, the lolling place, the picnic spot, the ideal viewing point from which to survey at leisure all the other delights of the garden.

* Ed Hume is a Seattle-based gardener with a regular television program and newspaper column on gardening.

Ferula communis
Giant fennel

Clematis alpina

C. macropetala

Fritillaria meleagris
Checkered fritillary

'Sweetheart'
Tulip

MARCHING THROUGH THE BORDER
Plants that take March winds in stride

The garden is awash with color, much of it contributed by the bulbs that are covering themselves with glory just now. A month ago each flower stood out, a treasure of color in a grey and quiet landscape. Now things are leaping out of the ground, the air snaps with electricity, and the garden is a vital, rapidly changing place. As the perennials wake up, their crowns are expanding daily. The netted, rough lace of giant fennel, *Ferula communis*, pours out of the ground in foaming, surging fountains of fresh green. The early clematis, dainty *Clematis alpina* and the bolder blossoms of the gay *C. macropetala*, clamber higher every day, throwing their garlands of burgeoning buds, pink and soft blue and cream, over anything too slow to escape.

The overall impression is of green, green, and more green, but color, both brazen and subtle, is everywhere. A spume of feathery bronze fennel makes a subtle backdrop for the pendant bells of the checkered fritillary, *Fritillaria meleagris*. These short (six to ten inches) plants with tesselated flowers charm every visitor; the bells really do appear to be checkered, in tweedy blends of cream, lavender, plum, and pink. The English have selected a number of forms as named varieties, many in heathery solid shades of purple, white, or subdued pink. These bloom even more generously than the type, and are well worth seeking out in specialty catalogs.

One of the best recent tulip introductions is the absolutely delectable 'Sweetheart'. Egg-shaped green buds soften to shimmering yellow, edges feathered with angelic white wings. The slanted light of spring makes them translucent, almost supernal. Despite this ethereal appearance, they have a blessedly robust constitution, lasting well both cut and in the border, and coming back strongly each year. Try grouping them with silky white poppy-flowered anemones and primroses in shades of

48

yellow and white. All have a pristine quality, delicate yet sparkling, pleasing in the grey rain or soft sun alike.

Another splendid new tulip is called 'Apricot Beauty'. East of the mountains, it is apricot indeed; here in Seattle, it is more of a peachy pink. Delectable anywhere, it should be planted by the bagful. Like 'Sweetheart', it is short and sturdy with terrific substance and finish. Clusters of 'Apricot Beauty' are repeated throughout the garden, each encircled by nosegays of soft pink primroses with a pale yellow eye. It is literally a traffic-stopping combination. Spreading carpets of creeping thyme and mats of felted grey lamb's ears (*Stachys lanata*) pull these and other repeated groupings together, creating a visual tie and some breathing space where colors are less than compatible.

Short but highly visible, a greigii hybrid tulip, 'Sweet Lady', has tangerine pink flowers with distinctive and lovely leaves. All the greigii tulips have patterned leaves, and these are boldly striped and stippled, burgundy on sage green. A bit farther down the path, the scarlet-and-cream 'Plaisir' spreads wide leaves of fresh green marked wine red. The leaves are marvelous together, like ikat-dyed tapestry, but the flowers must not be neighbors.

A tiny red primrose has petals neatly rimmed in gold, like banded dinner plates. The red exactly matches the emerging shoots of the Japanese peony as they spring strongly out of the ground, beet red at the base and bronzy green at the tops. The new leaves are dark green suffused with purple, each edge tinged with bronze. Those of the tree peony are even prettier, powdery pink-and-bronze leaves on dusky plum stems. Tree peonies differ from the bushy ones in having a permanent stem, almost a little trunk, which over the years gets gnarly and interestingly twisty. Those lucky enough to stroll through Seattle's Arboretum this month should go beyond Azalea Way and discover the little grove of tree peonies up past the Visitor Center. Pick up a guide map at the Center if you have trouble locating the grove; three hundred acres is a lot of arboretum, and it's easy

'Apricot Beauty' Tulip

'Sweetheart'

Stachys lanata Lamb's ears

'Sweet Lady' Tulip

'Plaisir'

Lychnis coronaria
Rose campion

'Gold Laced'
Primrose

Astrantia major
Masterwort

A. carniolica

Anemone sylvestris
Snowdrop windflower

to get lost. My own garden doesn't rise to groves of anything, yet the tree peonies with their great, elegantly cut leaves add tremendous distinction to the narrow border they will soon have outgrown. Till then, the rippled rosettes of silver-leaved rose campion (*Lychnis coronaria*) accent the ashy, muted colors of these unusual peonies.

The little red primrose was selected from a batch of seedlings out of an old-fashioned strain aptly called 'Gold Laced'. The original seedling has increased and been divided many times; there are dozens of them throughout the garden and all over the neighborhood. The ruby blossoms with their gilded lace and fresh green doily make a Victorian valentine of each clump. Properly placed, this primrose draws the eye powerfully to details like the peony stems or the copper-colored and lacy new leaves of the masterworts (*Astrantia major, A. carniolica*, and others). The odd flowers of this family reward close inspection; flat daisy-rays form a scalloped plate for an airy puff of tiny flowers, each on a slender stem. The flowers last for months, silver, white, green, or pinky rose. Masterworts are easy to please, but hard to find (try Lamb Nursery; see Appendix A), and a plant in bloom always brings requests for seed from other gardeners.

From a flurry of dissected leaves rise slender stalks surmounted by wide blossoms of pleated white silk; this is the snowdrop windflower (*Anemone sylvestris*). The satiny, scented flowers are rather like poppies, and the feathery seedheads which follow are as attractive as those of certain clematis. The heavy buds pull the thin stems down in drooping curves that straighten as the blossoms unfold until at last they are up-facing, little cups of light for a shady spot. March winds will shake them, but these delicate flowers are not as frail as they look.

Along the sunny south wall, a new note is introduced in late March by the appearance of the first iris, usually the old blue flags. Even before the first flowers of spring are withered, summer is announced. The iris, with their height and strong form, herald the overflowing riches of June. They toss their proud heads in the rowdy winds of March, and face the April rain unbowed.

Viburnum plicatum
tomentosum 'Mariesii'
Double file viburnum

THE RIGHT STUFF
Terrific trees for urban gardens

I nteresting bone structure gives definition, character, and sometimes beauty to a face from youth into old age, and so it is with gardens. Garden "bones" are delineators: paths, edgings, hedges, and certain plants, whether massive, solid, or tall. Such things direct the eye and guide, entice, or beckon the visitor on. Even the tiniest garden has need of such structure and will benefit appreciably from the judicious use of non-plant material as well as those special plants which give panache without overwhelming the smaller scene.

In small, urban gardens, the most common focal points are trees. It feels good to plant trees; they give us feelings of stability, maturity, security. When asked what to do on the last day on earth, Martin Luther said, "Plant a tree." Sound advice, with one caveat: perhaps the hardest lesson to learn is that scale must be preserved to make visual sense out of anything. How delightful to tumble head over teakettle in love with a beautiful tree, demure in its ten-gallon nursery bucket. However, it is imperative to ask the crucial question: "How Big Will It Be?" Practice saying that to yourself several times before you shop for trees; forget to ask and you can kiss your yard good-bye.

Which trees will perform well in the city, where plants must cope with pollution, poor and compacted soil, and generally adverse growing conditions? Which can be relied on never to outgrow their positions, to be healthy and sturdy, and furthermore to look elegant and distinguished all year? There are numerous fine choices for such sites; following is a very partial list, for trees are surprisingly adaptable and plenty of plants will thrive even under dubious conditions.

The most beautiful tree in the world is the double file viburnum, especially Marie's variety (*Viburnum plicatum tomentosum* 'Mariesii'). Slow-growing, it may eventually reach fifteen feet, each year bringing greater character to the graceful tiers of horizontal branches. Smothered in large white flowers like nesting doves in late spring and early summer, the heavy crop of subsequent blood red berries is just as decorative. The general effect is similar to that of dogwood, but the viburnum is a more arresting plant. The shapely leaves are large and deeply veined, stained in autumn with tones of burgundy, claret, and hock. Viburnums aren't fussy about soil, and they actually like a rich clay very well. This is good news for many Puget Sound gardeners, since our typical stodgy clay soil can be amended to suit this glorious tree right down to the ground. Viburnums need ample water but must have sharp drainage—relatively few plants like a boggy soil—and will take sun or shade in stride. Marie's viburnum has a gracious presence, powerful in a small setting without overwhelming its lesser companions. It is compellingly attractive at any season, a grand focal point for any garden.

As for dogwoods, let me make a case for a wonderful red-barked Siberian, *Cornus alba* 'Elegantissima'. A shrubby little thing well under ten feet tall, it will grace the smallest garden. One of its beauties is the bark, ripe-cherry red in winter and brightest on young growth. This dogwood responds well to an annual thinning of up to a third of its branches, which guarantees that there will always be lots of brilliant young growth. The leaves are delicious, variegated in cream and fresh green, far showier than the relatively small flowers, which are the color of old ivory and pleasantly fragrant. The leaves are warmly hued in autumn—amber and gold, pink and bronzy green.

Dogwoods tolerate a wide variety of soils and conditions, including pollution, heavy clay, sun and shade. They grow best in moist shade, where the lovely leaves will lighten gloomy urban shade. An elegant and graceful relative, the tricolor dogwood (*C. florida* 'Welchii'), slowly achieves its mature height of perhaps eighteen feet. It has an understated, Quakerish charm, its fine leaves variegated in pale and rosy pink, ivory and green.

Cornus alba 'Elegantissima'
Siberian dogwood

C. florida 'Welchii'
Tricolor dogwood

53

Prunus

P. serrulata
Flowering cherry

'Shogetsu'

'Sieboldii'

'Pendula'

'Krauter Vesuvius'
Plum

'Thundercloud'

Pieris japonica
Andromeda

They deepen delightfully in autumn to tints of verdigris. The typical dogwood blossoms are creamy pink, the bark is grey, and the whole plant is lovely at any time.

If your heart yearns for a flowering tree, try to resist those overplanted cherries, plums, and whatnot that look so very dull eleven months out of the year. Oversized specimens planted in small sites require frequent and skilled pruning which they seldom get, and are subsequently more than usually prey to a whole horrible host of pests and diseases. If you simply must, remember the size rule. *Prunus* is a big family, including peach, plum, apricot, cherry, and other stone fruits, most of them making quite large trees.

Flowering cherry, *P. serrulata*, has some daintier forms, such as 'Shogetsu', which carries quantities of soft pink semi-double flowers, is less graceless than some, and reaches perhaps fifteen feet over a number of years. 'Sieboldii' is similar, a little smaller and earlier blooming. The one real smasher of the family is 'Pendula', the weeping cherry, generally under ten feet in height at maturity. These are engaging and attractive, but slow to develop (often not a drawback in urban settings). They will eventually create areas of dense shade that require careful under-planting to avoid scraggly spots from October till April (hardy cyclamen are choice in such sites).

Among plums, a smallish purple-leaved variety, 'Krauter Vesuvius', opens pale clouds of pink flowers in late winter before the smoldering leaves unfold. 'Thundercloud' has brassy leaves and soft pink flowers; with an ultimate height of about twenty feet, this is the best bet for copper-and-pink fans with small yards. Under normal circumstances, such compact varieties should need only light aesthetic pruning.

Andromeda, or lily-of-the-valley shrub (*Pieris japonica*), is a finely textured evergreen of lilting, rhythmic construction. Arching leaves form whirling clusters handsome all year round. In spring they are set with foaming strands of white bellflowers rimmed with buttery yellow, which gleam splendidly amid the tender pink new leaves. Pieris is compact and disciplined in habit, tending to be upright and narrow. It makes a lastingly attractive foundation (house-side) plant. A particularly dashing relative is a hybrid of *Pieris forrestii* called 'Forest Flame', in which the typical rubicund spring growth is transformed to a pure and singing pink. As they age, these new leaves pass through a series of color changes, the unfurling infants a light biscuit beige, nearly white. This deepens to creamy yellow, which in turn achieves that invigorating pink. At this stage the shrub looks like a poinsettia in full fig, or an old-fashioned valentine, the dangling bunches of flowers like creamy lace. As spring becomes summer, the pink becomes lime green, deepening to the normal glossy rich color by July, a prolonged and fascinating show. None of the andromedas get much over eight or ten feet tall, and all may be kept trim with light pruning. The exact shade of youthful pink can vary a good deal, so select the color you prefer by cruising the nurseries now. Many forms will not be at their best just now; too many are burdened with new growth of that sullen shade so mistakenly admired in that sadly overplanted shrub, photinia, of which we will speak no more.

A choice and diminutive tree with particularly good form is *Parrotia persica*, seldom grown though easily suited. If you find shrubby specimens at the nursery, they can be trimmed of lower leaves to encourage the development of a dramatic plant with multiple trunks. In whatever form, this tree has flair and all sorts of style on a manageable scale, since it seldom exceeds a dozen feet in height in the city. In summer, the elongated leaves are a jaunty green, more than acceptable, and in autumn their garb will rival any maple. Gold, yellow, orange, pink, scarlet, they are streaked and splashed with all the warmest fall colors, a radiant show piece in any setting.

The fringe tree, *Chionanthus virginicus*, is a native American with tremendous purity of line. It has a grace, a felicity of detail which sets it apart from commoner things. Over the years, it may slowly reach a height of ten feet (west of the Cascades), a lavish and precocious

Pieris forrestii
'Forest Flame'

Parrotia persica

Chionanthus virginicus
Fringe tree

Styrax japonica
Snowdrop tree

S. obassia
Snowbell tree

Betula pendula 'Youngii'
European white birch

bloomer. The individual flowers are wispy and insignificant, but arranged as they are in feathery plumes, they have considerable impact. Close at hand, the flowers shimmer like strands of flossy silk. Each icy flower is touched with green, virginal and appealing. As the blossoms mature they deepen, dangling feathers of pale gold. As the lively green leaves color warmly as well, the gilded flower-feathers are well displayed.

Once rare, but now appearing with regularity at better nurseries, are a pair of plump and splendid snowdrop or snowbell trees, *Styrax japonica* and *S. obassia*. Both are shapely deciduous trees with pendulous, spreading branches embellished in early summer by most fetching flowers. Those of the fragrant snowbell (*S. obassia*) hang in long, dense clusters, so tightly packed that they form a herringbone pattern. The sweet white bells, slightly reflexed, are like flared porcelain bells with tiny golden clappers, and merit close examination. The leaves are large and deeply veined, clear, strong green with the gleam of health on them.

The snowdrop tree (*S. japonica*) has rounder, scalloped leaves of a particularly vivid green, dark but clear, a dramatic setting for its more open, shorter sprays of rounded bells. They droop elegantly from the uptilted branch tips in rhythmic symmetry. Both trees are endowed with that special quality, almost charisma, found only rarely in plants or people. Both deserve a special position in the garden, perhaps above a seat or on a slight slope where passersby can gaze up at the bobbing flowers and catch their scent. They need sun, water, and good drainage, and will reach about twenty feet in the average urban setting.

Weeping trees always fascinate; perhaps it is the opposition of the rather mournful posture with the energetic, invigorating sweep of the branches, and the sense of life imparted by their frequent and frolicsome motion. In any event, weeping trees are well placed in urban gardens. The European white birch, itself a fine tree, is often planted, but many of its most desirable varieties are neglected. One of these, *Betula pendula* 'Youngii',

'Purpurea'
Purple birch

Arbutus unedo
Strawberry tree

is enchanting at any season: when its catkins dangle like enameled green and gold earrings in winter, when unfolding the pleated fans of tender new leaves, cool as a plashing fountain in summer, rippling with every movement of air, and when coloring soft warm gold in fall. A majestic cousin, seldom grown but utterly commanding, is 'Purpurea', the purple birch. Its leaves are suffused with beet-juice purple, its twigs wine-dark. Long streams of afternoon sun turn the leaves as lustrous as glass in twenty tints of Tyrian purple. The trunks of both forms are wrapped in peeling golden bark which whitens with age, when the stark black scars of forgotten branches make the classic black-and-white birchbark patterns. With any weeping tree, there is one caution to observe: once trained (bent) to weep, the tree won't grow significantly taller, though it will fill out in maturity, so choose a plant that is already approximately the size you want. This is not true of trees with a natural weeping branch habit; whether birch, spruce, pear, or willow, they can and will get enormously tall, thus are not suitable for small gardens.

The strawberry tree, *Arbutus unedo*, though native to Ireland, has adapted nicely to life in the Northwest. Given a site with good drainage, it takes on most city conditions with aplomb. One of its chief attractions is the rough and shaggy bark, rustier in color than the similar bloody orange bark of its local cousin, the madrona. The arbutus has evergreen leaves, dark and shiny, which effectively frame the fat bunches of white flowers like coarse heather bells and the round, pimpled fruits. Both appear simultaneously, the flowers of one year jostling the fruit of the last. These are the "strawberries"; beige-yellow flushed and flecked with rose when unripe, they ripen to an eye-catching rosy red. The taste is bland rather than awful, but the Latin name, *unedo*, is supposed to be derived from the phrase meaning "I only eat one"; after you've tasted a fruit, that seems wholly probable. Taste aside, the strawberries make a cheerful winter feature in the dull grey garden. These trees can vary a good deal in habit; select the most compact plants with smaller leaves and shorter leafstems, for a rangy youngster will be a straggly adult.

It is wise to view the tree of choice in a garden or park before you make the final decision. Seattleites can be musing about type and variety while strolling through the thousands of examples in their Arboretum, many of them full-grown specimens. All are labeled and the visitor's center staff can answer questions and sell you a locating guide ($2) to what's growing there. Jot down what appeals to you, but when you get to the nursery with your list, remember to reiterate the Master Question. A tree that looks appealingly small against a canopy of mature giants might become appallingly huge in your yard.

APRIL

CROWN IMPERIALS

These architectural fritillaries are royalty among spring bulbs

I n April, people often stop by the garden to ask what "those enormous flowers out front" can possibly be. Tall strong stalks rise from rosettes of basal leaves, each bearing a crown of large, dangling bells topped with tousled crests. They look a little punk, like a pineapple that just discovered mousse, yet they have an undeniable dignity. Despite intense competition, these queenly blossoms are the showiest in the garden.

The crown imperial (*Fritillaria imperialis*) is certainly a commanding plant. The brilliant lemon yellow bells of 'Lutea Maxima' are the most often seen, but several other forms are increasingly available as these bold flowers regain popularity. 'Aurora' has bells of deep tomato bronze, and 'Rubra Major' is a toasty cinnamon red; both are lovely and fairly easily found these days. Crown imperials were once cottage garden staples with many named varieties, some with variegated leaves or flowers, that are now lost to cultivation. Long neglected and still too little known, the crown imperial is one of the easiest and certainly the most spectacular of spring bulbs.

Happily, these striking fritillaries are enjoying a new vogue. Plenty of regional nurseries (including those in Safeway grocery stores) now offer at least one or two forms, and several sorts are showing up in nursery catalogs as well. Crown imperials will grow strongly in sun or shade and will perform well in most soils. Like most bulbs, they do not tolerate standing water or boggy ground, but where drainage is fast, they are likely to succeed. Although they are large and appear dauntingly exotic, they are not prima donnas, and will give generously in return for ordinary care. When their moderate requirements are met, these fritillaries can multiply surprisingly quickly. In certain English gardens, where plantings have remained undisturbed for many years, they

Fritillaria imperialis
Crown imperial

'Lutea Maxima'

'Aurora'

'Rubra Major'

have achieved great colonies which are understandably famous attractions.

Crown imperials have a strong, architectural shape that makes them particularly effective focal points in garden beds or borders. They may be grouped in out-sized containers as well, for an uncommon patio or door-way accent. Lined along a shady path, the yellow kind gleams like lost sunshine amid the leafy murk. Thickly clustered, these oversized fritillaries lend a tropical air to an otherwise undistinguished planting. A single plant will look a little forlorn, towering over everything else like the tallest kid in gym class, but put three together and you get a dominating focal point that can unite an undefined, haphazard garden scene. Place them be-tween deciduous shrubs, in spots that are full of lush foliage in summer but may look a bit thin in spring. Feathery herbs like dill and fennel or the steely blue Jackman's rue make stylish companions with contrasting foliage that will help mask the fading fritillaries later on.

One might expect a big, showy plant like this to have a powerful scent, and indeed it does, an interest-ing blend of skunk with subtle undertones of garlic and wet dog. It is most noticeable when the plant is han-dled—the scent doesn't come and get you—so it isn't really much of a drawback. However, you will definitely not be picking them; these are not flowers for the table, even if the menu includes *aioli*. Forget it. Garden books frequently encourage us to tilt up the great bells and peer inside. Each bell holds a lingering drop of nectar which defies gravity by hanging at the throat of the blossom without spilling out. Few people view this won-der of nature more than once, fascinating as it may be.

The bulbs, which are suitably enormous, are planted in fall along with the other spring bloomers. A bulb this big wants a generous hole, about eight inches deep on clay, ten to twelve inches where soil is light or sandy. Put a handful of well-rotted manure in the bottom of each hole; the kind sold in bags is aged and will do very well, but avoid fresh or "hot" manures, which can cause virus and rot problems. Add another handful of bone meal, a tablespoon of kelp meal (if you have it), and a scoop of grit, gravel, or builder's sand. Mix it all together with a little soil until no streaks of grey are left. Cover this mixture with another scoop of sand before putting the bulb in, to ensure quick drainage. Big bulbs like this are prone to rot, so set them in place at a slight angle. You don't want them flat on their sides, just tipped a bit to keep water from pooling in the necks as the foliage dies off in the spring. The stalks will still come up straight unless you get really carried away. When the plump buds emerge from the cold ground in February, a mulch of aged manure or compost blended with a good sprinkle of bone meal will act like carboloading to strengthen and encourage the plants.

After the flowers fade, most books recommend cutting off the head to prevent seed set, which can weaken the plants and may discourage the production of offsets. Unfortunately, that leaves you with an ungainly stump of stalk that looks terrible. To avoid such frumpiness, remove only the moribund bells and leave the crest and stalk to wither. When the plant yellows and is definitely on the way out, you may amputate the remains to the ground. If the basal (ground-level) leaves are still flexible, leave them to dry out further; it's perfectly O.K. to tuck them out of sight under a light mulch or behind surrounding foliage to finish the job discreetly. Many gardeners neglect this important part of bulb culture, feeling (quite rightly) that it is unsightly and (quite wrongly) unnecessary. Bulbs benefit appreciably from being allowed to dry off this way, stalk intact. It isn't pretty, but use a few disguising tricks and let nature take its course. Given proper soil preparation and aftercare, these willing workers can begin producing offsets in their first season, so take the time to start them out right. Think of it as investing in future bulbs, future spring displays, with an unusual form of garden interest.

Cytisus praecox or
C. scoparius

MOONLIGHT BROOM
Well-mannered members
of a vilified family

As a kid, I dreaded the first day of school. The teacher would always eye me severely and say, "I remember your brother. You sit right here where I can keep my eye on you." Naturally, my brother was simply brilliant and misunderstood, but the bad reputation stuck all the same. Some of it even rubbed off on me, till I proved myself to be as docile and meek as. . .but that is not the point. I want to draw your attention to a wonderful plant from a family with a bad name, and I want you to consider its claims without prejudice. Agreed?

The most delightful spring-flowering shrub of all has got to be the 'Moonlight' broom. Long described as a hybrid form of *Cytisus praecox*, it is now classified as a form of *C. scoparius*, so you may find it listed differently at various nurseries. It's a small shrub, quickly reaching its mature height of about four feet, and spreading perhaps five feet wide. It is at its peak from April into May, a perfect explosion of popcorn flowers in butter yellow—but that doesn't do it justice. Prom-gown yellow, lemon-ice yellow, moonlight yellow. . .it's definitely not pastel, but if ever a color was both pale and bright, this is it. The shrub seems full of light, the flowers bubbling off the arching sprays in such abundance that the branches are invisible.

Let me hasten to add that this hybrid is not the nefarious Scotch broom. It will not seed itself ferociously into every garden bed, though you may find a seedling now and then (I have found two in four years and am very glad to have them). It is not rampant and scrawny, it does not combust spontaneously, and does not generally evoke the strong allergic response caused by its black sheep cousin. Besides, the assertively clean, spicy scent is worth a sneeze or two. Admittedly, it has an awkward period as the flowers fade, but it is a brief one, and the shrub is less repellent in this state than camellias or those huge white rhododendrons which decay so very obtrusively. With so many virtues and no real faults, this bush deserves to illuminate many more gardens. It is a shame that all brooms get labeled Bad Plants for the sins of their relatives.

Summer and winter, the densely packed twigs look gracefully windswept, making wild swirls of lively green. The slim, leafless stems are as spiky as a trendy hair cut and charged with the same youthful energy. Brooms can be rather straggly shrubs, at best interestingly angular, with great character but sparse bloom. 'Moonlight' is a notable exception both for flowering exuberance and for its tidy growth habit. This is lucky, because it does not appreciate being cut back. Occasional judicious thinning won't disturb it, but the shrub clearly resents hard pruning.

'Moonlight' is a wonderful plant for poor soil in full sun with good drainage, a natural for a slope or steep bank. The small, round leaves and similar appetites of the bushy smoke tree, *Rhus cotinus*, make it a splendid companion in such a situation. There are reddish- and purple-leaved varieties which make an attractive contrast at all seasons, notably 'Royal Purple'. This Dutch hybrid has leaves of plummy purple, almost black, each with a blood red edge. When the sun pours through them, the effect is of multicolored silks. The leaves of 'Royal Purple' differ from those of other dark forms in keeping their strong color through the summer until fall turns them russet flame. When the 'Moonlight' is out, the flat, cool yellow is the perfect foil for the smoldering, muted glories of the smoke tree.

If you can't find 'Moonlight' at the nursery, look for Warminster broom. This is *Cytisus praecox*, or at least it was when this book went to press. The classification and reclassification of various garden plants is a source of frustration to everyone in the field. To the ordinary gardener, such squabblings are as inscrutable as the challenges of grand masters, pushing chess pieces around the board. For many people, the simple use of

Rhus cotinus
Smoke tree

'Royal Purple'

Cytisus praecox
Warminster broom

Cytisus kewensis

C. praecox
'Hollandia'

Cytisus x
'Lucky'

Genista hispanica

Latin or Greek proper names for plants is bad enough, though the necessity for a system of nomenclature is generally accepted. Frequent changes of these already-difficult names seem abstruse, arbitrary, effete. To nursery people, it's a problem of labeling and information to the customer; try explaining that what you sold in the past as *Lithospermum diffusum* is the same as what you are now selling as *Lithodora diffusa*. Furthermore, you weren't wrong then, but you aren't wrong now, either.

Anyway, Warminster broom is another compact, relatively tidy bush, with a similar abundance of flowers and absence of obvious leaf. It too is creamy pale and well behaved, but to my eye it lacks the charismatic zip of Miss Moonlight. Another broom that looks attractive tumbling down a slope is *Cytisus kewensis*. This one is prostrate, sending out wide and vigorous arms to cover quite a good area, as much as seven feet, though it stays quite flat as it does so. Its fresh green is sprightly among somber prostrate junipers; in a mixed planting it will catch and magnify the gleams from gold-tipped junipers and lighten the overall effect considerably.

Many members of the enormous broom family make good choices for steep banks, seaside gardens, or any open, dry places where other plants can't cut it. *Cytisus praecox* 'Hollandia' is a rosy pink edition of 'Moonlight', and *Cytisus x* 'Lucky' is soft peach flushed with pink. The closely related *Genista hispanica* is another generous bloomer, a low creeper which will cover a slope with short, spiny twigs, most discouraging to invaders, and will blaze with bright gold in late spring and early summer. If you have avoided planting any kind of broom because of the bad manners of a few, try a little 'Moonlight'; it could be the start of something good.

PINCHING CHRYSANTHEMUMS
Steal a march on fall; pinch now for future pleasures

I n so many young gardens the fading spring bulbs are hustled away early to make room for summer bedding plants. A frequent and rather sad sight is that of half a dozen infant chrysanthemums in full flower, jammed together into a space suited for perhaps one mature plant. Earnestly tended and scrutinized, the poor things do the best they can, till one by one they succumb to adversity. In the end, pansies or petunias will provide the summer's display. By fall, the remaining chrysanthemums look less than prepossessing, their blooming brief and inglorious. One can only hope that the sorrowing gardener has learned an important lesson; chrysanthemums are not meant to bloom in April.

Most nurseries carry rooted cuttings of chrysanthemums in the spring, which is an excellent time to plant out anything that blooms in the fall. The fact that these plants are already opening buds is due to the average gardener's reluctance to buy flowering plants that aren't flowering. Strictly speaking, such forcing of bloom is poor cultural practice, even mildly deceptive, but who can blame the supplier for playing a few chemical tricks? Chrysanthemums are very popular plants, very easy to sell when heavily budded, but unless they are blooming, they just don't move off the nursery shelves till fall. Transplanting large, flowering plants into the garden in fall is not satisfactory; heavy with bloom, they shock easily and are more likely to die outright than go from strength to strength. Spring is the time, all right, and if the plants need flowers in order to sell well, that can be arranged.

These early-bird flowers are a bit misleading, however, since their proper season is a good six months away. It is rarely indicated at the nurseries that the flowers are for display purposes only, meant to show the color and form of the eventual blooms. The size

67

of the full-grown plant is not always given either, and it can be quite a surprise when that little snippet of a chrysanthemum turns into a young shrub. The most satisfactory way to deal with the whole question would be to post large and accurate pictures, showing over-all scale, flower size, and color. The promising cuttings, nestled in their six-packs, could be pure green potential, with no buds to dissipate their energy.

Keeping this in mind, select well-branched, deep-green plants with as few buds as possible. Avoid plants with roots dangling from the bottom, with drooping lower leaves or discolored foliage. When you get your chosen ones home, you must harden your heart and pinch off every last bud. If you don't, chrysanthemums will seldom fulfill their true function as they might. Worse yet, these possibly perennial plants may be so exhausted by trying to bloom for seven straight months that they would rather throw in the towel and die than stick around where the expectations are so high. After all, they are intended by nature and the hybridizers to bloom heavily from September till frost. It is asking a lot to expect them to do this well if they have been at it since April.

This doesn't mean that forced plants are not a good buy. Go ahead and pick out the colors and shapes you like, paying attention to the eventual size. If the labels don't indicate these things, ask the nursery people (if they don't have a clue, perhaps it's time to check out a few other nurseries). Before transplanting your chrysanthemums, a good going-over will ensure that they give of their best at the proper time. Pinch out the growing tips (the last pair of leaves and the tiny tip between them) on each stem to induce ample, bushy new growth. Cut straggly stems back even further, to just above any pair of leaves, to make your plants symmetrical. Directing the plant's eager spring energy this way results in a healthy, sturdy specimen, improved from its root system to the tips of its last leaves. Repeat this pinching and grooming whenever the plant makes about five or six inches of new growth, with the last session in early

July. At that point, you may allow the buds to set as thickly as you please; your renovated chrysanthemums will bloom generously all fall and reappear to repeat the performance.

Even well-pinched specimens can develop impressive bulk that will demand support. If you would rather not lose your handiwork to the wind and rain, give all the plants their own stakes, short but stout, when you plant them. As they fill out, secure them loosely to their supports, using double loops of garden twine. It is easy to tell if you are doing this right; if plants are secured too loosely, the wind will whip them over anyway. If secured too tightly, the trussed-up sacrificial victim is throttled. An inch or two of play is about right. By August, the stake should be invisible. By October, when the plants' volume has quadrupled and our wet and windy weather sets in, these minor efforts will pay off generously. Blossoms last a lot longer with their faces out of the mud, and look better, too. So go ahead, load up on chrysanthemums, and don't hesitate to pinch your purchases; those precocious flowers are a small price to pay for months of autumn color.

'Pleniflora'

KERRIA JAPONICA
Country charms in a city tough

F ew small gardens can afford the sheer dead weight of the average spring-blooming shrubs. Incandescent for a few flaming weeks, they relapse like dowdy dowagers, dull in summer, dim in fall, and positively subfusc in winter. It is well worth seeking out the golden few which carry their own for a greater part of the year. One such stellar plant is *Kerria japonica*, an old-fashioned shrub with easy ways and many beauties, something pleasant for every season. Each of its several forms has some outstanding qualities and, despite their air of country simplicity, all are well suited for life in the big city. Kerrias adapt nicely to sun or shade, containers or cramped quarters, and flourish unconcerned in nearly any kind of soil.

The ordinary garden form of kerria makes a smallish bush, ranging from three to perhaps five feet in girth, depending on how it likes the local conditions. In spring the arching wands are generously spangled with charming yellow flowers rather like buttercups. These appear off and on all summer, and with fall a second, paler flush of flowers may occur. Autumn also brings a change to the tapered, toothed leaves, which turn from rich green to clear gold. The branches keep their fresh green coats through the winter, adding a refreshing bit of color to the cool neutrals about them. The new growth is brighter still, and the unfolding young leaves have a fluttering grace which seems to be a common feature of Japanese plants.

A larger kerria, sometimes called butterballs, bachelor's buttons, or globeflower, has double flowers, fat little pompoms more golden than yellow (*Kerria japonica* 'Pleniflora'). There is a delightful spot in my neighborhood where this taller kerria leans over a white picket fence atop a slight rise. The long, pendant branches bend to mingle with the dandelions which thickly stud the grassy bank, and the color and form of the two tufty blossoms are nearly identical. Double kerria belongs where it can dangle and spread, since when happy it may send out branches ten feet long. Its width is not correspondingly bulky; it tends to be rather small at the base, sending out long wands in a loose cascade. Double kerria can be very effective planted at the back of the border, where the shoots can curve down to make a see-through curtain over the plants in front. It is also attractive grown along a fence or trained against a wall, especially when woven into the company of true climbers like variegated ivy, climbing hydrangeas, or roses.

Variegated kerria (*Kerria japonica* 'Variegata') is undeservedly uncommon, and could bring cool elegance to many a hot, dull garden in August. The flowers are single, a paler lemon than the type plant, and the leaves are streaked with white or cream. Some forms have a fairly even border of the lighter color, while others carry an irregular splash of rich green on a chiefly cream leaf. It makes a small, rather open shrub, rarely over two feet tall, yet spreading as much as six. Pruning can easily control this spread where room is tight, resulting in a more compact shrub suitable for small borders. Open and airy, it will not smother smaller plants it may overlie, and indeed can look smashing with clumps of sword ferns and lilies growing through the shelter of its arms. In a large tub, variegated kerria makes a strong character plant, decorating patio or poolside with élan. Under-planted with small bulbs and a creeping mat of woolly thyme, the shrub will be presentable any day of the year.

All kerrias have few, but basic, requirements; sadly, this very ease of culture has worked against them. Once widely planted, they became old hat, and now they are easier to find in old gardens than in nurseries. The double form is most commonly available, but only a few enterprising Northwestern nurseries carry other forms (which seem to appeal most to the more sophisticated eye). If you are fortunate enough to locate one of these kerrias, give it the best-prepared bed you can, since it will be with you for a very long time. When you dig up the soil, add a generous amount of damp peat moss, all .the compost you can spare, and a good handful of bone meal. Water deeply at least monthly during the first summer and fall; once kerrias have settled in, they tolerate drought fairly well. An annual mulch of compost, manure, and bone meal will keep things rolling along nicely.

Kerrias that seem unshapely or sprawling may be pruned to your taste, but the better the site and the soil, the more compact and thrifty the plant, so you get what you give. They are rarely troubled by pests or disease, and the most basic care will be rewarded by ample and long-lasting bloom. Gardening books (written with the eastern USA in mind) often remark on the short bloom season of kerrias, but the milder maritime Northwest brings out the best in these unassuming plants. Here they bloom for many long weeks in spring, and the scattering of flowers that appear sporadically throughout the summer is often intensified in the fall. Kerrias grow especially well in a partially shady place; since the entire Northwest coast can be so described, it is logical that they should perform with such a right good will here.

In their native Japan, the kerrias are still held in high regard. In ancient times, the pith of kerria stems was mixed with fish oil to make the traditional fuel for garden lanterns. The flickering light, warm gold on grey stone, is still an important feature of the night garden. Without going to such lengths, we too can enjoy the kerrias as they illuminate shady corners of our modern gardens all year long.

FULL MANY A ROSE

Revamping the traditional rose garden for year-round interest

'Peace'

Sarcococca ruscifolia
Sweet box

Azara microphylla
Boxleaf azara

T he first rose to open in this neighborhood is a hoary old bush of 'Peace'. The buds are formed by early April and a flower or two will open within the week. These first flowers are creamy yellow faintly blushed with pink, gentler than the hectic flush that develops later in the season. This rose was much planted in the post-war fifties, and still is, though not by me. While in accord with the sentiment, I find the rose itself unsubtle, not to say coarse. It is, however, a marvelously sturdy plant, and that counts for plenty. This earliest of bushes is planted against a wall facing south and west, sheltered from winds and frost, and equally from the first rays of morning sun, which can destroy a frosted bud by too sudden an awakening. In such a spot, roses will revel.

Even where conditions are less than ideal, roses can be made to thrive; it's a matter of choosing the varieties with great care. A rosery may be fitted into the smallest of gardens, provided only that there is adequate light (four or five hours of direct sunshine). Just a block or two away from the 'Peace' rose, there is just such a tiny plot. Open to the east and south, the promising buds are often blasted by the morning sun. It would be so easy to give this hopeful patch the needed shelter from wind and weather by hedging it around with box, or better yet, with sweet box (*Sarcococca ruscifolia*) or the boxleaf azara, (*Azara microphylla*). Both have potently scented winter flowers and neat leaves, as small hedges should. Room could be made for a little bench, and the windswept and forlorn plot would be converted into a snug suntrap.

"But I hate rose gardens," I hear you say; indeed, they have many faults. For six or eight months of the year, most rose gardens are less than prepossessing. These havens of horticultural horror are packed with

73

'Maytime'

'Nathalie Nypels'

'Nymphenburg'

'Just Joey'

harshly pruned bushes that are unattractive till covered with bloom. If the pruning is poorly done, they are never lovely. On the other hand, roses are difficult to blend into the small mixed border, as their shape is stiff rather than shrubby. Where space is not a restriction the shrub roses are a delightful border element, but they look hopelessly out of scale in little borders. How, then, should this queen of flowers be incorporated into the average smallish garden? A cautious segregation answers best.

The roses we invite into such a bower must have numerous strengths, since as a family they have so many weaknesses. The main qualities we seek are of course color, form, and perfume. Furthermore, we want a prolonged or repeated season of bloom, a vigorous habit (yet an easy one to prune), as few thorns as possible, stalwart health, and resistance to disease. We are interested in a variety of forms as well, wanting contrasts of height and shape of plants and both large and small flowers. Not every rose we choose will combine every virtue, but let's shoot for as many as possible.

Some excellent candidates include 'Maytime', its blossoms a lovely full apricot tinged with peachy coral, its scent warm and lingering. The bush is relatively shapely, just over three feet tall, with lustrous and handsome foliage. By our bench, let's have 'Nathalie Nypels', a low-growing and prolific little bush. It will be covered from late April until sharp frost with exquisite buds of coral pink. The flowers, arranged in loose sprays, are quite large and well formed for this type of rose, and exceptionally fragrant.

Beyond these diminutive sprawlers, the precisely chiseled buds of 'Nymphenburg', softly apricot, could be opening into bowls of blended salmon, pink, and cream. This rose has an insinuating, fruity scent, lovely pinky green new leaves, and makes a healthy three-foot shrub. We can't overlook 'Just Joey', the hands-down favorite in our yard. His flowers are large and utterly perfect, unfolding from elegant buds into ruffled doubled chalices of buttery orange sherbet—a subtle yet full and carrying color. The sturdy plants are short, just under three feet, and the fragrant flowers open for months. The bronze green foliage of 'Wild Ginger' makes a good backdrop for Joey's peachy charms, its own winsome flowers in complementary golden melon colors.

Nothing is lovelier by moonlight than white roses, and we could easily fill our little plot with these alone. This time we'll surround our bench with 'White Pet', her full skirts spreading in low swirls and spangled with hundreds of tiny roses in continually opening sprays. Behind her, we will place 'White Wings'. This taller, upright bush is smothered with dainty, quivering single blossoms with an ineffable fragrance. Wide and satiny petals hold a cluster of ruby red stamens cupped in the heart of each blossom. If we only have room for one more, let it be 'Iceberg', an older variety never surpassed for vigor, abundance, and snowy perfection of bloom.

Unfortunately, grouping roses (or any single plant) together can lead to all sorts of nasty complications. Any plant is more attractive to its special pests when temptingly arrayed in the mass. In the past, this was done to facilitate care; it is easier to carry out complicated spraying and pruning routines when the subjects are closely grouped. Unfortunately, this in turn makes the spraying even more necessary as the pests and diseases multiply in these ideal conditions. To avoid this syndrome, and incidentally add a great deal of interest to the little garden during the off-season, be creative and generous with the companion plants. Thoughtful additions can give the smallest garden such character that it remains an enticing retreat even when the roses fade. The path, however humble, can be delineated with lacy ruffles of dusty miller, sage green and silver, or low-growing lavenders such as 'Munstead', 'Hidcote', or the baby of the family, 'Compacta Nana'. Use mats of creeping thyme, the wooly grey kind mixed with rich green carpets of *Thymus serpyllum* and gold-edged pools of variegated lemon thyme. Let them spread over the path a bit; your feet will release pungent combinations of scent even in winter. The roses won't mind such shallow-rooted competition, and the lovely patterned

'Wild Ginger'

'White Pet'

'White Wings'

'Iceberg'

**'Munstead'
Lavender**

**'Hidcote'
Lavender**

**'Compacta Nana'
Lavender**

Thymus serpyllum

Lemon thyme

Viola 'Sylvia Hart'

'Stella de Oro'
Daylily

'Raindrop'

rug will please the eye all year.

Work in some early spring bulbs as well; dwarf narcissus and tulips, crocus and scillas, all on the smallest possible scale. Add clumps of violets, not the rank and weedy kinds, but little treasures like *Viola* 'Sylvia Hart', barely three inches tall, its pink flowers nodding above minute leaves of celadon green heavily veined with silver threads. The dusky Labrador violet or any of the scented ones would do nicely. Find room for some dwarf daylilies, long bloomers like the golden 'Stella de Oro' or the soft yellow 'Raindrop'. A few clusters of the tiniest iris could be easily tucked in along the edges of the beds and paths. In winter, the round and shining leaves of hardy cyclamen will add luster to the thyme blanket, and the perky butterfly flowers will lure you into the rose garden even when there is not a rose to be seen. If you have used sweet box or azara for your hedge, the scents of wild honey and vanilla will fill the chilly air. Let our small bench face the south to trap whatever thin winter sunshine there may be. A plot with such a mixed planting will quickly develop enough character to remain an enticing retreat even when the flowers fade. A comfortable and well-placed seat will encourage lingering visits and the sort of sociable interludes that rose gardens are all about. Romantics may twine a jasmine plant or two through the sheltering hedge behind the seat for a peerless midsummer experience; when rose meets jasmine, the result is pure magic.

Would you like such a secret garden in your yard? To support such magic, the soil will need all the extras you can muster, and this is a good place for Milorganite or other inexpensive conditioners that are not suitable where there is any question of edibles being raised. Add manure, blood and bone meals, ample quantities of peat and compost, and when you get it all dug in, cover it with a good thick layer of mulch to keep the animals and rain from undoing all your labor. Mark out the paths, and lay them with brick, cement, or whatever you had in mind. Did you think this would be the work of but a moment? It takes hard work to make magic, but a good foundation will last for years, and well-started plants are very long lasting, needing only routine care to keep them flourishing. Hedged in, filled with bright companions, such a rose garden need never languish ashamed or blush unseen.

MAY

BETTER BEDDERS
How to tell the dogs from the dynamite

The nurseries are full of flowering things these days, from arabis to zinnias, and we gardeners know no restraint. We wander happily up and down the crowded aisles, filling up our carts with pretty things. Among so many plants (and so many people), it's easy to get distracted and it can be hard to identify the best choices. If you've been disappointed in the past by plants that didn't perform up to expectation, a few basic tips may help you get home with a carload of winners this time.

Sturdy, compact plants are always your best bet. Taller plants (anything over about eight inches) are fine if they are in their own good-sized pots (at least four-inchers) and don't look pale or lanky. Examine the lower stem; it should be well furnished with closely spaced leaves and branches. Drooping, yellowing leaves at the base are stress signals; leave those plants right where they are. Roots should not be growing strongly out of the bottom of the container, nor should they be exposed by inadequate soil cover on top. Any of these trouble signs point to problems that will take their toll in reduced vigor and indifferent performance.

Tall, scrawny-looking plants with sparse leaves or few branches may have been brought up in a plant ghetto with no elbow room or raised too far from the light source. Sometimes good aftercare and frequent pinching can bring such a plant to greatness, but it wouldn't be a sure thing. Light green, yellowish, or mottled foliage can be symptoms of starvation, poor access to light, overcrowding, or disease. Check around under the leaves for aphids or other pests, too. Pick the plants with the deepest green leaves, even if those plants are smaller or have fewer flowers. (Many plants will flower themselves to death under stress, trying to achieve the biological imperative to reproduce.) Naturally, a variegated plant is going to look a bit different even when healthy, but in general, off-color is undesirable.

Limp, wilted, or tired-looking plants may be water-stressed. This can happen easily if the soil-less mix they are growing in has dried out even once. It is difficult to get the stuff properly wet in the first place, and once dry, it is unlikely that ordinary watering will ever penetrate to the roots. Check the size of the pot, too; in general, the more soil and room a plant has, the better its chances for transplanting and growing on well. If it has outgrown its pot, there may be too little soil left to hold water. This is a fairly common problem with those amazing spring bargains, so resist them if the plants don't look spanking fresh. In the long run, it is usually cheaper and less painful to pay twice as much for fewer but healthier plants.

An actively developing plant can fill up a small container pretty fast. Look underneath for dangling strands of roots which indicate that the plant is overdue for a change of place. If there are a lot of roots, just walk on by. Remember the times you pulled a little plant from its pot to find a white maze of tangled roots running frantically around the sides of the rootball? Such plants rarely recover well enough to justify planting them. You are going to spend a summer—perhaps even years—with this plant. Who needs more stressed-out companions?

Some "six-packs" really only have three plants, so investigate under the leaves to be sure of what you are getting. Choose the kind of container with little dividers making four or six places in preference to the kind which houses several plants in one larger soil pan. As one tears the plants apart, the root systems are invariably damaged; the resulting shock prolongs the dangerous adjustment period while the plant adapts to new surroundings. Plants grown in flats (rectangular shallow trays) often transplant badly for this reason, though a skilled, careful gardener can hand-separate the plants with little trauma. Slicing the plants apart is really not good horticultural practice, despite book advice.

Freshly transplanted plants that are heavily budded

may seem torn between the urge to renew and expand their roots and the conflicting drive to flower and set seed. If the root system is well developed and disturbed as little as possible, the transition from container to open ground will be less difficult. However, opening flowers will slow post-transplant growth, so plants already in bloom are a much better buy if they are potted individually or in divided containers with a good-sized soil pan, usually two-packs. Bearing the above information in mind, look for annuals which have many buds and flowers. They are short-lived, high-energy plants, and those displaying the most promising early growth are usually the most rewarding later.

Good follow-up is at least as important as choosing good stock in the nursery. When you put the plants in the car, protect them from direct sunlight and provide some ventilation to avoid baking your investment. Once home, leave them in a shady place until you are ready to plant. It helps to gather all your supplies in advance to minimize the running back and forth hunting for the bone meal or the beer opener while the plants lie parching, exposed to the sun and wind. When possible, it is a good plan to prepare the ground in advance, but unless these plants are going into a separate new bed, it is seldom practical. Spring bedding usually consists of setting young plants among established ones, so it makes more sense to prepare the individual spots as you plant them. Load the wheelbarrow with all the gear you might possibly want. Trowels, one big, one small. A container of bone meal, another of damp peat moss, a sack of aged manure, a small bag of lime for the lime-lovers, a bucket of builder's sand. A pail of plain water and another mixed with very mild (⅓ strength) fertilizer, which lessens transplant shock. Oh, and the plants.

A rule of thumb as well applied to small bedding plants as to trees is to dig a ten-dollar hole for a one-dollar plant and so on up the economic ladder. When this little excavation is accomplished, stir in some manure, some peat moss and a little bone meal (a tablespoon for a six-pack plant) until the dirt turns greyish.

In clay or heavy soil, be generous with the peat moss, and dig in a good handful of sand at the bottom of the hole to lighten and open the soil around the root zone. Now pour in some water, and while it soaks in, slide the baby gently out of its pot and tuck it in the hole. Spread the roots a bit, cover them with the fluffy peaty soil, and pat them in firmly. Put your two hands around the plant's neck (very loosely) and lean into it, getting those roots in good contact with the dirt. Finally, water it in well with a dilute fertilizer solution.

Once all this is done, the magic word is WATER. It is crucial to water transplants often, perhaps even twice a day in hot, dry weather, until the plants are established (showing new growth). After that, water thoroughly and deeply at least weekly; don't wait until you see flagging flowers and drooping foliage. Container-grown plants are especially vulnerable. Even with plenty of rain, mature plants can shed so much water off their large leaves that little or none reaches the soil. You may feel silly wandering around with the hose, watering in the rain, but your garden will love you for it. Besides, the right to be eccentric is practically constitutional. Given the above prescription for installation and care, most plants will settle in most satisfactorily. Assuming you have selected well, weeding the dogs from the dyna-mite, you may now rest on your laurels, reveling in the flowery rewards of a good job well done.

CONTAINED PLEASURES
Gardenless gardeners have choices too

I n Europe, where cities are old and yards are rare, flowers and vegetables are raised anywhere possible, public or private. The tiniest plot will be terraced for grapes and olives; each kitchen has a window box for herbs and geraniums; every alley is bright with bird cages and tumbling flowers. Rabbits in their small hutches share shed space with the inevitable motor scooter, and boxes of greens (for the rabbits and their owners) sit on top of the sheds.

Gardeners without gardens can do more than just dream; if you have only one window, you can still have a window box, a hanging basket, or a pot or two on the sill. (There are metal rings which hold pots securely if cats share your sun.) The rooftop, if accessible, can hold an oasis in the hot tar desert. A fire escape, fire code permitting, can host a whole container garden. Where there are walls, drainpipes, fences, even junked cars in the alley, there can be gardens.

You can buy or build planting containers or use nearly anything from old sneakers to a paper box lined with a plastic bag, a few holes punched for drainage. Thickly planted with salad or flowering favorites, the container can be practically invisible, so a less-than-dapper one is just fine. To get started, the simplest and cheapest containers are suitable. If you are making a long-term commitment to this kind of gardening, it is certainly worth investigating the various types of permanent planters for those best suited to your setting. In any case, what matters most is that the container be sturdy enough to last as long as you intend it to, whether months or years. It also needs a few drainage holes, unless you are fond of bog plants.

The soil mix you use is crucial; don't try to use dirt unless you are prepared to sterilize it in your oven, a messy, smelly job. Bagged planting soil will be adequate

85

for single-season use and can be beefed up for permanent planters by adding one cup of bone meal and half a big bag of steer manure to each twelve quarts. "Soilless" mixtures, despite claims to the contrary, are not appropriate for container planting without some significant additions. Unaltered, they can't support the growth of beneficial microorganisms necessary to healthy soil and proper plant growth. They are too light, and for large plants this can prove fatal when wind blasts the branches and the roots are ripped right out of the fluffy "soil." Furthermore, in winter these lightweights can't insulate roots as well as dirt does, so normally hardy plants may suffer extra frost damage. However, with the addition of at least twenty percent (by volume) garden soil, such mixes can be a boon for oversized containers and wherever weight is a concern.

Whatever mix you use, be prepared to feed plants more frequently than you would if they were in the ground. Use less than the full-strength formula, rotating several kinds to get a variety of trace elements. An annual top dressing of compost mixed with manure and bone meal can replace the upper few inches of soil each spring. During the dog days of summer, a refreshing drink of manure tea (dilute solution of manure and water) will gratifyingly revive flagging specimens. For any contained planting, water is of the essence. These plants will need water early and often, before signs of distress occur. Plan to water deeply at least weekly, possibly even daily for smaller pots or baskets in full sun in July. Even after rain, a well-grown container can be bone dry; bountiful big foliage may shed more water than it lets in.

Before buying anything, analyze your site; what conditions does it have? Is it full or part sun or always shady? Is it dry (under eaves, etc.) or will it be partly watered by rainfall? Is there a hose or water source nearby? Next, define your desires: flowers, herbs or vegetables, one bold accent plant or a variety? A blaze of many colors, the severity of one, or a quiet theme played on two or three notes? Now develop your mission state-

Fabia 'Tangerine'
Rhododendron

'Hotei'
Rhododendron

Myrtus communis
Myrtle

Fatsia japonica
Fatsia

Leucothoe fontanesiana
Broadleaved leucothoe

ment: "Window box, north-facing, plant for year-round interest," or perhaps, "Large half-barrel, full sun, major accent plant, permanent." How about, "Bucket and trellis, half sun, quick-growing annual vine, screen view, add privacy"? The permutations are endless, but following are some samples for several common situations. For more ideas, the large and well-illustrated paperback *Right Plant, Right Place* by Nicola Ferguson is highly recommended. Sunset and Ortho both put out useful basic books on the subject as well.

Sometimes all it takes is one big "statement" plant to pull things together. This may give you the clean, strong look you want for your entryway, by the pool, or on the patio. Visually, the container will carry almost equal weight in such a spot, so it too should be distinctive, appropriate in scale and theme with both the site and chosen plant. A trailing or weeping juniper develops distinctive character with age, and suits an earth-toned wood and tile setting down to the ground. Certain small hybrid rhododendrons like *Fabia* 'Tangerine' or the canary yellow 'Hotei' have forceful personalities and a spreading, twisting habit that has terrific impact against a smooth, flat wall, dramatic in the most minimal of modern environments. For a traditional, formal look, elegant and fastidious little shrubs like sarcococcas or a pair of glossy-leaved standard camellias in brass-banded tubs strike the correct note. An exotic substitute for a sheltered position would be a trim pomegranate tree decked with tubular fuchsia-like flowers and the familiar globular fruit in dusty red.

Larger areas may be filled with an enormous pot of shrubby myrtle (*Myrtus communis*) with aromatic leaves and pale and pungent flowers. The huge, splay-fingered leaves of fatsias (*Fatsia japonica*) make an imposing display, especially in winter when the enormous umbels of ivory florets open, followed by glossy midnight blue fruits. For Japanese-influenced architecture, a whispering stand of black-stemmed bamboo or a group of drooping broadleaved leucothoes (*Leucothoe fontanesiana*) will add luster to their setting.

87

'Tom Thumb'
Fuchsia

'Goldheart'
Ivy

'Tricolor'

'Buttercup'

'Ivalace'

'Galaxy'

'Anne Marie'

Clematis tangutica

C. flammula

'Pretziosa'
Hydrangea

'Forever Pink'

Cyclamen coum

Viola 'Clear Crystals'
Pansy

Sarcococca humilis
Sweet box

There are hundreds of striking plants for the shady site. Hardy (perennial) fuchsias thrive without direct sun; 'Tom Thumb' stands a foot high and carries lacquered pink and purple flowers from early summer till severe frost. Evergreen ferns bring a luxuriance to the nether part of your little scene; perhaps a small lettuce-edged polypody or a lacy dwarf maidenhair, the tall and prominent sword ferns, or the deep curly pile carpets of selaginellas.

Ivies contribute tidy good looks in all seasons, especially the miniature or smaller-leaved kinds. Where sun is scarce, variegated types like 'Goldheart', the pink-bordered green and cream 'Tricolor' or the lemon and lime 'Buttercup' are cheerful. Delicate texture comes from the ruffled 'Ivalace', starry sprays of 'Galaxy', or the undulating, reflective leaves of 'Anne Marie'. Let some of the ivy dangle and some climb the walls to add depth to the overall design.

You could trail a shade-tolerant clematis through the ivy as well: perhaps *Clematis tangutica*, heavily hung with little orange lanterns and fluffy seed heads, or *C. flammula*, its pale, sweetly scented flowers small but profuse. Most lilies prefer half-shade and adapt wonderfully to pot life. Smother their feet with violets and begonias or New Guinea impatiens, many of which have interesting leaves, variegated or textured for contrast.

For deeper shade, try a small hydrangea, perhaps 'Pretziosa', with gentle faded pink flowers which turn mysterious tints of verdigris and verde antique in fall, or the brighter, rosy 'Forever Pink'. Underplant the hydrangea generously with fall- and winter-blooming hardy cyclamen (maybe *Cyclamen coum*, with either red or white flowers) and clear-faced pansies in lemon or sky blue, raspberry velvet, or whipped apricot (*Viola* 'Clear Crystals'). These bloom abundantly, and if lightly pinched and pruned may live for several years. They will clamber into the hydrangea and spangle it with blossoms through fall and winter, or cascade gracefully over the tub.

Sweet box (*Sarcococca humilis*) is a dapper dwarf

evergreen with gleaming tapered leaves, neat as a band-box in every season. The sarcococcas open minuscule wispy flowers from December through March, filling the winter air with a wild, sweet fragrance. Good tub-mates would be checkered lilies (*Fritillaria meleagris*) in soft purple and ivory houndstooth tweed, the dainty rayed stars of wood anemones (*Anemone nemerosa*), and the choice creeping evergreen, *Gaultheria procumbens* with glistening leaves, small but vivid, and engaging white bellflowers succeeded by ruddy berries. With a tiny cut-leaved maple or a sprawling prostrate juniper, each feathery wing tipped with gold, this grouping would have a changing loveliness every day of the year.

A salad tub is perfect for a sunny spot. Lime green butter lettuce with ruffled pink radicchio, ferny fronds of dill and fennel, delicate sprays of salad burnet mingle pleasantly. Aromatic garlic chives, their huge white flower heads humming with bees, trailing oregano with rosy blooms, wide mounds of tiny-leaved basil, or bushy sheaves of the taller kinds all do well in such a position. Further color and scent come from lemon thyme, grey tarragon, and vigorous 'Whirlybird' nasturtiums. Train some 'Sweet 100' cherry tomatoes up a little trellis with 'Patio Pik' cucumbers and a few 'Scarlet Runner' or tender haricot beans. Some of these things, chiefly let-tuces and spinach, will clearly look worse for wear with use. One good way around this is to plant such things in smaller (six- or eight-inch) pots which are then sunk into the bigger container. Pull a depleted pot and drop a fresh one into the hole, three lettuce or spinach plants to a pot, mix or match. If you don't have much room, stick to longer-season things that earn their keep. For us, spinach ('Mazurka', or 'Bloomsdale Savoy') will always be worth growing, for others it might be artichokes (striking, but prickly) or ten kinds of basil for pesto experimentation.

The multicolored tissue paper flutters of portulaca cover dry hot spots lavishly, and newer types like 'After-noon Delight' will still be open when you get home from work. Interplant it with a fascinating variety of sedums,

Fritillaria meleagris
Checkered lilies

Anemone nemerosa
Wood anemone

Gaultheria procumbens

'Whirlybird'
Nasturtium

'Sweet 100'
Cherry tomato

'Patio Pik'
Cucumber

'Scarlet Runner'
Bean

'Mazurka'
Spinach

'Bloomsdale Savoy'

'Afternoon Delight'
Portulaca

'Beverly Sills'
Iris

'White Queen'

Parthenocissus lowii
Boston ivy
(Miniature)

Lobularia maritima
Sweet alyssum

'Antique Fantasy'
Sweet pea

tall or trailing, creeping or sprawling, for a grouping that will take drought and heat with aplomb. For a stronger, more emphatic shape, a stiff sheaf of yucca or any of the New Zealand phormiums will give the impact and drama you want.

Iris love sunshine, and the spreading fans of sword-like foliage are more attractive as specimen plants than when crammed into the border. Perhaps you would enjoy the flamingo pink 'Beverly Sills', heavily ruffled and fragrant, or that slender, refined Siberian, 'White Queen', all icy purity. Deck the feet of either with emerald Scotch moss, grey mats of woolly thyme, or long tendrils of the miniature *Parthenocissus lowii*, which will color brilliantly, come fall. For contrast and long-term color, add an airy geranium in pink or rose, and some exploding puffs of royal blue agapanthus.

Patio plantings can be a wild jumble of flashy colors, a fireworks blaze of blossoms, or an understated composition further muted by an abundance of grey and silver foliage. However you want it, fragrance deepens the pleasure; you find yourself wandering outdoors just to drink in the mingled odors. Nothing beats the pure honey scent of sweet alyssum (now called *Lobularia maritima*), and a thick planting in full sun will have you humming bee songs. The scent is most pronounced in white flowers, doubly valuable for adding zest to solid lumps of color, softening harsh tones, uniting multicolored groups, softening container edges, or accenting those deep-toned plants that smoulder dully by themselves. Add a touch of light, whether white or silver or grey, and sullen shades become as clear and glowing as dark jewels.

The soft spires of snapdragons are often very fragrant, as are old-fashioned sweetpeas (grandifloras). Many newer forms are not, and if you have bemoaned this lack, try the 'Antique Fantasy' strain this year. Although they are on the small side and their form and colors are less splendid than those of the modern hybrids, their overwhelming perfume is the genuine article, and will knock your socks off. Plant a few seeds every few weeks to prolong the bloom, and pick off dead flowers assiduously; once they set seed, the party's over. Run these twining climbers up a drainpipe covered with plastic netting or chicken wire, train them to cover a fence, or drape them about a window where you can enjoy their gentle colors and fresh, clean scent.

The potent fragrance of sweet stocks (*Malcolmia maritima*) is well known. These fluffy flowers come in a range of soft candy colors, decorative in pots or out, but unless you stake the taller kinds, they will waste their perfume on the desert air—or at least on the ants and slugs. Night-scented stock (*Matthiola* species) is just that. Mostly of a washed-out lilac color, they are not the most striking plants in the garden, but their scent is heavy and haunting and they carry on the good work after hours at no extra charge. By moonlight, they look just fine. Another dim little plant with a far-ranging perfume is mignonette (*Reseda odorata*). It has small creamy greenish flowers of no particular distinction, though they have charmed people for centuries with their unique, intense sweetness. In Europe, the scent has gradually been bred out of these unassuming flowers, and they had nearly been lost to cultivation when the true strain was rediscovered here in America some years ago. It is well-paired with the odd, fluted blossoms of flowering tobacco (*Nicotiana* species). Both 'Lime Green' or 'Green Domino' complement the cool coloring of the mignonette, and will send out insinuating trails of fragrance at night to enhance those candlelight occasions.

An astonishing number of plants will thrive on the mixture of sun and shade offered by most yards. Only experimentation and time will tell you the perfect combinations for your particular site. Happily, the process is very stimulating, the disasters relatively cheap and quickly hustled away. Faced with a newly emptied container, you sigh, you fondly remember, and you start again. Visits to other gardens lead to fresh ideas, trips to local nurseries leave you with a new treasure trove, a wave of the gardener's trowel makes all good, and if it doesn't, well, you have the joys of endless new beginnings ahead.

Malcolmia maritima
Sweet stock

Matthiola
Night-scented stock

Reseda odorata
Mignonette

Nicotiana species
Flowering tobacco

'Lime Green'

'Green Domino'

SMALL IRIS
Bearded dwarves make good company

L overs of those opulent bearded iris that so enrich the June garden need not despair if their garden plot is too small for such fulsome beauties. Even a diminutive window box can make a fitting home for certain dwarf iris, little versions of the tall bearded belles. These dwarves resemble their fair sisters in most ways, with one important exception; they are none of them over fifteen inches tall. The flowers, which are available in a great variety of colors and markings, come into bloom rather earlier than the larger lovelies: from April through June, depending on the cultivar.

Ideal for edging a walkway or brick path, many of these perfectly shaped miniature iris are only six or seven inches tall. A tiny variety called 'Brass Tacks' shines out with true cheerfulness, just the thing to light up any pathway. It opens numerous good-sized flowers with great good will, golden blossoms gleaming with a brassy splotch on each broad fall (the petals that go upward are called the standards, those that go down are the falls). 'Navy Doll', a crisply ruffled white with a bright navy blue mark or thumbprint on the falls, is pretty as paint with forget-me-nots and California poppies (*Eschscholzia* species). More exotic looking, 'Be Dazzled' is bumblebee yellow with a burgundy splash. That sounded awful to me, and the plant (a gift) was consigned to an out-of-the-way corner until it bloomed; this plant has flair.

Small, late daffodils like 'Hawera' and 'Little Gem' make flattering partners for the luminous flowers of 'Rain Dance', a ruffled, saturated blue with soaring falls. 'Crystal Bright' echoes the cool yellows of the daffodils, a sparkling little whirl of white with sun-splashed falls. Clumps of primroses, tender pink and yellow, nestle appealingly beside 'Inscription', palest yellow with soft lavender-pink markings, and the delicate 'Betsy Boo', the same suffused lavender-pink all over, but with a fuzzy light coral beard. In these combinations and groupings, everything charms but the names on the labels; apparently, cutesy appellations are irresistible to the talented but schmaltzy hybridizers.

Many bicolored flowers are more showy than attractive, but there are some lovely two-tones among these dwarf iris. 'Peppermint Twist' is what is called a plicata, each white petal rimmed with a wide, even band of purple stippled markings. 'Pixie Princess' is similar, its smooth white petals precisely outlined in china blue, cute as a bunny and multiplying nearly as fast. 'Sunny Heart' is a piquant flower, Purex white with sunny thumbprints, a zesty, energizing companion for a cluster of late tulips; the fringed tulip, 'Maja', is the same lemony color. A tall billowy columbine nods its yellow, clustered dove-flowers between Sunny and 'Clap Hands', an ice yellow plicata marked with blue, and twining trails of the glossy miniature ivy-leaved toadflax with lipped blue flowers (*Cymbalaria muralis*) weave all together in a pleasing way.

A biscuit pink iris, 'Fortune Cookie', is ruffled as an apron, delightfully tucked among the scalloped leaves and rosy flowers of coral bells (*Heuchera* hybrids). Some of these dwarves are a bit harder to place; 'Stockholm', for instance, has large, clear yellow flowers with bushy blue beards that look almost artificial. This iris looks fetching with velvety, sky blue pansies and a carpet of creeping phlox or thyme in a window box. 'Laced Lemonade', with icy, lacy petals, and 'Twink', a perky plicata of spanking blue and white, are stylish container-mates that often cause visitors to ask, "Are those real?"

Darker and dramatic, 'Nanny' is a dusky wine color that needs sunlight and the company of foamy white sweet alyssum to bring out its highlights of chestnut and mahogany. It is planted in front of a young Japanese tree peony that bears enormous buff-yellow flowers, each petal with a thin line of oxblood red which is picked up and intensified marvelously by the little red iris at its feet.

'Peppermint Twist'

'Pixie Princess'

'Sunny Heart'

'Maja'
Tulip

'Clap Hands'
Iris

Cymbalaria muralis
Toadflax

'Fortune Cookie'
Iris

Heuchera hybrids
Coral bells

'Stockholm'
Iris

'Laced Lemonade'

'Twink'

'Nanny'

93

Dwarf or Lilliput iris love sun as much as their larger counterparts, though they are far more tolerant of partly shaded situations. Some will flourish even in deep shade, so it is worth experimenting even if you don't have much sun. They are an ideal edging plant for small beds, neat and unobtrusive when out of flower, or will wind in colored ribbons beside paths. Try them in pots, containers, or window boxes, combined with bright, small annuals, or to cover the feet of larger accent plants in such positions. They associate pleasantly with dwarf daylilies and miniature roses, and groups of all three are effective at the front of the border, or wherever they can be easily appreciated.

All iris have good appetites and will enjoy several feedings during their growing season. This can be difficult to achieve with the larger iris, which are often inaccessible, clear at the back of a big border, but nothing could be easier with these little edgers, since they are right at one's feet. It is fine to use an ordinary commercial fertilizer, taking care to apply it after a good watering session to avoid burning tender roots (fertilizer should always be given to already-wet plants). Iris borer is not the problem in the West that it is in the East; out here, few pests trouble iris, but slugs can disfigure the blooms by nibbling on the buds, so it's worth the trouble to scatter slug bait or diatomaceous earth every few weeks.

These iris multiply fast but seldom need as frequent division as the big ones; in hearty soil, dwarves can be left for five or six years without reduced bloom. The best way to minimize the need to divide your iris so often is to enrich the soil well before you plant. Adding several inches of well-rotted manure and generous dustings of bone meal and cottonseed meal with a smaller amount of kelp meal will repay your efforts with better flowers for years. If your soil is acid, which in Western Washington it probably is, a little lime is a good idea: about a teaspoon per plant (and the same amount of the kelp meal if you use it). Mix all in until the soil is uniform in color, water generously, and set in the plants.

It is traditional to use small groups of three or five of the same type, placed in rough triangles facing the front of the border or bed. In very small gardens and strips where these small iris are most suitable, don't hesitate to use one or two of each. They will soon increase anyway, and if you like variety, the more, the better. The rule about planting broad, solid sweeps of everything is a fine one for large gardens and beds, but in a tiny plot, even one or two plants can have an impact.

Dwarf iris can be placed quite close together, six inches for an immediate effect, up to a foot apart if you aren't in a hurry. Scatter some seeds of gay annuals: poppies, pansies, godetia, or nemesia, to plump out the picture this first year. Rhizomes (the fat storage roots of the iris) are usually placed in a fan, a triangle, or in staggered rows to make a pleasing display as they mature. The top of the rhizome should be just under the soil; they usually push themselves out of the ground, enjoying a good baking in the summer sun. It is helpful to set each large rhizome on a ridge of soil between two shallow trenches. Spread the long feeder roots out in the trenches, cover with soil and pat them in firmly. It's better to let the rhizome emerge too far than to cover it too deeply, but the finer feeder roots must be covered completely.

Iris need both a good deal of moisture and a quick-draining soil. The starchy roots will rot if planted where the ground stays soggy, so tight soils and heavy clays need the addition of coarse gravel or builder's sand and an ample helping of peat moss to open the soil and improve both texture and drainage. Raised beds, even if only a couple of inches above the path or lawn, can greatly improve performance; iris hate wet feet. In this part of the country, established beds rarely need supplemental watering. Newly planted beds require a fair amount of water while settling into their first season. In unusually dry years, where long rainless months create a demand for extra water throughout the garden, your iris will appreciate the attention as much as anything else, established or not.

**'Beverly Sills'
Iris**

Next time you find yourself cursing the greedy big iris as bed-hogs even as you seek space to try just a few more fascinating varieties, stop and take a deep breath. Flip a few pages further on in those glossy iris catalogs, and turn to the section marked "Dwarves" for relief. You can fit two or three of these small fry into the same space required by one good-sized root of 'Beverly Sills'. In small gardens, the dainty dwarves are far more practical and more lastingly welcome than the blowsy charms of their taller relatives. Plant them practically anytime, and watch these sturdy and willing plants develop; almost before your eyes, a scrap of root becomes big enough to bloom. As the earliest flowers fade, well before the onset of the big iris boom, these dwarves will cover themselves with glory, a flowery link between the tulips and the roses. Instead of feeling bereft at the passing of the daffodils, you could be basking in the company of your own bushy-bearded dwarves.

AKEBIA QUINATA
A climber for trellising

Nearly every garden has places where a soft screening effect is wanted, one which will modify a problem view or block an unsightly one, yet not shut out the light entirely. Vines and climbing plants can perform such a task to perfection, making lacy curtains which part slightly in the breeze, creating half-seen vistas more alluring than any obvious scene, filtering light through leaves of green or gold or pink or bronze to create an unusual atmosphere.

For a generous, trailing open effect, five-leaf akebia (*Akebia quinata*) is a likely candidate. A strong grower, it has smooth purple-red stems that twine themselves around anything that doesn't move fast enough. When it can't reach any higher, it throws out loose fans of tendrils in abundance, a waterfall of light fluttering leaves. The divided leaves are like widespread hands with five oval fingers, each with a little scallop or notch at the end. Akebia grows cheerfully, tossing its sprays of spumy leaves with light-hearted grace, and obviously enjoying the defiance of gravity. It makes arching leaps across the air to the next support, its seeking tendrils curling with a carefree elegance.

Akebia is not noted for its flowers; indeed, though charming, they are hardly obtrusive. The competition is intense in spring, and such subfusc blooms are easily overlooked. They are fascinating little things, however, deserving a close examination. The buds form grape-like clusters of dull purple balls, the size of peppercorns. Each in turn unfolds three dimpled petals which widen and reflex like blown-out umbrellas. As they ripen, the petals relax and flatten, round as violet-colored plates. The stubby stamens are tightly clumped, ribbed mauve and purple balls centering each flower. When a blossom opens fully, the stamens pop apart, each tipped with a trembling drop of nectar to entice pollinating insects.

By midspring you may find flowers in all of these stages on your akebia. Mature blooms are an inch or more across and give off a wonderful fruity, complex perfume. It suggests grapes to my nose, but that may be simple association of color and form. It is a subtle rather than a pervasive scent, most powerful on warm, sunny days. The nectar lure must be designed to attract some Oriental insect unknown to the Northwest, since akebia only rarely sets its curious fruit in this area. The fruits look like warty, rounded purple bananas, perhaps four inches long. They are edible, if not precisely gourmet fare, though jam may be made of them by the enterprising.

Hardy as a rock, this little-known vine is evergreen in mild climates, but sheds most or all of its leaves in a hard frost. It comes back into leaf quickly; by earliest spring, akebia is spangled with light green leaves and tiny flower buds. This is one tough plant, dealing competently with drought, neglect, terrible soil, and any amount of light, but most luxuriant when given ordinary conditions. It requires stout support of some sort and should not be allowed to make a giant snarl. The lacy, airy quality of akebia is accentuated when the vine is used to cover arbors or fencing, and it may be trained to grow in patterns as easily as ivy.

A trellis or fan of strings, wire, or wood gives this graceful climber a chance to strut its stuff, and it will willingly clamber up fifteen or twenty feet in a single season. It can decorate a chain-link fence, a tree, or a wall, climb a pipe wrapped with chickenwire, or cover a garage in no time. If you have a problem area which you want to minimize, you can amuse yourself by creating an akebia cover screen. Training a vine to grow in patterns is rather fun, and very useful for distracting the eye from ugly views. It involves taking the seeking shoots gently but firmly in hand and explaining your ideas to them. Introduce them to the support you have ready; you may need to twine the tendrils around the wire or strings a bit. It's hard to work with very short shoots but the longer ones can be coaxed into position easily and shouldn't need tying to stay in place. Be

vigilant about your reminders and you will reap a rich reward; this plant is most eager to please and takes suggestions readily.

I am ashamed to admit that after planting my own akebia one bright spring day, I forgot all about it. It came through a long, dry summer very well, making, however, an irrepressible tangle and sending questing shoots under the porch and into the front garden where it had no business to be. There was nothing for it but to cut the whole mess to the ground and start over. It took such harsh measures with such good grace that now I never hesitate to thin or shape it heavily with the clippers, knowing that it will come back better than ever. I certainly don't recommend that you treat your akebia this badly, should you decide to try one, but be assured that this is a fine plant, not invasive or too rudely healthy, yet with an energy and delight in life that is really quite infectious.

Kurume azalea

Hino azalea

Aubrieta

BRIDGE OVER TROUBLED BORDERS
Flowers that take us from tulips to roses

A recent visitor made the incautious comment that there wasn't much color in the garden in May. Incensed, I rushed out and in short order found him ninety-three different plants in bloom. I will spare you the entire roster; suffice it to say that May is not a floral desert. The gardening literature makes much of the great floral gap that exists between the fading of the last tulips and the onset of the tall bearded iris, the peonies, and the roses of early summer. It is perfectly true that such things as are now in bloom are not as showy or powerfully formed as tulips or iris. The problem is not, however, an absence of color so much as a lack of drama, coupled with a failure on the part of certain garden writers to appreciate any flower smaller than a breadbox.

May is a month of blobby bloomers, shapeless but willing. There is, however, great beauty in the flowing rivers and spreading carpets, low mounds and creeping mats of midspring color. The scene as a whole is soft-edged, gentle, promising with the fast-developing shoots of burgeoning perennials. This makes for quiet charm rather than high and vivid contrast; lovers of the over-blown must wait till June for opulence.

If there are few flowers with enough oomph to carry visually clear across the garden, an examination of individual humble blossoms reveals piquant details that can only be appreciated at close range. There are indeed May bloomers which could be classified as spectacular —those rigid rows of tightly pruned Kurume and Hino azaleas lined along the house walls like electric pink tennis balls, or the incandescent juxtapositions of brashly brilliant deciduous azaleas—but "spectacular" has several meanings.

All the unassuming charm of the cottage garden is gathered in the tumbling masses of aubrietas, rich tangles of purples and lavenders, blues and magenta pinks. "Magenta" makes refined gardeners cringe with horror, but a surprising amount of this reviled shade may be found in their gardens all the same, masquerading as hot pink, warm red, fuchsia, or rose. Whatever you call it, magenta is a perfectly good color that simply needs careful placement to be effective without overwhelming less stalwart shades. In some cases, nature seems to know this; the hot, heavy flowers of rose campion are artfully set off by their own rippled leaves of fuzzy silver. Any magenta blossom is better for such treatment; surround it with greys and silvers, a touch of baby-ribbon pink, slate blue, and some lavender, and you have transformed the harsh into the stunning. The bold chrome yellow florets of basket-of-gold (now called *Aurinia saxatilis*) are also of an intense color, and benefit from the company of dusty miller or silvery artemisias. Like the rose campion, they are displayed to advantage amid the dusty grey-green of their own leaves. Basket-of-gold can look splendid among the darkest aubrietas; red as smoking embers, midnight or Prussian blue, and saturated purple-black, these need the brighter tones of gold and silver to catch fire and glow like stained glass.

Where a gentler yellow is wanted, another ex-alyssum, *Aurinia saxatilis* 'Luteum' (sometimes sold as 'Citrinum'), makes pools of creamy lemon sherbet, smooth and satisfying with quieter tones of blues, whites, and rose pinks. This cooler yellow does wonders for smoky blues, velvety purples, and clear oranges as well, well grouped with catmint (*Nepeta mussinii*), dusky pasque flowers (*Pulsatilla* species), gay poppies, and calendulas. Later in the season, the flat umbels of a Greek yarrow, *Achillea taygetea*, carry on this invaluable color for months on end.

Arabis has many popular forms, mostly unrefined and far too rowdy for a choice position, but the double form would be welcome anywhere. Those sold as "pink" tend to be an indefinite lavender, or a dirty mauve, but the white form is spanking clean and crisp. The delicate

Rose campion

Aurinia saxatilis
Basket-of-gold

'Luteum'
'Citrinum'

Nepeta mussinii
Catmint

Pulsatilla
Pasque flower

Achillea taygetea
Yarrow

Arabis

101

Arabis fernandi-coburgii 'Variegata'

Corydalis lutea Fern-leaved fumitory

Dicentra cucullaria Dutchman's breeches

and appealing flowers massed on sturdy stems eight or ten inches above the sea green leaves have every good quality but fragrance. A neat-leaved sort that makes an unusual accent plant is *Arabis fernandi-coburgii* 'Variegata', which carries its plain white flowers above tufts of dark green leaves, each heavily bordered with irregular white markings. A similar variant is called 'Variegata', its leaves rather bitty but pleasantly combining pale gold and green, the flowers an unassuming pink. Either of these behaves well enough to be placed in window boxes or smallish planters where they can be readily appreciated.

Such low, sprawling plants, best suited to slopes or rockeries, are not prime border candidates. For the garden proper, fluffy mounds of *Corydalis lutea*, the fern-leaved fumitory, have the same airy grace as maidenhair ferns. They are utterly content in full dry sun or damp shade, sowing themselves into cracks in walls or between rocks with determination. They are easily pulled out where not wanted, however, and an unerring instinct for the dramatic guides them to place themselves in some very attractive positions. The glaucous leaves are finely divided, a good background for the curving stems bearing sprays of warm yellow flowers. The blossoms are lipped and spurred; they perch and bob on the thin stems like odd little birds on a wire. This corydalis is almost evergreen in the Northwest; a sharp frost may blacken the outermost leaves, but with the protection of an overhanging shrub, it will carry on unscathed all winter. A close relative, the Dutchman's breeches (*Dicentra cucullaria*) always captures the fancy of visiting children; it deserves a choice spot where the curious flowers can be properly observed. They look exactly like miniature inflated pantaloons, freshly washed and hung out to dry upside-down. They are ivory white, tightly cinched at the waist with a yellow sash, and dangle from slender stems above much-dissected foliage of subdued green, the whole plant under eight inches tall. This loves a shady spot, and naturalizes nicely—a bit too nicely for some—though it is easily removed where not wanted.

Although I personally would not invite it into the border, the bold, handsome leaves and purple or lavender flowers of the moonwort, *Lunaria annua*, come into their own in May. Where soil is poor, or in odd rough corners where a pleasant plant or two would improve appearances, this old-fashioned flower will more than fill the bill. It has many common names: honesty, silver dollars, money plant, moonflower, all relating to the seedpods which succeed the flowers. They are gay in a mass, but undistinguished in themselves, being plain and mustardlike. The flowers give way to rounded seedpods which persist, silvery as coins, well into winter. In fall, the big, toothed leaves take on tints of Tyrian purple splashed with red; the combination is pleasing, if ragged. Certain upscale nurseries offer named English border varieties, some with white flowers or variegated leaves, but most of us are content to transplant a few of the ordinary sort from the alley. They self-seed abundantly, requiring vigilant weeding in spring. Although they become quite coarse plants as summer rolls on, lunarias bring welcome color and interest at two difficult times. If a spangled money plant introduces itself into your yard, let a clump or two stay, by the garage or along the back fence, and see if it doesn't win you over with its unobtrusive charms.

A splendid plant frequently found growing in old walls and along the alleys is *Centranthus ruber*, or red valerian. Garden snobs treat it as a perfect weed, yet it gives unstintingly of its very flashy flowers for much of the year. These appear early and often, airy globes of clustered florets, most often a light crimson, rising tall above neat rosettes of fleshy blue-green leaves. Stalks keep forming nearly all year, and there will be a flower head or two in all but the coldest weather. This strong-minded plant needs careful placement and certainly does not belong in any self-respecting border, but is terrifically useful for borderline spots where choicer things fail. Properly positioned, valerian will not cause problems; on the contrary, it will bloom most vigorously and

Lunaria annua
Moonwort

Centranthus ruber
Red valerian

enjoy total health while entirely independent of the gardener. It will do this practically anywhere except in boggy shade, and makes a wonderful prolonged display in dry, poor soil where little else will even try. Our alley boasts three distinct shades, a deep crimson, a softer shade of crushed raspberry, and a dull, faded pink, all very free-flowering. There are better pinks and several white varieties available from many nurseries. It is a snap to transplant seedlings, but older plants would rather die, and often do, so they aren't worth trying to divide unless you really intend to conquer.

We have said nothing at all of the columbines, the flax, the poppies and the meadow rue, the coral bells, the pansies, the London pride or the anemones, the rockroses, the sunroses, the shrub roses that fill the beds and borders, or the clambering vines that cover the house walls with bloom. Arch and trellis are smothered with rapidly expanding leaves, swelling buds, and tentative, half-opened flowers. The paths and borders are filling to the bursting point; don't sigh for April or pant longingly for June, simply look at May and be glad.

JUNE

TALL IRIS

Border queens with funny hats

'White Lightning'

I s there anything more spectacular than the bearded iris in their short season? The newer varieties
command our attention, as compellingly attractive
as royalty. In fact, they have much the same air of gracious majesty as the Queen Mother, and much the same
taste in hats. Perhaps it's that they look rather like her
hats, especially those enormous, ruffled ones worn at
the famous summer teas. Like the Q.M., the new iris
draw a crowd of admirers the moment they appear, and
nearly everyone who passes the garden comments on
the progress and quality of their bloom. Some people
seem doubtful that these huge and exotic blooms really
are iris. Clearly, iris hybridizing has resulted in some
spectacular plants; those of years past are left in the dust.

Modern iris are very large indeed, carried on stout
stems so loaded with buds that each stalk requires its
own stake. Such high bud counts mean that these iris
open bloom after bloom, prolonging the show considerably over the traditional two or three weeks. In another
striking improvement, the muddy pinks, dirty yellows
and flat, dull reds of old have been superceded by clear,
ringing tones of all those colors and more. Development
of stylish form has led to the rise of several distinct types;
some iris are ruffled, some fringed, while others have
recaptured the flaring, arching purity of shape so delightful in certain species iris. All bloom with great good
will, and the multi-branched sorts can keep it up for
more than six weeks. With more early and late bloomers
introduced every year, it is increasingly possible to have
iris in bloom for nearly two months.

In my yard, 'White Lightning' starts things off with
a bang. It is heavily budded, each sparkling white petal
deeply finger-ruffled and wide spreading. The fragrance
is intensely clean, the beards are intensely lemon yellow,
and the whole thing is intensely pleasing. It's on the

107

Meconopsis cambrica
Welsh poppy

Mimulus species
Monkey flower

'Lacy Snowflake'
Iris

'Lady Madonna'

'New Moon'

'Debby Rairdon'

'Acapulco Gold'

'Sapphire Hills'

'Sailor's Dance'

'Victoria Falls'

short side, about thirty inches tall, and looks fresh and energizing with yellow Welsh poppies (*Meconopsis cambrica*), soft mounds of sweet alyssum and golden orange monkey flowers (*Mimulus* species). It is a superlative cut flower as well, smashing with an armload of lilac.

Among white iris, 'Lacy Snowflake' stands out, a feathery, fluffy thing with scalloped falls (the part that goes down) and crisp, tightly closed standards (the part that goes up). The beard is touched lightly with buttery yellow, giving this snowy flower a glowing throat. The brand-new 'Lady Madonna' is the color of fresh cream, its petals more ruffled, laced, and fringed than a Fifties prom gown. With rounded, arched standards and full, tumbling falls, this flower is simply outrageous. It gets stolen faster than anything else in the yard, the hands-down favorite of the neighborhood.

Clear yellows are invaluable as buffers and blenders of stronger colors. 'New Moon' is a saturated chrome yellow, clean and showy. Winner of many medals and awards, it has splendid finish and substance, a long-blooming showpiece in any setting. The famous 'Debby Rairdon' is palest butterscotch with a large cream splotch on the center of each fall. Miss R. has been a garden classic for many years and is highly regarded as a pleasing intensifier of nearly any deep color. For sheer pizzazz, 'Acapulco Gold' can't be beat. It has remarkable form and sends up stem after heavily budded stem of luminous, brilliant blossoms heightened with white at the throat, gleaming and glorious.

Among the hundreds of blue iris, a magnificent few stand out. 'Sapphire Hills' is one such; true sapphire blue, huge and shapely, it is a dazzling flower. The falls are waved and finger-ruffled, the standards are stiff and crisp, the beards are powerfully blue, and the whole is very fetching indeed. 'Sailor's Dance' has a definite and cheerful personality. Its line is clean and uncluttered, wide-flared and fluted, and in color it is deepest sea blue with a paler beard. It has a distinctly lilting manner, and is highly approved by the you-pick crowd (they have good taste, if poor manners). 'Victoria Falls' is another award

'Lovely Kay'

'Storybook'

'Love Duet'

'Beverly Sills'

'Ovation'

'War Sails'

'Black Dragon'

'Warrior King'

winner with character, that quickly builds a big clump. Clear-water blue flushed white, it was named after the great African waterfall, and captures something of the feeling of a huge mass of tumbling water, touched with white foam and lightened with spray. It is heavily ruffled, with strongly upright standards and wide, spreading falls, pleasantly fragrant and totally beautiful.

True pink iris are splendid additions to the border. Though they were once rare, there are now so many good ones that it's hard to choose a favorite. None are lovelier than 'Lovely Kay', smooth orchid pink and most elegantly formed. She has nearly horizontal, flaring falls and standards arched like a ballerina's arms, the whole flower poised *en pointe*. The raspberry cream of 'Storybook' finds echoes in the charming faces of the strawberries-and-cream pansy 'Love Duet' at its feet. 'Storybook' is a romantic, lacy blossom that looks too ethereal to be a good garden plant, though in fact it is very strong and healthy. The flamboyant 'Beverly Sills' is appropriately bubbly, a top-notch performer and very fast on her feet. Coral pink with effervescent highlights, she multiplies incredibly quickly and sends up an astonishing number of irresistible flowers—at least, in my neighborhood they are. On a completely different scale, 'Ovation' is a smaller flower with unmatched subtlety of markings. Nothing else comes close to this depth of pink. Each blossom is beautifully sculpted, with a texture like heavy silk and a fine fragrance.

The play of light and color in a mixed border is enriched by those heavy, dark colors that give depth and weight to the brighter, lighter tones. Well placed, 'War Sails' glimmers like a bowl of rubies, rich and rare. It is a sumptuous clear red, smooth and gleaming, with lovely full form and many fat buds. 'Black Dragon' evokes the paintings of Georgia O'Keeffe; it has unmatched presence, and, backlit by the morning sun, it takes your breath away. 'Warrior King' has similar strength of character. Tall and powerful, it seems carved out of mahogany. In full sun an inner flame of searing red bursts in its heart, cooling to smoking embers at the

'Modern Classic'

'Dover Beach'

'Bubbling Over'

petals' tips.

There is a price for such wealth, and it is a stiff one. The plants themselves are not particularly costly, but they require a great deal of room with their vigorous, questing roots and spreading ways. Bearded iris have far too much energy for the average small garden; in a large border, they can be left undisturbed for three to five years, but in little beds, they are likely to need division every other year. They are gross feeders, wanting the best soil, the best and most food, a great deal of arduous hand-weeding, and all the sun they can get. In a word, they are hogs, these great queenly things, and greedy as children.

One solution is to confine them to half-barrels, choosing new kinds every couple of years and distributing the old plants among your friends. This will give you lots of variety and make you very popular. Once you let the iris loose in the border, you are doomed to give up a lot of space for what, despite improvements, is still essentially a rather short period of bloom. It is annoying to have large patches of unexciting leaves all summer and fall where prime border turf is given over to these immoderate creatures. Unfortunately, they do not share well, and nothing they are partnered with in an attempt to prolong color and interest in their area can stand up to their overbearing habits. They are royalty, and will not be gainsaid.

There really is no perfect way to control these magnificent plants, and every few years I tear them all out in disgust and give them away, declaring that from now on we will grow only the better-mannered Siberians, the dwarf varieties, and the several quietly spectacular species that thrive here. Yet somehow, these voluptuous, blowsy iris always charm us again. How can anyone resist the ravishing 'Modern Classic', a bold white with neatly embroidered stitchery outlining each petal in violet? It is too beautiful to pass up. And 'Dover Beach', so modestly cheerful with standards as white as sheets and falls as blue as the summer sky. 'Bubbling Over', an energetic frenzy of ruffles, can scarcely be contained, it grows so strongly, yet its quality is outstanding. . . . What is one to do? Sigh, and buy, and start again. Iris have that magnetic, fatal attraction for fond and foolish gardeners. Weak of will, we can't do without them; before we know it they are back, more than ever. We grumble and complain endlessly until for a few magical weeks, they bloom. And bloom. And bloom. We are silenced. Quietly we resume the endless round of chores, but this time with a heart full of praise. After all, there is nothing like an iris.

TEENY ZUCCHINI
Vegetable infanticide could be for you

There is something rather touching about the first tiny zucchini. It is so small, so tender, so innocent-looking. It is the harbinger of full summer, the herald of wonderful things to come, and like many a cutie it can develop into an oversized monster overnight. The obvious course is to eat it before it multiplies. When people whine to me about how nobody wants their wonderful zucchini and then produce a huge blob like a swollen baseball bat, I have no sympathy for them at all. If those dreadful gross objects had been picked in their prime, you can bet there would be plenty of takers.

The problem, of course, is greed. Greed and pride. Don't I know it? It takes a real effort of will to force oneself to pick vegetables in their infancy when we all know that the neighborhood kudos goes to the guy whose cucumbers weigh six or eight pounds and who complains that picking snap peas one at a time is giving him a bad back. The answer, of course, is education. Education and greed.

Greed enters the picture when a fellow decides that more and bigger gives him a better return on his sixty-nine–cent seed packet. If he can get three or four hundred pounds of food from it, he's way ahead, right? Spare me. On the other hand, properly introduced (education), greed saves the day. This is how it's done. Go to the garden together, knife in hand. Select several of the smallest, tenderest zucchini you can find and cut them off (five inches is just about right). Now let Mr. Big choose one of the giant leather ones, a two-footer. Hack that one off as well, and repair to the house. Ready?

Put a teaspoon or so of good olive oil in each of two frying pans (saute pans O.K.). While the oil heats up, rinse zucchs and pat dry. Trim ends and put the babies into one pan whole. You may slice or dice or cut jerky-like strips off of grandad, whatever you like, and put an equivalent amount into the other pan. Coat both sets with the oil, gently rolling and tossing to cover evenly. When this is accomplished, cover both pans and let them steam for a moment or two. You may spend this time profitably by stepping out the back door and pinching a bit of tarragon, chives, thyme or basil, but be sure to put the same amount, very little, in each pan. Now, the big moment. You and Big-is-better both do the taste test, and you have just converted your first practitioner of vegetarian infanticide. Way to go!

The same idea holds true for many strong growers. Lettuce, for instance, ought to be buttery, and softly, not aggressively, crisp. This perfect condition is quickly outgrown, so that salads made from row thinnings are often better in delicacy, texture, and taste than the over-developed grown-ups. Spinach too can be picked as soon as it has six or eight leaves. Don't strip the plants, of course; choose a leaf here, a leaf there, thinning and shaping as you go. Raw pattypan squash are tasty in salads if picked when just a few inches across, and beans and pea pods are tenderer and most sweetly flavorful when under three inches long. Tiny beets can be quickly steamed whole and marinated in a light dressing while still hot. With beets arranged in alternating rows with a mixture of sliced baby cucumbers, fresh red onion, and yogurt, this salad is pretty and cool on a hot night.

Young salads and vegetables need lighter, fresher dressings than the heavy, oily kinds which serve to disguise and minimize the texture and taste of winter produce. You might as well be eating Mexican iceberg lettuce in January if you toss a handful of baby greens with creamy ranch or blue cheese. The best way to appreciate produce from your garden is with the simplest dressings. Fingerling carrots and new potatoes need only butter and a dusting of fresh dill or a sprig or two of fennel to achieve perfection. Almost any young vegetable tastes splendid if quickly steamed and drizzled with fresh lemon juice and butter, but the subtle addition of tarragon or savory to the steaming water makes a pleasant change, very effective with sweeter things like corn, carrots, or peas.

If you pick more small fry than you can use right away, go ahead and steam them, then plunge them, still warm, into a marinade of olive oil and herb or fruit vinegar. Add a few snippets of dried apricots, fresh peach slices, or something of that nature, and the next day the results will lend mixed greens an unusual grace. Don't feel bad about robbing your plants, either, for the best way to keep annuals of any kind productive is to pick steadily and thoroughly throughout the season. Who wouldn't rather gather sixty or eighty tiny, succulent little courgettes over the course of a whole summer than harvest ten or even a hundred baseball bats? True, those great hulking things are impressive, but think how silly they'd look in a salad bowl.

DIMINUTIVE DAYLILIES
Generous and prolific border babies

'Stella de Oro'

D aylilies have been subjected to perhaps the greatest hybridizing push any plant has experienced, and the results are fantastic. This is not always the case with manipulated "improvements," but daylilies have such sunny dispositions that all the tinkering in the world can't sour them. Some are as exotically breathtaking as orchids, while others retain the old-fashioned charm of the species. Most interesting of all to city gardeners are the dwarf (short) and miniature (small-flowered) varieties. Compact and free-blooming, they are wonderfully suited to the smallest gardens, container plantings, or even window boxes.

One such shorty, 'Stella de Oro', is getting lots of good press lately as a front-of-the-border plant with style and charm. In the Northwest, Stella is famous for having the longest continual season of bloom of any daylily around, and that is saying something. Generally between ten and twelve inches tall, depending on local conditions, this prolific creature has warm yellow petals, slightly ruffled and curled, a tiny grass green heart and a soft, fruity fragrance that smells of summer. Stella has won most of the prizes known to the daylily world, and with good reason. Dependable and lovely, she is untroubled by pest or disease, and daytime workers will appreciate her thoughtful habit of holding her flowers open all evening. Stella is widely available at widely varying prices; one very reasonable and practically local source is Donna's Lilies of the Valley (see Appendix A).

There are a whole flock of similar small daylilies which will contribute strongly to the garden picture through the summer months. These shorties tend to be long-blooming, but their garden usefulness doesn't end there. Their fresh, green leaves burgeon just in time to conceal late-fading bulb foliage, and in fall they take on warm tones of tobacco and rust, attractive with the late sedums and asters. Most of the dwarf daylilies will range between ten and fifteen inches in height, but will vary from garden to garden, reflecting local conditions. Cultivars can be chosen for a long succession of flowers from April through October—and beyond, in a mild year.

The first daylily to bloom in my garden is 'Gold Dust', sunny and fragrant. This one dates back to the turn of the century, but doesn't show its age a bit. Like many hybrids, it is a "repeat bloomer," sending up additional bud stalks later in the season. Soon 'Double Cutie' opens greenish flowers, each with an extra ruff of petals tucked into its heart. This one looks charming in front of late tulips like the icy yellow 'Maja' or the elegant 'Court Lady' in cream and green. Another daylily that suits such company is 'Eternal Blessing', a warm near-white splashed with palest green at the throat. It has particularly good finish, smooth and cool-looking, and makes a delightful understory planting for that dapper grey shrub, Senecio greyi (also sold as S. laxifolius, or even S. 'Sunshine').

Early summer brings another award winner, 'Little Grapette'. This fetching and fragrant flower is as purple as ripe grapes, its small, neat throat intensely green. This greenness of throat is an attribute currently much prized by daylily fanciers, and indeed it is most attractive, enhancing as it does so many colors. Lovers of green flowers will join me in admiring 'Sweet Pea', with blossoms the color of a half-ripe lemon deepening to unusual pea green throats. It is evergreen, so the leaves are pleasantly rushlike all year, except in a real cold snap.

For a warmer wash of color, pair 'Squeaky', bedecked with starry, deep yellow flowers, and 'Tiny Pumpkin', this one covered with round rich orange blossoms. Combined with low, sprawling nasturtiums like 'Whirlybird', with Latin-bright flowers of flame and coral, orange and scarlet, gold and singing yellow, they are cheerful indeed. For greater and long-lasting effect, back the entire group with spangled cosmos in the heavy, hot sunset colors of Cosmos 'Bright Lights' mixture, and the whole area will glow.

Double flowers are often coarse and clumsy, but 'Pojo' is very pretty, its ruffled multi-petaled blossoms like deep yellow rosebuds. 'Double Sunset Glow' is perfectly splendid; peachy beige streaked with evening tones, it seems to go with everything in the garden. The petals are tightly whorled at the center, the wider outer sepals relaxed. With burnt orange monkey flowers (*Mimulus* 'Calypso Gold') in front and tangerine-colored Peruvian lilies (*Alstroemeria* species) behind, this brocade of interwoven texture and tone is a knockout for nearly three months.

The dog days bring out the best in 'Thumbelina', a sturdy multi-branched plant with flowers of smooth, glossy cantaloupe. Little 'Raindrop' also likes the heat, opening fragrant butter yellow flowers, ruffled and round, and quickly making a satisfying clump. This cool, pale yellow makes a perfect foil for the taller 'Prairie Blue Eyes', a stellar cultivar of royal purple with a shallow, cup-shaped heart of glowing lemon and a faint eye of incredible blue. This one is worth rising early to see at its bluest and best. In partial shade, the heat of late summer just seems to intensify the blue of this uncommon cultivar.

A delicate beauty, the orchidlike 'Buffy's Doll' is appropriately baby pink with a rosy eyezone (a band of color between the throat and the outer edge of the petals). Clumps of this dainty flower are delightful among the spreading skirts of the low-growing rose, 'The Fairy', with multitudes of palest pink roses in tiny sprays. Interspersed with all this frothy pinkness, the vivid 'Fox Grape' adds a piquant note. The big blossoms are dusky purple with a silvery "watermark," pleasantly fragrant and very different.

There is a good deal of controversy in daylily circles over the relative size of flowers on dwarf plants; some like them big, others prefer them tiny, in scale with their height. The miniature daylilies have blossoms that are less than three inches across, though the bud scapes may be quite tall in some cases. 'Melon Balls' is a good

'Pojo'

'Double Sunset Glow'

Mimulus 'Calypso Gold'
Monkey flower

Alstroemeria species
Peruvian lily

'Thumbelina'
Daylily

'Raindrop'

'Prairie Blue Eyes'

'Buffy's Doll'

'The Fairy'
Rose

'Fox Grape'
Daylily

'Melon Balls'

'Simple Gifts'

'Little Wine Cup'

'Red Mittens'

'Little Much'

example; it carries a seemingly endless bouquet of little, ruffled flowers on twenty-inch scapes. 'Simple Gifts' has round and peachy blossoms of a similar size, but on twelve-inch scapes. Many of the mini-flowered varieties bloom so heavily that their garden impact equals or exceeds that of their bigger-bloomed buddies; 'Little Wine Cup', a heady burgundy, 'Red Mittens' in clear, light scarlet, and the citrus-colored 'Little Much' all rival 'Stella de Oro' in energy and performance.

There are a number of regional nurseries specializing in modern daylilies, many of which offer a mail-order catalog. This is a fine way to discover the new daylilies, but if at all possible, try to visit a garden or nursery where some of these recent cultivars are grown. For one thing, it is always best to see a plant growing before you buy it, as catalog descriptions rarely coincide with our own perceptions of color. For another, daylily fanciers tend to be friendly, generous, and knowledgeable; you will probably leave with more than just a few new plants. You will certainly gain some solid cultural information, and you may make some lifelong friends. I must add a word of warning, however; these diminutive daylilies are impossible to resist. But why try? The new daylilies transplant well any time of the year, quickly building up to good-sized clumps. This girl-next-door made over can outperform many a sulky border beauty, returning a minimum of care with a generous outpouring of bloom year after year.

FERTILIZING FLOWERS
Sex and the single alstroemeria

Ligtu hybrids

A spray of alstroemeria in a tall glass is a wonderful thing. The blossoms, shaped like ruffled champagne flutes, come in a full range of clear, luminous colors. What we buy for the table are generally the Ligtu hybrids, which can be rosy red or lavender cream, bright coral or tawny buff, soft pink or silky apricot, cool grapefruit or pale lemon, warm pinky gold or hot fuchsia, all dappled with deeper tones of chestnut or mahogany. Lovely and long-lasting as cut flowers, they are even more spectacular when blazing away as a thriving clump in the garden.

Confusingly called Peruvian lilies (they are native to Chile), alstroemerias have a hothouse look belied by their tough constitution. For Northwest gardeners, alstros are hardy perennials, easily grown from seed or nursery stock. Many regional nurseries carry the Ligtus now, and there are more mail-order sources each year. A number of seed houses, notably that of Thompson & Morgan (see Appendix B), offer a broader range of species and hybrids.

Like many strong and persistent plants, alstros can be a bit tricky to get started, and many good gardeners have come to grief over this mercurial perennial, chiefly through an excess of zeal. It can be so puzzling to fail repeatedly with such a plant, and then to hear others complain about how the plant in question is taking over their gardens. If you have found alstroemerias difficult in the past, read on and be heartened.

One problem can be that of expectation; alstros will contribute little or nothing to the general scene in their first year. Impatience must be curbed, however, and the alstros left to settle in despite their poor performance. If they survive that first winter, they improve rapidly, often blooming freely but at half-mast in their second year from seed. Nursery plants should perform normally

119

Alstroemeria aurantiaca 'Moerheim Orange'

A. pulchella

in their second season in your garden, and by the third summer, both seedlings and transplants will achieve a triumph of trumpeting bloom at their full mature height. The Ligtus bloom from late May through the summer; the older the clump, the longer it will bloom. Other varieties, especially *Alstroemeria aurantiaca* 'Moerheim Orange' and *A. pulchella*, will carry on well past Thanksgiving in a mild year. Often, budded stems may be picked in late November; brought into the house, they may still be opening at Christmas. Whatever the variety, an established clump is breathtaking over a long period, and well worth the patience and mild effort required.

Whether sown in spring or fall, alstroemerias germinate freely from seed. This is good, because while many species and varieties are available as seed, locating plants of anything other than the Ligtus is difficult. Both plants and seeds are generally offered as a blend or mix, and it can be impossible to find just that particular shade you really love. Since all are beautiful, it may not matter to you, and the luck of the draw may bring exactly what you want. If not, why not try something completely different?

Buy a sheaf of your favorite kind, cut an inch off the bottom of the stems, and put them in a deep vase. O.K. Get a Q-tip. Pour yourself a glass of wine. Relax. O.K. Now, take the Q-tip, and gently swoosh it around inside the flower. The idea is to transfer pollen from the anthers to the stamen (see diagram). Do this several times, going from flower to flower. Look at pictures of honey, buzz softly, establish the mood. Stay loose. Remember, it should be fun for everybody.

If all goes well, in a few days you will notice a swelling in the base of the flower, and the petals will fade and dry up sooner than is usual. When the seedpods are puffed up and full as little ribbed balloons, reduce the water to about an inch and let the stalks dry out naturally. This will quite often produce ripe and fertile seed. When the pods are fully ripe, they begin to explode violently, casting the seeds far and wide. Pull the

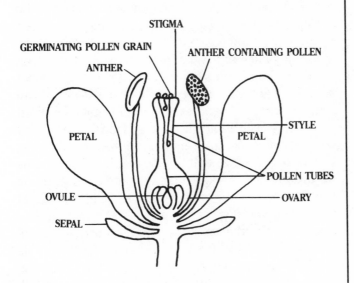

pods off the stems and put them in an envelope or a loosely closed paper bag. They go right on shattering but the seeds stay put.

The seeds resulting from this curious act may be sown either in spring or fall. If possible, it is well to sow them *in situ*, digging the soil deeply and adding peat, aged manure, bone meal, and compost. Alstros really love fish, so if you know any sportsmen, beg some heads and tails and plant them Squanto-style. Bury those fish deep, or every cat in the neighborhood will know your name. Seeds may also be started in good-sized peat or plastic pots, using a nice, fluffy, light soil mix.

There are a few simple tricks which help in getting the seedlings through their first winter, the hardest time of their long and useful life. Most failures with alstros result from mistakes at this stage, since, properly established, they are rarely troubled by weather, pests, or disease. Because the seedlings resent transplanting, handle them with care, and avoid disturbing the brittle roots when setting them out (this goes double for nursery transplants). If seeds are direct sown, it is

Dianthus
Pink

Stachys lanata
Lamb's ear

crucial to mark the spot very clearly. A few twiggy sticks strategically placed will discourage lounging cats and cruising dogs, and possibly even prevent us from planting something else in an apparently bare spot. This is especially important because most alstroemeria seedlings have a trick of apparently dying back in late summer their first year. No amount of water, fertilizer, or coaxing will bring them back. Don't despair, and definitely don't dig them up to see if they are dead, as I used to. Just leave them alone—with a good mulch for the winter—and they'll come home and bloom for you the next year. Be vigilant about keeping their places marked so you don't try to put daffodils there in October. Root disturbance, especially in this dormant stage, is generally fatal.

In the spring, the little whorled stalks will reappear, often only about a foot tall. These wimpy-looking shoots may well give you a mini-preview by opening a spray of two of blossoms, some of which may even set seed, which of course can be gathered and dealt with all over again. During this stage, the small, fingerlike root fattens up and dives down, burying itself ten or more inches deep. This great depth of root effectively protects the established plants from frost damage, and once they have achieved this step, they are practically permanent. A well-prepared soil really pays off, making this burrowing stage easier for your alstros, and resulting in healthy, sturdy plants which are better able to withstand wind and rain.

Once a clump is established, you can carefully introduce shallow-rooted plants with earlier and later bloom for prolonged color. When dry, the tall stalks of the alstros can be pulled cleanly out of the ground, and whatever is interplanted will take on a ground-covering role. In deeper borders where low-level planting would be ineffectual, use taller late bloomers in front to hide the gaps. Silvery foliage plants like pinks (*Dianthus* species and hybrids), the various dusty millers, or lamb's ear (*Stachys lanata*) make attractive companions, as do late-blooming daylilies and the taller hardy geraniums, perhaps *Geranium pratense* with soft blue flowers and large, lacy leaves, mixed with the early purple *G. tuberosum*.

Most alstros are born floppers, needing at least moderate staking. They are not heavy plants; a few bamboo wands and some twine should give sufficient support. Such props can be quite low, and as the new leaves lengthen, the network of string and sticks becomes invisible. An excellent way to use alstroemerias in a low-maintenance setting is to place them among groups of small shrubs. Low-growing junipers or salal, for instance, will lend their unobtrusive support and provide attractive contrast as well. With its airy, open structure, slender grey leaves and clusters of blue flowers, 'Bluebeard' (*Caryopteris* species) fills the bill nicely too.

Alstroemerias want all the sun the Northwest can offer, though they will accept an open, partly shaded position. In full sun, and where drainage is very free, they may need additional water during their spring burst of active growth. Where full sun isn't an option, improving drainage and soil will do wonders. At no time will they tolerate standing water, and in partial shade, good drainage in the winter months can mean success instead of failure. The typical Seattle clay should be well amended as usual, with the addition of a good handful of fine gravel or coarse builder's sand to loosen up tight soil. Mix it all in, nice and deep, so those probing roots can find what they need. As clumps mature and spread, they seem to adapt to whatever soil is around, but improving conditions initially really pays off when getting those first plants established.

When you feed these eager bloomers, juggle a variety of fertilizers for greater range and balance of trace minerals. Alstroemerias have a good appetite, and appreciate a monthly feeding when in active growth. Commercial preparations are fine, but as a general rule it is better to use them diluted, at about half the suggested strength, to avoid shocking or burning young shoots. Any plant should be well watered before being fed, since fertilizers can burn even mature specimens if applied

Geranium pratense

G. tuberosum

Juniper

Salal

Caryopteris 'Bluebeard'

**A. aurantiaca
'Lutea'**

to dry roots. Compost and manure tea can be added anytime without harm. One ardent local gardener feeds her collection of alstroemerias dilute fish emulsion each Friday and is rewarded by legendary bloom. An annual fall mulch of aged manure mixed with a handful of bone meal and plenty of compost can be laid on quite thickly; as much as a six-inch layer would be welcome. Such care will reward you in both amount and quality of bloom; a patch treated this way may last over ten years without renewal.

It is possible to find robust old specimens of alstroemeria in older gardens throughout the Northwest, most commonly the superhardy species *A. aurantiaca* (orange) or its yellow form, 'Lutea'. Check out plantings in abandoned lots or neglected gardens in older neighborhoods. These alstros are often free for the asking. These toughs transplant very easily; just take a shovel and chop out a good, deep chunk. They will flop and droop at first, but perk up amazingly fast with lots of water. These are survivors, but be warned by their very hardiness; if happy, they are rampant spreaders, and will take all the space they can get. Other species, and the Ligtus, are not quite this bold, but they are all spreaders by nature. As clumps mature, controlling their spread may become a concern, but established plantings can be judiciously thinned when going dormant. Bare patches in the interior of an older clump can be filled by tucking seedlings in peat pots into the gaps.

Since every root will send up numerous stalks, there should soon be plenty to cut for the house without diminishing the backyard display. Some of the hardier types act like cut-and-come-again annuals, sending up a second flush of budded shoots after the summer's show is over. Don't be put off by the admonitions to take care; alstros really are simple to raise, given gentle handling. Once established, a minimum of care will net you a maximum return; a few seedlings sown now could bring you years of pleasure as you savor these bright trumpets indoors and out.

JULY

WAR
Guerrilla gardening at its best

I t's time to loosen up the old throwing arm and get out the binoculars. Spring is back, the flowers are flourishing, and the war is on. Urban gardeners may not have to worry much about deer or rabbits, but there are other forms of fauna quite as bad from which city gardens need zealous guarding. Cats, dogs, squirrels, and other terrorists abound, each worse than the other. Would-be guerrilla gardeners need a wide-ranging arsenal to be ready to face the foe of the hour. A stock of whiffle balls, perhaps kept in an attractive basket on the back porch. A whistle, the louder the better. Bird glasses, if you are part of a neighborhood Garden Watch network. Various repellent sprays, like Chaperone, Doggone, or Katscat.

For cats and squirrels, whiffle balls are tops. With practice, you will quickly develop the skill of hitting the creature while sparing the plant it is doing unhelpful things to. My husband is especially good at this, and one prime shot remains golden in my mind. A fat little brat was digging up my hardy cyclamen corms under the lilac, a tasty salad for a city squirrel. It had already tossed several crocus out of the bed, replacing them with peanuts and seeds of its choice. (Since they all invariably sprout like the weeds they are, I consider this a bad habit.) Our hero not only nailed the little thug on the first shot, but when it ran along the fence and hid behind the up-turned wheelbarrow, he sent another round which crashed resoundingly on the metal barrow. That particular squirrel has not returned, though it comes right up to the sidewalk and says rude things.

Cats, too, dislike being pelted with whiffle balls; it is a distinct blow to their pride. Their excavations cease with remarkable abruptness when whiffle balls appear. Frisbees are not in our arsenal, since they can really hurt both plants and animals. We are not out to destroy

127

wildlife in the area, after all, but merely putting on a display of power, marking our turf. Cats are also not fond of being squirted with the hose, especially if you cover most of the opening with your thumb. You can get quite accurate at directing a good spray this way, but unless the hose is on and handy you lose the element of surprise, which is half the battle. Squirt bottles are easy to carry on reconnaissance missions; a few tablespoons of alcohol (rubbing, not brandy) in the water gives you garden clout. If you miss the dog and spray your plants, that's O.K. too, since the stuff works pretty well on aphids, and makes a killer spray for slugs (killer in both senses of the word).

Water is the weapon of choice for dogs as well, as long as you are right on the scene. If you miss the chance to soak the animal (or its owner), turn your attention to your lawn and flower beds; dogs are easily habituated, and any spots that are consistently being used as a poop deck must be scrupulously cleaned up and carefully rinsed, since the scent of past misdeeds encourages them to repeat the offense. Sprays like the above-mentioned Chaperone are moderately effective but need frequent replenishing (at least daily), and they will wash away in the rain. Repellent-saturated ropes can be put around beds, shrubs and trouble spots, but aren't safely handled by small children. Perhaps the oldest remedies are still the most effective. Large quantities of ground pepper sprinkled over problem areas can teach an old dog new tricks. Mothballs or moth crystals certainly work, even against cats and squirrels. These are not good for children either, but can be used deep in the border where cats make their nests, or buried shallowly over freshly planted bulbs.

Talking to dog owners can be surprisingly useless. It's odd that some very nice people with very nice dogs have no sense about manners and common courtesy out of doors. Sometimes I suggest that sending undiapered small children into the offender's living room would very likely be construed as unneighborly. The graphic picture is best. Since I like most animals, and actually most people even, my initial manner is always friendly and polite. BUT. If negotiations fail, it's war. Chocolate Ex-lax, left where the dog likes to leave his night deposit.

Dealing with incorrigible animals and their recalcitrant owners is one thing; the essence of the battle is thoughtlessness rather than actual malice, or so I'd like to believe. Far worse is coping with children—and adults—who like to break plants just for the hell of it. Most of these characters will desist if you can catch them at it and give them a thundering scold. Trickier yet, however, are the cases involving flagrant theft by plant plunderers who arrive armed with scissors or knives, clearly intent on their business. I could hardly believe my eyes when I found our lilac bush being systematically denuded by two old women. It was clearly not a case for whiffle balls, and I am hampered by a traditional New England upbringing which forbids rudeness to my elders. Well, mostly. In any case, that particular sortie met with a vigorous repulse. "Oh, honey, such lovely flowers, and so many, and our apartment is so small. . . ." Well, all right. But ALL the lilac, in such a small apartment? And is it too far-fetched to want people to ask permission before they clean out the yard?

No gardener would resent the loss of one or two of practically anything, if that's where it stopped. Who would even notice such discreet borrowing? Many of us cut flowers for passers-by who admire them, getting pleasure from the thought of brightening up city apartments and lives. However, it is always a shock to find that all the daffodils have been carefully cut down in the night. It is a curious sensation to be called a capitalist running dog when requesting that a total stranger refrain from uprooting lilies in one's own yard. I don't always want to share with Krishna, either, and finding a rosebush brutally stripped in his name, broken past healing, does little to promote ecumenical understanding.

Even with a fence, it's not a good idea to plant anything you have an attachment to near the edges of your property. Fences just seem to add piquancy to the challenge, and the plants will suffer even more for being fallen into, tugged at, and sliced off from a distance. In our neighborhood, we use whistles and the telephone to alert one another and to let saboteurs know that they are being observed. Kids usually respond really well if you explain how to pick things without hurting the plants, and hint that discretion is the greater part of survival. Adults, and some surprising ones, are another story. But retaliation is a losing game, and flowers are for pleasure, after all. Some years ago, our garden had a small sign that read: Please Leave the Flowers for All of Us to Enjoy. Now, I might expand the message: Take a few, if you must, but leave something for the rest of the world, not to mention the gardener, to enjoy. Otherwise, watch out for whiffle balls!

CLASSIC DAYLILIES

The girl next door made over belongs in every garden

America is universally acknowledged to be hybridizing heaven for daylily fanciers. Over the past twenty years or so, American enthusiasts have succeeded in producing thousands of gorgeous flowers in colors far removed from the raw oranges and yellows of the species. People who are still thinking of daylilies as tawny terrors with major takeover propensities may not even recognize the newer cultivars as belonging to the same family.

Modern daylilies can be pure pink, silvery buff, ivory to near white, palest green, vivid clear yellows, oranges with no trace of brick or rust, velvety reds, near blacks, wine-dark purples, coral, tangerine, grapefruit, and everything in between. True blue is still on the horizon, but lavenders abound, and many newer flowers have blue markings. Sound incredible? How about diamond dusting, which gives petals a glittering luster, ruffles which can be deeply waved or as tidy as the fluting on a pie crust, petals crimped and curled, narrow and twisted, or wide, flat, and round as a sand dollar.

Skeptical? Perhaps these new beauties need to be seen to be believed. There are regional nurseries and display gardens throughout America, most of them open from midspring through fall. Perhaps a western Washington vacation could include a detour to Donna's Lilies of the Valley in Tonasket. (See Appendix A for this and subsequent addresses.) Oregon? Stop by Caprice Farms in Sherwood. And in California, look for Alpine Valley Garden in Santa Rosa. All these places have mail-order catalogs, too. For other states, an inquiry to the American Hemerocallis Society (c/o Ainie Busse, Route 2, Cokato, MN 55321) will bring you addresses of display gardens and nurseries across the country. If your travel plans don't pan out, send $2.00 (credited to your first order) to Wild's of Missouri, and you will see for yourself

131

'Ruffled Paradise'

'Big Buster'

'Moon Jet'

'Little Tyke'

'Bright Lights'

'Classic Simplicity'

'Hyperion'

'Master Touch'

'Summer Wine'

that it is the greatest daylily nursery of them all. Their catalog listing hundreds of modern daylilies is accurately illustrated, with meticulous descriptions of each plant.

The newest cultivars can cost $100 and more for one small division, but don't panic. Wild's carries several hundred daylilies for under $5, including several pages of "Space-Savers", a close-out of older models at five plants for $6.50. Among these cheapest ones are some personal favorites, exceptional bloomers with garden presence. 'Ruffled Paradise' blossoms are apricot pink, as smooth as silk, each heavily ruffled and spangled with diamond dust. In a mild, wet year, it repeats generously (in daylily talk, this means it blooms again in the fall). 'Big Buster' is a tall fellow, producing great quantities of eight-inch-wide flowers the color of canteloupe sherbet. 'Moon Jet', creamy lemon-curd yellow, has wide petals with crimped edges, stylish and energetic. The floriferous 'Little Tyke' is on the short side, bursting with bouquets of miniature scarlet flowers with grass green throats. Add 'Bright Lights', strong azalea pink trumpets with throats of glowing apricot, and you've got your money's worth.

Some of the most popular daylilies in my garden cost less than $5. 'Classic Simplicity' has elegantly formed blossoms of primrose yellow, and easily surpasses that old standard for yellows, 'Hyperion'. Another aristocrat that gets a lot of attention is 'Master Touch'. This one is a warm, mellow pink, the creped, broad petals having frilled edges and a lovely substance (what fabric dealers call "hand"; it means roughly the "feel" of the petals). This was the first $100 daylily and the first true pink, introduced back in 1968. Now under $5, it is still supremely beautiful.

You don't have to spend a fortune for a real showpiece. Everyone who sees 'Summer Wine' wants it in his garden too. This one has big, rounded blossoms, waved, ruffled, and crimped, fresh from the beauty salon. The color is equally remarkable; intense, saturated purple, a bit redder than plums, the flowers smoulder sumptuously, a real color breakthrough in daylilies. Backed by tall, feathery spires of the fluffy grey artemisia 'Silver King', it is highly effective. Prices range widely for the more expensive daylilies; 'Summer Wine' lists between $8 and more than $20. If you fall for the pricier plants, get several catalogs and shop around. Smaller nurseries often have very simple catalogs but great prices and big plants. The fancy, glossy catalogs help us see the possibilities, but you generally pay for the privilege. Wild's is unusual in offering bargain collections where one chooses the varieties and receives labeled plants. Some very reputable nurseries are still passing off older, inferior varieties at inflated prices, and the average low-cost collection is a grab-bag. Unless you have no color or seasonal scheme in your garden, miscellaneous plants are rarely worth buying.

Given your choice of color and bloom season, it's hard to go wrong with these flowers, whether you choose the most expensive cultivars or stick with the lower-priced collections. One good way to make selections is to learn to read the descriptive key included in all specialty catalogs. Most growers use the same abbreviations, and they generally make sense: "dor" is dormant, "ev" is evergreen, etc. For maritime gardeners, this distinction is not critical, but evergreen cultivars are not perfectly hardy in colder climates, notably in areas subject to frequent thaws and refreezes. Often a deep, loose winter mulch of straw can compensate for temperature fluctuations and reduce losses from frost heaves.

Other points to consider are season, indicated as "E" (early), "M" (mid-), or "L" (late), so that you can stagger bloom times over a longer period—it is possible to have daylilies flowering from April through fall in much of the Northwest. Cultivars marked "O.E." will be open evenings to be savored when the rigors of the day are past. Modern daylilies stay open longer than the species (whose early collapse earned the common name), and there are now many which open later in the day and remain open overnight. The letter "F" denotes fragrance, which can be considerable; one of my favorites is 'Ice

'Silver King'
Artemisia

Carnival', a crisp lemon-juice white with a small, brilliant, enamel green heart. The petals are as stiff as heavy silk, ruffled and fluted and diamond dusted to boot. 'Ice Carnival' blooms for most of the summer and opens late to perfume the evening air with its deep, sweet scent.

Daylilies have gained so many excellent attributes from the hybridizing process that they bear small resemblance to their now-distant species cousins. Perhaps the most remarkable aspect of all this hybridizing (which includes genetic manipulation, treatment with colchicine and other substances to alter genetic patterns and double the chromosome count) is that, despite numerous changes, modern daylilies are nearly all as easy to grow as the species. Their hardiness is one of their greatest assets, making them among the best of choices for anyone who wants to reduce garden work and be guaranteed success.

Daylilies have suffered somewhat from being labeled "easy care" plants. Too often, plants billed as requiring low maintenance are treated as if they needed *no* care, and this simply isn't true. I hate to see daylilies treated this way, starved and improperly placed, bravely blooming anyway, but far from the visual feast afforded by a well-grown clump. Although a daylily might well survive being planted in raw clay with no further help from the hand of man, that doesn't mean that such treatment is a good idea. Any plant will benefit from a good beginning, which in this case means digging a hole large enough to fit the roots without bending or cramming them in any which way. Fan the roots out and pack the soil carefully to avoid air pockets; daylilies have fat storage roots with finer feeder roots attached, and these finer roots need to be in good contact with the soil to get nutrients to the plant.

Where the soil is less than perfect, adding some peat moss, aged manure and bone meal at planting time would be a thoughtful touch. A mulch of compost, renewed once or twice a year, is another useful long-term investment. It is also worth taking the trouble to see that the crown of the plant isn't smothered with soil and that all the roots are well covered; tuck the plant in nicely, water it in generously, and all will be well. None of this is particularly difficult, yet it is often stinted, leading to disappointing results that are quite unnecessary. A very little care—but perhaps I shouldn't start that again.

Daylilies need lots of water before and during their blooming time; this is probably the single most important aspect of their culture. More than any fertilizer, adequate water will ensure a good crop of flowers and, more than any other stressor, lack of water will produce a paucity of blooms or even no flowers at all from otherwise healthy-looking plants. Many professional growers water abundantly but do not artificially feed their daylilies at all. Others feed once a year, usually in late spring, using a fertilizer with a high middle number (5-10-10 is fine). Most of them have soil that is kept in very good heart, however, which too many home gardens do not, so it is worth repeating that annual renewal of such soil amendments as bone and cottonseed meals, manure, peat, and compost will greatly benefit the soil structure and nutrient content. This can't help but benefit the plants in ways that no chemical fertilizer, however balanced and complete, can hope to match. Use both approaches if you like, but feed the soil first and the plants will pretty much take care of themselves.

It is probably worth mentioning what may seem to be obvious: first-year plants are unlikely to stun you with a floral explosion. Even these very willing creatures have their limitations. This doesn't mean that they won't bloom at all; it is not uncommon for a daylily set out in April to put up a bloom scape quite soon, and open a few flowers that same summer. This is so tantalizing; each bud of a new plant is eagerly inspected as the buds swell, and it is practically a sure thing that you will be out of town on the day that the first one opens. However, the real displays come after the plants have had a year or two to settle down. In my yard, for instance, a new

'Three Bars'

plant of 'Three Bars' carried 7 blossoms its first year. The second year, it had 42, not bad at all. In the third year, it produced 287 flowers on upwards of thirty scapes. This cultivar blooms over a long period, more than three months, and I've long since stopped counting the flowers. I consider that a pretty good return on my $1.35 (it was part of a collection from Wild's).

You can get a lot of enjoyment from daylilies without going to extremes (or so I've heard), but it isn't easy—with this year's additions, our daylily collection includes well over one hundred different kinds. We enjoyed them just as much when we only had half a dozen, but it's a bit like eating peanuts; one thing leads to another. If you can't manage a visit to a modern daylily garden or nursery, do investigate Wild's—it's the next-best introduction to these fresh classics which no garden should be without. I will issue a challenge, however: I'll bet you can't choose just one!

WHILE YOU WERE AWAY. . .

Techniques and troubleshooting to minimize post-vacation trauma

The morning mist burns off early; it's going to be another scorcher. Vacation time is just around the corner and you hustle around the house packing the beach bags, locating the lotions, the shades, that fat book, and the cooler. There you are, the beach umbrella over your shoulder, your arms full of big towels, when it suddenly hits you; the garden is going to get fried. Don't throw in those towels; there are several things you can do, even at the penultimate minute, to avoid garden burnout.

First, review the neighborhood. Can you get on a buddy system? Are there any trustworthy teenager-types who can help out? If so, it's a breeze. Arrange for a short intro session, My Garden 101. Keep it simple; no one else will do it all your way, and most details will get ignored. Bow to the inevitable, choose your top three or four priorities, and leave it at that. It doesn't hurt to write things down; list anything that needs special attention, perhaps a container that's apt to dry out, or a batch of young fall salad greens that will wilt without extra care. Better yet, move the container to a partially shady place, and screen the greens with a piece of muslin or an old window screen, propped up on the sunward side. Simplification will inevitably lead to better results for all concerned. If your buddy is not a gardener in his or her own right, be very specific and very simple in your directions. Very.

If you are on your own, the prep process is a bit more complicated. You will need to budget several pre-departure hours for summer-proofing the garden, but don't panic: although the process sounds difficult, it actually breaks down into a few simple tasks. As long as you don't break down first, no worries. Here's the main point; in truly hot weather, most plants are only staying active because your care is keeping them awake. Unless you want to come home to premature brownout, some part of that care needs to continue while you are gone. The most effective technique involves long, slow soaks for the week (or at least a couple of days) before you leave. If all you have is an overhead sprinkler, try using it on very low pressure, so that the foliage is not kept wet, but the ground beneath is drenched. Those soaker hoses with lots of little holes are just the ticket; thread them through the beds and turn the pressure down till just a trickle of water emerges. Leave them on overnight, all day, or for at least three or four hours, whatever you can manage. The ground must be deeply saturated, so that you can dig down eight or ten inches and still find wet dirt. Now, cover that soil with a good layer of mulch, shredded bark, or dried grass clippings, compost, newspapers, anything you can hustle up. Soak the mulch as well, and it will act as an insulation blanket, keeping things cool and moist for a week or ten days. Even during those long spells of dry but overcast weather of recent years, this treatment can hold the garden together for weeks on end.

If you use grass clippings for the mulch, be advised that a couple of inches of fresh grass will begin to compost, heating up alarmingly, and this is not at all what we had in mind. Dried clippings are terrific, and you can pile them as thickly as you like. Strew green (wet) clippings on a tarp (or the grass) in the hot sun for an afternoon and they will be as dry as you please. Keep any mulch from covering the crowns of the plants, however, since the aim is to insulate and protect, not to smother. In our generally benevolent climate, one great problem with mulch is the fascinating way it can increase the slug and snail population. This too is not our goal, but for a week or so, we can get away with it. To be on the safe side, sprinkle a healthy dusting of slug bait around each plant before laying on the mulch. Baits which use metaldehyde are not environmentally damaging (except to the slug's environment, I suppose) though there may be valid societal objections to increasing alcoholism in any strata.

To ensure something to look at when you get home, get out the secateurs (pruning shears) and give the most floriferous things a light pruning. This is especially important with annuals and plants with short-lived blossoms; a good trim now will stimulate all sorts of nice new growth while you are gone. If all goes well, another crop of flowers will await your return. Where there are fading perennials with ratty-looking leaves, cut these back as well, to stimulate another round of fresh leaves. When you get home, give everybody a good drink, and a treat of manure tea or dilute fertilizer to reward their good behavior, or at worst, their effort. You may even get a fall encore in the flower department this way.

You can perform similar acts in the vegetable patch, but if the crops are fairly well advanced, there is no holding them back. Invite the neighbors over to harvest the ripe stuff, or take a load to the Gospel Mission on your way out of town. Win some, lose some. At least somebody can enjoy it.

When you finally get started on that vacation, keep your eyes open for garden tours, and make a point of visiting nurseries wherever you go. It can be fascinating to see how foreign familiar plants can appear in another climate or setting. There is always the chance of seeing plants read about but never seen, or discovering flowers you've never even heard about. Each locale seems to favor certain plants and treatments, and it is refreshing to see new choices. Gardeners in the Pacific Northwest are fortunate enough to be able to grow practically any plant commercially available in the U.S.A., so the chances are fair to good that you can reproduce that stunning effect in your own yard. Besides, it is nearly always fun, or at least instructive, to try new things, plants not excluded.

Garden-hopping gives you a great opportunity to see unfamiliar plants in a garden setting, important because a specimen in a pot at a nursery is still essentially an unknown. It isn't until you see an established plant in a garden, among companions, that you get a real sense of its potential, how it relates to other plants, its presence or personality, and where it might appear to greatest advantage in your own garden. We can all learn a lot by visiting gardens, big or small, and each gardener has something unique to show us. Keep your eyes open for lovely varieties of native plants, new ways to treat old favorites, delightful combinations of plants, or trouble-shooting ideas. How is that awkward north wall handled, what is done to mitigate an ugly view or maximize a cramped lot? There is much to learn even from gardens we don't enjoy; try to analyze why you don't like it, what went wrong, what could help.

Once you get home again, you may well find that things did not go totally according to plan. If disaster has struck, there is an excellent troubleshooting resource for residents of Washington state: the Master Gardener program. Despite funding cutbacks, it is going strong locally, and the continuation of Master Gardener Clinics is cause for celebration. These clinics bring information and assistance of professional quality to the public, providing on-the-spot diagnosis and culture tips to anyone who stops by. They take place throughout the spring and summer, in useful places like shopping malls and local branches of the public library. For a schedule of this summer's clinics, consult your local County Extension Service Agent. Master Gardeners undergo rigorous and lengthy training; by the end of it, they know a good deal about lawn care and vegetable gardening, care of ornamental and fruit trees, typical garden shrubs and perennials, common pests and problems, and so forth. It's wonderful to be able to call a Master Gardener and say, "I have these repellent little black things all over my poppy stems. . . ." and to be briskly reassured, "Aphids. Spray them with the hose, good and hard, and be nice to your ladybugs."

Do stress that you prefer organic or non-toxic alternatives if the suggested treatment sounds aggressively lethal; the one serious drawback of this program is the emphasis on pesticides and chemical warfare. Master Gardeners generally can offer several ideas, and if you ask for "organic" or less toxic treatments, they try to deliver. However, the initial response will nearly always be to suggest a chemical solution to your problem. This is still regrettably standard practice, and will only change when gardeners demand alternatives. The fact is that there usually *are* good, practical alternatives, but you must probe a bit to find them. Make a point of asking for less dangerous techniques and solutions to what is, after all, a very minor problem in the grand scheme of things. What may (debatably) be necessary for large-scale farmers is quite often horrifyingly out of place in a family garden; if you wouldn't want your kids or your cats to eat it, don't use it. After all, we don't need to wipe *every* caterpillar off the face of the earth.

You can call up Master Gardeners year-round most places (check with the county agent for schedule) and get sound, locally appropriate advice for free, but these summer clinics are especially valuable, since you can take a piece of your plant in for instant diagnosis or identification instead of trying to explain over the phone. The training and the program vary somewhat from state to state; in Washington, the Master Gardener program has been developed by the Extension Service using volunteers who train under W.S.U. Cooperative Extension Agents and horticultural specialists. These generous plant-minded people give a lot of time unstintingly, and their reward is in seeing more and better gardens springing up all over the state—not a bad return on a pretty hefty investment.

'Regale'
Lily

'Pink Perfection'

'Green Magic'

HIGH SUMMER IN THE BORDER
Shrubs and perennials that look great when things get hot

As summer matures, the border achieves ripe fullness and all the work of fall and spring shows results, good or bad. It's time to take a few pictures and to analyze—just a little—the overall effect. Make note of favorite combinations, and try to figure out just what makes them so good: color, texture, shape, contrast, or just plain delightful plants. If there are large blanks in the border, gaps or dull spots, note that too, so you can arrange some excitement for next year.

The hybrid lilies pass their peak in late June, following the bearded iris in quick succession. For later bloom, plant a collection of aurelian hybrids, and as the summer heat builds, the trumpets will sound. Stately and towering when supported, they lurch about in a most undignified fashion unless each tall stem has its own bamboo cane. Properly staked, the aurelians have enormous presence and their heavy perfume haunts the garden well into the evening. The 'Regale' lilies begin to open large purple buds into blossoms of purest white, refreshingly cool in the warmth of July. Their throats are splashed with warm yellow and filled with big golden stamens bobbing on celadon green stems. The pollen stains dreadfully, and those who stop to inhale the ineffable scent are branded with streaks of gold dust.

Quick on their heels comes 'Pink Perfection', rose satin with a green throat and dark cinnabar pollen that persists for days on your hands. If you cut lilies for the house, clip off the stamens first or the pollen will be everywhere. 'Green Magic' can reach five or six feet and looks especially magical rising up between small shrubs, backlit by long streams of rich summer sunshine. Not exactly green, it is a creamy, satiny, butter yellow overlaid with green, excellent with the steely blues and grey-greens of many herbs. The association of lilies and herbs is a very old one, recorded in garden books that predate Christ, and is well worth repeating in modern gardens. Two golden girls who look especially striking among a feathery sea of herbs are the very tall 'African Queen', a sumptuous cantaloupe, and her companion, 'Golden Splendor', deep yellow with a hint of tangerine juice. These statuesque lilies bloom for weeks, their architectural strength perhaps most obvious by moonlight, when the whole garden glimmers pale, fragrant, and mysterious.

Bedding annuals can be counted on for a good show at this time, but they do need lots of attention to keep them fresh and productive in the heat. Some of the best midsummer effects in my garden come from low-maintenance combinations of hardy perennials with dwarf shrubs. These add a pleasing solidity to the borders without weighing things down, yet are open and airy enough in structure that their neighbors are not smothered. Especially good for foundation plantings, such natural dwarves never outgrow their positions and need only the simplest pruning to keep them shapely. Some that begin to bloom in midsummer carry on till fall, and even those that aren't evergreen bring structure and color to the border year-round.

A particular favorite, bluebeard (*Caryopteris*) is a splendid small bush, light and loosely built. It is easy to grow and care for and most generous with its flowers from a tender age. There are quite a few forms, all rather similar, and it doesn't much matter which kind you get, since all are lovely. Caryopteris has narrow leaves in opposite pairs, slightly toothed, and silvery to quite dark green. The flowers appear in little poufs at the leaf nodes, diminutive individually but arranged in such dense clusters that they gain considerable visual impact. 'Heavenly Blue' has powdery sky blue blossoms, an excellent foil for the sharp oranges and golds of calendulas, particularly the compact 'Fiesta Gitana' blend. The flowers of 'Dark Knight' are cobalt; surround this one with the heavy reds of dianthus or roses, and mix in plenty of white and silver for sparkle. 'Kew Blue' flowers are almost royal blue, and a planting of this with the

'African Queen' Lily

'Golden Splendor'

Caryopteris Bluebeard

'Heavenly Blue'

'Fiesta Gitana' Calendula

'Dark Knight' Bluebeard

'Kew Blue'

143

Tanacetum haradjanii
Tansy

Perovskia atriplicifolia
Russian sage

Shirley
Poppy

flat plates of achilleas in mustard and cerise, lightened with the soft, creeping feathers of grey tansy (*Tanacetum haradjanii*), is synergism illustrated.

All three caryopteris varieties reach a height of two or three feet by late spring and are blooming their heads off by midsummer. In the fall, the leaves take on numinous tones of purple, mauve, slate blue, and gunmetal grey. Later, the silver-brown stems trimmed with fat seedpods enliven the winter garden, a favorite feeding ground for chirping, bustling small birds. Caryopteris are not for shady gardens, though they take partial shade in stride. Tolerant of most soils, they thrive even in wretched dirt, as long as the drainage is sharp (quick). They need only one hard pruning in midspring when frost danger is past; this is rather fun, as you simply chop them down, nearly to the ground. If there are lots of buds at the base of the stem, cut just above those. Just don't try to prune them too early, or they may succumb to a late frost.

Another good performer for the sunny border is Russian sage (*Perovskia atriplicifolia*), a silver blue bush with aromatic, downy leaves used to flavor vodka. Like caryopteris, Russian sage is delicate and light in appearance, a gentle haze of lavender blue billowing out perhaps three feet in all directions. The violet flowers are small, grouped on whorled spikes which contrast vividly in both form and color with the finely dissected smoky leaves. Russian sage can have its skirts planted with purple and white lilies for an elegant effect. For a bolder look, give it a bright embroidery of sun-colored calendulas, splashy Shirley poppies or mounds of shrub roses. In fall, the leaves vanish quickly to reveal white stems that gleam like miniature birches among the subtle soft colors around them. Like bluebeard, this shrub wants only a hard pruning in midspring to regain its distinctive good looks each year.

Both bluebeard and Russian sage provide an excellent opportunity to bring orange, that most underused color, into the high-summer border. There is no pleasanter sight than a caryopteris in full blossom, surrounded

144

by frail, silky orange Iceland poppies, or that ubiquitous local poppy the color of orange crush. Nobody seems to know what this is; possibly *Papaver lateritium*, escaped from some earlier garden, it has numerous gentle orange flowers on fuzzy grey stems above rosettes of long, toothed grey leaves. It is a lovely plant, but far too generous a seeder to be allowed into the garden proper. If there is a rough place, rather dry and sunny, where few things will grow, either shrub, partnered with this most willing poppy, will do you proud. Orange can be difficult to use without tremendous clashing, but greys and silvers tone any brashness down. Clean oranges can brighten and intensify cool, pure blues like nothing else. A rather ordinary combination of blues, yellows, and whites will be stronger for a dash of orange, and the richer purples gain sparkle from a judicious bit of orange nearby, well mixed with green.

These two small shrubs are stalwarts, but there are loads of fine perennials that bring striking color to the high-summer garden. Daylilies come into their own at this time, the backbone of many a famous border. Try 'Hot Toddy' in zingy azalea pink, interplanted with a dozen herringbone shoots of the hardy Byzantine gladiola (*Gladiolus byzantinus*) in ringing, resonant magenta. This color is even further out of favor than orange, but coupled with feathery mounds of artemisias or dusty millers, it is as impressive as stained glass against grey stone; the cathedral effect, I call it. If you prefer a cooler scheme, consider a group of incredibly prolific daylilies, 'Three Bars', creamy apricot warmed with peachy overtones, the fragrant lemon sherbet blossoms of 'Ice Carnival' and the twisting, spidery curls of 'July Gold'. All are long-lasting border beauties *par excellence*.

Tiger lilies come in many colors now, though the old-fashioned yellow and orange freckled flowers are still welcome in my high-summer border. The mysterious silver pink flowers of *Lilium tigrinum* 'Rose' look lovely next to the tall achillea, 'Cerise Queen', with its flat plate-flowers of cherry pink. As Queenie fades, she turns all sorts of muted pinks and mauves, looking most attrac-

Papever lateritium
Poppy

'Hot Toddy'
Daylily

Gladiolus byzantinus
Byzantine gladiola

'Three Bars'
Daylily

'Ice Carnival'

'July Gold'

Lilium tigrinum
'Rose'

'Cerise Queen'
Achillea

145

tive for months on end. The open trumpets of a butter-scotch tiger lily, 'Torino', provide satiny contrast for the apricot buds of a delightful old rose, 'Gruss an Coburg'. A species achillea, *A. taygetea*, makes a suitable companion for this rose, and is equally stunning with sun-roses (*Helianthemum* species) and shrubby potentillas. This yarrow is itself a silvery plant, with woolly grey leaves and flat umbels of the coolest buttery flowers, more delicate and subtle than its well-known cousin, *A.* 'Moonlight'.

There is no need to let the garden decline after the great crescendo of early summer. Keep your eyes open as you visit other gardens, parks, and nurseries, and make note of plants that catch your attention, whether for beauty of flower, fruit, leaf, or structure. Things don't have to change all at once; plants are added, moved around, and discarded each year. As we look, and learn, and evaluate, the garden develops different facets of its character with each season. Making a year-round garden is a lengthy process—it takes a lifetime of experimentation. Gradually you adjust your collection to include things you admire, editing out the dull or unsuccessful, allowing time for plants to mature, to display their full potential. The net result is an intensely personal statement, a living, changing, breathing garden.

AUGUST

ALLEY AMBLE

Old-fashioned plants of historical interest linger on in the alley

Vinca minor
Periwinkle

London Pride
Saxifrage

Bergenia

Most of us have some sentimental favorites among the old-fashioned plants. Hollyhocks may remind us of making dolls in grandmother's garden. The roses and violets, lavenders and mints that grew in the neighborhood are the very stuff of childhood, forever linked with our discovery of scents, textures, flavors. As a child, I loved to sip the honey drop of nectar from the curved horn of a columbine. My brothers waged flowery battles, pelting each other with the prickly balls of globe thistle. Later, when victory was clear, we gingerly gathered the seed because it brought bright goldfinches to the birdfeeder in winter. Who hasn't stuck maple seeds onto his small nose to emulate Pinocchio, or sent the double propellers twirling in miniature helicopters? Chewing spruce gum, the viscous, aromatic sap picked lovingly off the rough bark, was frowned upon by adults, but gave deep satisfaction to the children. To this day, tall blue spires of veronica, nodding clumps of daylilies, fat clusters of lilac, the puffy clouds of hydrangeas all bring a little rush of nostalgia, and I grow them as much for my children's delight in discovery as my own reminiscent pleasure.

Early Seattle gardens had some delightful forms of these old-fashioned flowers. Many can still be found on the fringes of older gardens, half hidden behind overgrown shrubs and tumbling off the property line into the alley, that wonderful repository of garden treasures from days past. There are at least six forms of periwinkle (*Vinca minor*) naturalized on Seattle's residential Capitol Hill, and one can quickly find several kinds of London Pride, that hardy, scalloped saxifrage. The floppy, leathery elephant-ear leaves of *Bergenia* are often seen in neglected lots and alley strips, as are many non-native ferns, sedums, and other die-hards. Gleaning from such a spot is not garden-raiding under the

Syringa vulgaris
Lavender lilac

S. vulgaris 'Alba'

Blue Flag
Iris

act, but common courtesy dictates that permission be sought if you have the least suspicion that someone is tending or appreciating these plants. I know several people who have bagged big shrubs and trees by asking contractors for plants growing on old gardens slated for new construction. Again, it's important to ask, since occasionally some plants are saved for landscaping. Daphnes, viburnums, rhododendrons, roses, they are out there in profusion, their accompanying houses long since vanished. It is true that older shrubs seldom transplant well, but what is there to lose? If nothing else, they are a rich source of cutting material. In fact, many gardeners report quite good luck in moving these large, established freebie plants; perhaps they like being rescued.

Next time you walk down an alley, take a good look at the plants there. You may be surprised by how many you recognize. Neglected and half wild, they tell a story about the area's early years. In my neighborhood most of the many lilacs are very old examples of *Syringa vulgaris*, the common lavender lilac or its unimproved white form, 'Alba.' These make shrubby trees or thickets along the fences and nothing on earth smells better. Lilac was brought to Seattle on the wagons of the earliest settlers and nearly every homestead had its bush. You can easily imagine rooted suckers being passed over the fence and shared around. It's amusing to speculate about distribution patterns: a blank space for a crochety neighbor or where there was no house, a whole cluster where a homesick bride tried to re-create her mother's garden.

Most older houses have a clump or two of the early iris called blue flag. Deeply fragrant and unfailingly cheerful, it often blooms from late March well into May and may be seen doing so throughout the older neighborhoods of the city. Of course it has been superseded a thousand times by improved forms of bearded iris, but I like to have a few around anyway. Clear purple-blue with deeper falls, yellow beard, and white netted throat, it is pleasant if undistinguished of form. It will do well anywhere you put it; my children planted a nearby traffic circle with this iris and are tickled with pleasure whenever we pass the thriving clumps.

I think every dooryard must have had some of that tall and tawny daylily, *Hemerocallis fulva*. It is nearly indestructible, another good plant for a traffic circle, where it can spread its rustling, grassy leaves as far as it likes without smothering anything. This vigorous performer will contribute many hot orange trumpets for long weeks, raising them as high as six feet in the air. At home, however, it needs an eye kept on it. Mine is—where else?—bordering the alley. There are other species (unimproved) daylilies which came west with the wagons too. The little lemon lily, *H. flava*, is far less rowdy, and opens clear yellow, citrus-scented flowers in early summer. It is well worth begging a start for your own garden if one of your neighbors has a patch of this one. *H. minor* is also fragrant, and is even daintier, just over a foot tall, with soft yellow flowers. It, too, lingers on throughout the city and is well worth restoring to garden status.

Tall spikes of velvety foxgloves are everywhere, purple and white; the younger specimens transplant nicely if well watered before and after. Canterbury bells and other bellflowers (*Campanula* species) still open their blossoms of blue, pink, or white long after their original gardens are lost to history. Seed gathered in summer can be sown fresh, summer and fall, for flowers next year. So can that of hollyhocks, and the old single types that bloom so freely out by the dumpsters seem less prone to hollyhock rust and other diseases that plague the fancy double forms in so many gardens.

Bushy *Iberis sempervirens* isn't called live-forever for nothing; there are some ancient plants of this snowy white candytuft around, with twisted, gnarled trunks like little bonsai. Basket-of-gold (*Aurinia saxatilis* or *Alyssum saxatile*) is often planted with it, and it too achieves a ripe old age, given the chance. Coral bells (*Heuchera* species) still spangle the sparse grass with vivid pink in shady spots. Ivy clambers up many a tree and wall, while old roses, tough and disease resistant, bloom gaily

Hemerocallis fulva
Daylily

H. flava
Lemon lily

H. minor

Campanula
Canterbury bell
Bellflower

Hollyhock

Iberis sempervirens
Live-forever

Aurinia saxatilis or
Alyssum saxatile
Basket-of-gold

Heuchera
Coral bells

on through the choking tangles of false bamboo and vine maple saplings.

These and others like them are real heritage plants, reminders of the first gardens in Seattle and of the spirit which defiantly creates a garden even in the wilderness. It seems tragic that they be abandoned and ignored; I often stop to pull the weeds away, to try and give these old geezers some breathing space. Isn't there anywhere they could go? Perhaps one of the city parks could use them, rehabilitated and planted up as a low-maintenance historical exhibit. Surely low-income housing would be more attractive if landscaped with such reclaimed shrubs. There must be hundreds of public places that would look better for a bit of local color. I cringe when I see old gardens crumble beneath the bulldozers; I want to take all those aging plants, like old horses past their work, to some last meadowy haven where they can bloom and fade in peace. They deserve a better fate than destruction or neglect, these unquenchable ghosts of the old Seattle gardens.

GOING GREY

Grey and silver foliage sparkles when the heat is on

Zauschneria
California fuchsia

Nepeta mussinii
Catmint

Senecio greyi

As waves of color come and go in the garden, the relatively stable framework of foliage which remains takes on greater significance. August is a difficult month for many gardens; what few flowers there are blaze away amid so much green that they look a bit lost. Furthermore, such flowers as are blooming are doing it in the hottest of colors; tiger lilies burning bright in orange, yellow, cinnamon; dahlias flaming in rose or rust or wine, those with jetty black leaves and blood red blossoms especially heavy looking. Hardy geraniums glow hot pink or bright purple. The California fuchsias (*Zauschneria* species) send up sparks of scarlet, coral, and flame. As the temperature rises, we turn to foliage with quiet contrasts of form and tone, green on green or grey or blue, for relief. Non-colors cool and soothe; floating white flowers shimmer in the still heat, the frosty haze of catmint (*Nepeta mussinii*) and the steely or slaty blues, greys, and silvers of the euphorbias, rues, artemisias and others calm the Mediterranean heat of the dog days.

These are the neutrals of the garden color scheme, playing the same role in the border that they do in our wardrobes. Plants with foliage of grey, silver, and white add sparkle and important contrast to strong color combinations. When the molten meets the smoldering, the result can be disappointingly subfusc. Bold colors often cancel each other out: instead of building heat upon heat to explosive visual fireworks, the picture fizzles, a sullen dud. It takes the greys of ash and smoke to set off the jets of hot color; diluted with silver and grey, bright colors are intensified and the scene achieves full strength.

A plant that makes every neighbor look better is *Senecio greyi*, an ever-silver shrub that is beautiful every single day of the year. Always elegant, its fascinating

153

**Clematis macropetala
'Rosy'**

**'Victoria'
Salvia**

**Cineraria
Dusty Miller**

Senecio maritima

'Diamond'

'Silver Dust'

'Cirrhus'

leaves are like folded taco shells made of sage grey velvet, the edges rimmed with silver. In early spring, it is the perfect host for the delicate pink blossoms of *Clematis macropetala* 'Rosy.' In summer, lilies are displayed to perfection between its branches. The deep blue spires of the farinaceous salvia 'Victoria' can disappear mysteriously into surrounding greenery; these plants will have all their intended impact and more when placed in front of the senecio. The crudest combinations of vivid oranges, yellows, and reds (those involved in zinnia mixtures, for instance) are gathered into harmony by this distinguished shrub.

When its own blossoms open in a smother of gay yellow daisies, the grey leaves set them off like little jewels. This senecio needs the sun to do its best, though it can take a bit of shade. Good, sharp drainage is equally important, as it will tolerate quite poor soils as long as they aren't soggy. This is an excellent plant for dry, difficult spots: along a driveway, by a hot, reflecting expanse of concrete or in a big tub by the pool.

The dusty miller clan is a composite group of low shrublets, usually under two feet tall. Named cultivars are varied in leaf form, which may range from broad and flat to the laciest cobwebs, but they are united in looking powdered with flour—thus the common name. All perform with excellence when mixed into the front of the border or in containers. Some call them *Cineraria* species and hybrids, others classify them as varieties of *Senecio maritima*, cousins to *S. greyi* though quite different in appearance. The most common sorts have dissected leaves flocked with silver or white hairs. 'Diamond' is intensely white, just the right accompaniment for the latin colors of portulaca or those salsa-bright mixes of cosmos. 'Silver Dust' has even more finely divided leaves, making a mounded filigree of lace which does wonderful things for carpeting junipers and sprawling cotoneasters, in the border with dahlias and roses, or shielding the feet of clematis from the scorching August sun. 'Cirrhus' ought really to be a storm cloud; its fuzzy uncut leaves are large and plain in shape, seemingly of velveteen, and of a color that in a real cloud would guarantee sleet or snow. The big leaves make a comfortable contrast to the round and restless leaves of the variegated helicrysum, *H. petiolatum* 'Variegatum', its wandering shoots trailing through the border most decoratively. 'Cirrhus' is also delightful when interplanted with metallic pink diascias (*Diascia rigescens*), tall sheaves of Tyrian purple daylilies, or feathery plumes of herbs like dill or fennel.

Usually sold and grown as annuals, the dusty millers can be perennial subshrubs in the Northwest. Left unpruned in the fall, they nearly always winter over successfully. Cut them back hard in March or April for dense, bushy new growth. Don't worry when the new leaves come in green: they will take on the proper color as they mature. Rain makes the leaves blotchy and green, looking like molting parrots, but only temporarily. This spring pruning also eliminates the rather ugly little flowers, small primitive daisies the color of ballpark mustard, that add nothing to the beauty of the plant. Like most grey-leaved things, the dusty millers prefer full sun, excellent drainage, and rather poor soil. They do not need fertilizers at any time, and only want supplemental water when first installed. After that, you may leave them to their own devices; all will appear at their whitest and best in places where most self-respecting plants would only sulk.

A deliciously weird little plant that is stunning in pots or at the front of the border is *Salvia argentea*. It looks exactly like a grey plush cabbage, the large thick leaves covered in silky down. Odd but extremely beautiful, it looks enchanting when planted at the foot of a rose; I like it with 'Shot Silk', great fragrant bowls of coral and apricot, textured like slubbed silk. A generous planting of this salvia makes a powerful foreground for burgundy lilies, perhaps 'Pirate' or 'Venture.' It is a very lovely foot cover for the ruffled sea blue clematis, 'Lasurstern', which will trail through low shrubs as happily as it climbs a more conventional trellis. This silver salvia is hard to track down, but it shows up now

Helichrysum petiolatum 'Variegatum'

'Cirrhus'

Diascia rigescens Pink diascia

Salvia argentea

'Shot Silk' Rose

'Pirate' Lily

'Venture'

'Lasurstern' Clematis

155

'Silver King'
Artemisia

'Silver Queen'

'Powis Castle'

'Lambrook Silver'

Artemisia canescens

Leptosiphon
Gilia

A. schmidtiana
'Silver Mound'

and then at plant sales and the more adventurous nurseries. Canyon Creek Nursery of Oroville, California lists it (see Appendix A).

Within the border, the artemisia family can bring plumes and curls of delightfully airy grey leaves to the scene. Certain types like 'Silver King', 'Silver Queen', and 'Powis Castle' can reach three or four feet, a splendid backdrop for flamboyant flowers that need cooling down. A particularly lovely tall form, 'Lambrook Silver' is exceptionally good-looking and vigorous. Since it was selected by the late Margery Fish and offered from her own nursery at Lambrook (in Somerset, England), one would expect nothing less.

Those who have not yet discovered Mrs. Fish's gardening books have an enormous treat in store. Like so many English books, they contain better advice for Northwest gardeners than anything written for the eastern U.S.A. Years ago, the complaint was that all the enticing plant varieties named in English books were unavailable to American gardeners, but that is far from true now. One simply needs to do some catalog and seed-exchange research in order to locate hundreds of famous English border beauties. Many regional nurseries carry such plants now as well, recognizing the suitability of these varieties to our beneficent climate. Check the catalogs of Canyon Creek, Lamb, and other regional nurseries (see Appendix A) if you don't find them locally.

For smaller spaces, there are many more modest artemisias, sea green, sage grey, or silvery. *Artemisia canescens* is a real beauty, under two feet tall and delicate as cobwebby old lace from an attic trunk. I like to use it with delicate flowers like the impertinent annual gilia, *Leptosiphon*. 'French Hybrids Mixed' is the only seed strain I've ever found commercially (from Thompson & Morgan, Appendix B). These make tiny open stars in pink and rose, gold and yellow, cream and white, all surrounded by fluffy greenery, the entire plant perhaps two inches tall. Absurd and delightful, they look just right flitting in and out of the filmy artemisia. An old standby in many gardens is *A. schmidtiana* 'Silver

Mound', a frosty heap of silk floss less than a foot tall. Its silver-grey coloring evolves into curious and wonderful hues of pale pink and metallic lavender as winter draws near, then fades to ashes till spring raises it up again. Or so one hopes. This, more than the others, is frost-tender, and exceptionally sensitive to standing water. The least hint of soggy ground is enough to send this ethereal creature to plant heaven. Fortunately, it can be found at any nursery, and very cheaply, so frequent replacement is not a problem.

All the greys want lots of sunshine, very little water, and no extra fertilizer or care. Isn't this just what you love to hear? All should be left unpruned until early spring, when they can be cut back hard, practically to the ground. Any new shoots will be obvious, and you may leave a stumpy inch or two of trunk if the main stems are thickly budded. These very moderate needs put the greys among the easiest things in the garden, the kind of plants dreamed of hopefully by busy but exigent gardeners.

Sorrel

Dandelion

Endive

Chicory

Italian parsley

Mustard cress

Rocket

Radicchio

SAVORY SUMMER SALADS
Look through the garden with fresh eyes and start munching

As children, my brothers and I had eclectic tastes, enjoying the flavors and textures of grass, spruce gum, twigs, almost anything, as long as it wasn't served on a plate. As adults, we abandoned this carefree attitude, so that the sour tang of cloverlike sorrel and the intensely *green* taste of young dandelion leaves were powerfully evocative the first time I tasted them in a salad. It was a curious sensation to be transported abruptly back to childhood while enjoying a mild flirtation and a sophisticated meal at a Roman restaurant. Once over the shock, I recognized a complexity of texture and taste amazing to one who regarded salad as a vehicle for blue cheese. That was many years ago, but it made a big impression. Italians like to savor everything, salad included, and the attitude stayed with me.

Italian markets sell mixed bunches of greens in great variety, and the idea is catching on in the Northwest too. Little baskets of sprouts, fresh herbs, and various greens bundled in small amounts are increasingly available. This is great, because some of us can't get through whole heads of endive, lettuce, chicory, and what not before decay sets in. Such variety is too expensive if half of what you buy ends up in the compost bin. For those with gardens, or even a good-sized window box, there is a logical alternative: grow your own salad bar. There are hundreds of kinds of greens and herbs available as seeds, and you can sow them a few at a time over a long season for fresh and varied salads a cut above what you find in the market.

Italian *insalate* are traditionally made of tender young leaves of something—several kinds of lettuce, perhaps spinach, wild greens, or flat Italian parsley—with sprigs of hot mustard cress or garlic mustard, seedlings of rocket, radicchio or corn salad, dandelions, and

Lettuce

Variegated sage

Borage

Radicchio

Salad burnet

Russian tarragon

Nasturtium

a sprinkling of fresh herb leaves. Served at room temperature and dressed with perfectly fresh olive oil and a good vinegar, such a salad is light-years away from what you get at Joe's Diner. No 'Iceberg.' No Thousand Island. No leftovers.

Recent American versions of such gastronomic enlightenment tend to incorporate large sprays—even young branches—of herbs, and flowers. Lots of flowers. Done well, it can be refreshing, appealing, and flavorful. It is possible to get carried away, however, and the salad becomes an incoherent mess, both to the eye and, where it really counts, to the palate. On the other hand, a Zen composition of three stalks of chives, a nasturtium leaf, and one rose petal is not a salad in my book. As usual, the Truth lies somewhere in between.

It's hard to go wrong with mixed greens, though three or at the most four types is plenty. Two lettuces with contrasting textures, like butterhead and endive or oakleaf, want only a few golden green leaves of variegated sage and some cobalt blue borage blossoms to be more than satisfying. Cos lettuce with ruffled red radicchio and ice white slices of bok choy needs very little help, but some feathery bits of salad burnet and Russian tarragon are a transforming addition.

Using flowers as ingredients rather than garnish is catching on, and gardeners certainly have the edge. Cruise the border in early morning and look for the irresistible. There are quite a few which are attractive and/or tasty as well as safe to use. If you think of a terrific visual combination but aren't too sure about the flower, call Poison Control first (206-526-2121 in Seattle). They can tell you if that particular bright idea is deadly —or illegal. There are certainly some fetching ways to use summer flowers; pinky pale shrimp tumbling from purple daylily cornucopias or Latin-bright nasturtiums floating in gazpacho can zip up a basic menu.

Stuffed nasturtiums make nice tidbits, too; run some ricotta and smoked salmon through the blender, chop in toasted hazelnuts and a sprig of fennel, add a squeeze of lemon juice—perfect! Use rosy orange and moonlight

'Alaska'
Nasturtium

Coriander

Hollyhock

Daylily

Geranium

Squash blossom

Calendula
Marigold

Monarda
Bee balm

yellow flowers with "plates" of their own round, peppery leaves. The leaves of 'Alaska' have the typical nasturtium shape and peppery taste, but are grey-green with creamy streaks and swirls, making elegant little wrappers for soft cheeses mashed with fresh herbs and bits of shredded crab or slivers of teriyaki chicken and Walla Walla sweets.

Larger nasturtium leaves make no-calorie tortillas. For taco fillings, thin strips of mesquite-marinated flank steak or turkey are great with fresh salsa. This can range from mild—blend red onion, Anaheim and red-ripened bell peppers with 'Sweet 100' or 'Sweetie' cherry tomatoes, nutmeg, cinnamon, and some orange juice—to very olé—try garlic, small, fiery 'Early Jalapeno' peppers, Italian plum tomatoes, and fresh coriander leaves (cilantro). Mash a bit of either salsa with yogurt and ricotta for an appealing summery taco filling.

Nasturtiums aren't the only flowers worth eating. Hollyhocks, daylilies, geraniums (pelargoniums), and squash blossoms all make colorful, edible, and reasonably tasty containers. A handful of baby beans, fruit slices, marinated vegetables, chicken or Russian salad, all look more exciting served between petals. Those petals can be strewn, too; the pot marigold (*Calendula*) adds a flash of gold dust or warm orange. Bee balm (*Monarda* species) blossoms may be rosy red or scarlet, pink or white, and a few of these can turn a plain plate into a blue-plate special (look out, Joe's).

When summer heat makes cooking a chore, look to the garden with fresh eyes. There is plenty to eat out there, and not just in the vegetable patch. Summery meals can be lovely and refreshing when you enjoy the garden to the fullest. Don't just smell the flowers; pile them on your plate and dig in.

BABY BLOOMERS

Small bulbs enliven spring gardens; spring for them now, fall for them later

I t's hard to think about the sprightly flowers of spring as you bask in summer sunshine. Nonetheless, it's time to get with the program. Stack a pile of catalogs next to your chaise and leaf through them as you lounge. Not yet on every mailing list in the country? Drop a line to some (or all) of the companies listed here, and I will guarantee you that by this time next year, you will be deluged with plant, bulb, and seed catalogs of every description.

As you meander through the bulb catalogs, keep an eye out for the pages devoted to the so-called "minor bulbs." A large and disparate group of bulbs are lumped together under this collective heading, united more by their size than by close family ties. Usually included are scillas, snowdrops, anemones, alliums, and numerous others. Gardeners with limited space can get a lot of mileage from these diminutive and wholly delightful creatures, less familiar than standard tulips and narcissus, but equally easy and colorful on a smaller scale. Tuck them in everywhere for brilliance from January on. These little bulbs are endlessly useful for filling in places which will be lush later but may seem dreary or empty in earliest spring.

Minor bulbs are most effective when generously planted in loose clusters by kind or color. A haphazard jumble is gay, but can't match the impact of structured color. Try planting dozens of 'Apricot Beauty' tulips in drifts amid sprawls of white creeping phlox (*P. subulata*) or creating a Mediterranean blue sweep of grape hyacinths (*Muscari azureum*) broken only by hefty clusters of lemony pale fringed tulips 'Maja'. Now, that is "impact." This is standard advice, but if you're not convinced, experiment; a few groups of five or ten bulbs carry better, make a bolder picture, than fifty bulbs thinly ribboned or dotted about the garden.

'Apricot Beauty'
Tulip

Phlox subulata
Creeping phlox

Muscari azureum
Grape hyacinth

'Maja'
Tulip

161

It can be hard to resist glossy catalog glories. Before we take the plunge, let me issue one caveat: not all that's glossy is gold. Lots of great-looking catalogs sell expensive failures and the price isn't so right after all. Here are some places you can safely order from: all back up their offerings with guarantees, and all send out the right stuff. Some of the best buys and biggest bulbs come from Van Bourgondien, of Babylon, New York (for this and all subsequent addresses, see Appendixes A & B). The catalog of Dutch Gardens of Adelphia, New Jersey, is essentially a book; the prices are nearly at wholesale, with a $20 minimum order, but it includes a bunch of order blanks so you can pass it around the office. Dutch Gardens offers exceptional stock, great tulip and minor bulb prices (Van B. is better for narcissus), and an annual red-hot special.

Gurney's, of Yankton, South Dakota, has a funky catalog like that of a fire-sale auction house, but their stock is fine, and sometimes choice. The Park Seed Company of Greenwood, South Carolina, offers bulbs and plants, as well as seeds; this catalog is pricier than the others, but the quality and selection of its merchandise are consistently good.

Well known to readers of *The New Yorker* (by which illustrious firm it is partially owned), White Flower Farms in Litchfield, Connecticut, has a beautifully designed catalog, well illustrated and informative. The prose, however, tends regrettably toward the precious. Wayside Gardens of Hodges, South Carolina, also has a lovely, informative catalog worth browsing. Both of these last catalogs are expensive, and their perennials can get tired in transit. The saving grace of both companies is their willingness to carry uncommon plants that will never enjoy huge, brisk sales. Such rarities are often unavailable elsewhere, which ensures the continued patronage of sometimes-infuriated gardeners.

Now, armed with some or all of these catalogs, think back to spring. Where were those blank spots, dull areas, disappointingly thin plantings? Wave the magic trowel, and all that can change. Spectacular spring color is so easy to achieve, and it's a rare garden that can't use an infusion of early bloom. The little bulbs are especially valuable in small, urban gardens and in any intimate setting where their charms can be appreciated: containers and window boxes, entryway plantings, mixed in with evergreen ground covers, and under deciduous trees where adequate light can penetrate early in the year.

Certain crocus species are called bunch-flowering, and the name is most descriptive of their generous blooming habit. These crocus make splendid, triumphant brushstrokes of early color, increasing within a few years to carpets of gold or blue or cream, sometimes blooming through snow. Silvery lavender Tommies (*Crocus tomasinianus*) colonize rapidly under trees, in short grass, or poking through a loose ground cover. They are very pretty and gay with the slate blue flowers and shining leaves of periwinkle (*Vinca minor*), spectacular amid the finely dissected grey feathers of the little Turkish tansy, *Tanacetum haradjanii*. The golden bunch (*C. ancyrensis*) throws abundant blooms like spilt sunshine among dull shrubs and sends up sprays of silky cups in bright beneficence between paving stones.

Bedding hyacinths look like puffy wands of cotton candy, reeking with their outrageous perfume. These pudgy charmers may last for years or disappear quickly, but are so cheap it isn't a heartbreaker if they do. Fall feeding makes a big difference to these and any bulbs; a good handful of bone meal stirred into the soil beneath the root zone before planting and another one mixed with manure and compost and scattered in subsequent falls makes many bulbs semi-permanent. Pale yellow hyacinths like 'City of Haarlem' or the ivory 'Carnegie', set among baby blue striped squills (*Puschkinia libanotica*) are deeply satisfying. They also sparkle in the presence of grape hyacinths (*Muscari* species) of which there are fluffy or feathery kinds available, less aggressively self-seeding than the type. 'Gypsy Queen', a hyacinth the color of salmon butter, blends delicately with clumps of the terrifically wind-proof and long-

Crocus tomasinianus
Tommies

Vinca minor
Periwinkle

Tanacetum haradjanii
Turkish tansy

C. ancyrensis
Golden bunch

'City of Haarlem'
Hyacinth

'Carnegie'

Puschkinia libanotica
Striped squill

Muscari
Grape hyacinth

'Gypsy Queen'

163

'February Gold'
Daffodil

Anemone blanda
Windflower

Hermodactylus
tuberosus
Iris tuberosa

blooming 'February Gold', that quintessential garden daffodil. By the hundred, they cost about twenty cents a piece; splurge on these, since repeated clumps of five or six bulbs, surrounded with spanking white or Greek blue windflowers (*Anemone blanda*) create a strong motif for path or border.

Tiny reticulated iris are electrifying in late winter, delicate yet bold. The flowers rise naked and gleaming in the thin winter sunshine, colored egg-yolk yellow, lustrous purple, gentle or lucid blue. If you pot up the bulblets in rich soil and keep them outside, sheltering in a cold frame or trench (or in the sandbox), you can bring these fragrant gems indoors when they bloom, the better to appreciate the delicacy of their fine markings.

Less common and hauntingly lovely, Iris tuberosa (*Hermodactylus tuberosus*) is as elegant as a tuxedo. This bulblet carries angular iris-flowers of smoky green, the rounded falls with the color and texture of black velvet. The blossoms emerge, tipped to one side, from tight sheaths of curling green rushlike leaves. They make stunning cut flowers, lending themselves beautifully to sparse, Oriental arrangements. I don't know why this widow's iris isn't grown more; the bulbs are very inexpensive, under three dollars a dozen, and it is very easily grown. It will persist best and even increase when happily placed; like most Mediterranean natives, it prefers a lean, well-drained soil and full sun.

Hardy cyclamen are miniature cousins of the exotic Persians we grow (or kill) in the house. Their scalloped, heart-shaped leaves are frequently marbled or stippled with soft patterning in cream or silver, making pleasant patterns when grown as a winter ground cover. The flowers open from whorled, tightly wrapped buds, as skinny as a stork's beak, and as they unwrap, they turn themselves inside out like little fluttering butterflies. The entire process is fascinating to watch, and you can often find flowers in all stages of bloom. Emerging bud stalks are coiled flat and tight as watchsprings. They straighten up to bloom, but as the seedpods ripen, the stems curl

Cyclamen coum

C. atkinsii

C. cilicium

C. neapolitanum

Veronica pectinata

back up and plunge the dry pods right into the receptive ground, at some little distance from the mother plant. Even if you don't spend weeks on your knees observing the vagaries of these curious plants, you will derive great and simple pleasure from the luminous flowers of red, or rose, or pink, or white.

Some few flower in winter, when they appear like lost butterflies bewildered by the snow, occasional as it is in coastal areas. *Cyclamen coum* is one such, with several varieties (sometimes offered as *C. atkinsii*) blooming from late fall through the winter. All are well placed among unfurling fern fronds or lacy trails of neat-leaved ivies. *C. cilicium* is of a softer pink, flowering from November into winter, as does *C. neapolitanum* in vivid magenta. These late bloomers are well placed among low mats of evergreen ground covers: creeping thymes, *Veronica pectinata*, or Corsican mint. All blossom with great good will once they settle in, which they might take a year or so to do. One of their best qualities is that of thriving in dry shade (they will need water till established, though), making them a great choice for those dark pits under weeping cherries and so forth. During the tree's off-season there is adequate light and moisture for these little toughs and they bloom when every bloom counts.

There are many more of these minor bulbs to delight the eye and the nose. Enjoy them among primroses and tidy ruffles of alpine forget-me-nots, in pots or baskets on the doorstep. Scatter them in broad sweeps and generous swales under shrubs or throughout the rose garden. Such willing, cheerful plants must rank among the easiest to grow. The only difficulty is cutting the list down to size; one must not only be able to pay for them, but also to plant them out (a few thousand is my absolute limit). Now get out the pen and paper, pass the iced au lait, and let's think spring.

SEPTEMBER

167

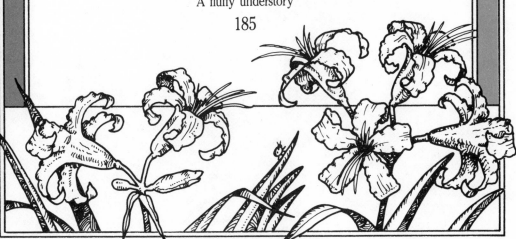

CITY COMPOSTING
Savvy soil building and garbage reducing works on any scale

As aging summer performers demand increasing grooming just to look presentable, we come to the unpleasant realization that even tiny gardens can generate an incredible amount of detritus. With garbage prices soaring, it makes less sense than ever to bag and trash this bulky stuff, and composting starts to sound pretty interesting. City people tend to dismiss the process as smelly, impractical on a small scale, and tedious, and it certainly can be all of the above. There are excellent alternatives to mess, however, and some are even appropriate for apartment dwellers.

Seattle is rich with practical information sources for the desperate, and perhaps the best place to find relief from the pressing problem of garbage disposal is the Good Shepherd Center in Wallingford. Seattle Tilth Association and the city, in the form of the Seattle Solid Waste Utility, have teamed up to offer a terrific array of composting techniques on their demonstration site at 4649 Sunnyside North. Master Composters (the equivalent of Master Gardeners) are on hand on Saturdays, but there is a very clear self-guided tour available anytime, which gives a splendid introduction to a variety of composting methods and materials. Folks from out of town—or even out of state—may still find Tilth to be a good resource; although they may not mail information out of the area (due to funding regulations), the folks at Tilth are developing a Master Composter slide presentation that they are able to take on the road. This will be an excellent program for garden clubs or other groups with environmental concerns. The details of remuneration for travel and so forth have yet to be worked out, but the Tilth people are willing to give any trip a shot, if practical.

The past few years have seen both an increase in interest in the "organic movement" and the disintegration of a regional information network that took years

169

to build. Evidently those earliest pioneers burned out before enough new people were ready to shoulder the immense work it takes to maintain such a network—and who can blame them. Say "organic" and most people hear "boring." That is where Tilth, in its present form, has great strength. The message is uncluttered, the approach direct and appealing. Composting is perhaps the most accessible of "organic gardening" concepts, and for city folks, it has immediate practical benefits. Through its Composting Hotline, (206) 633-0224, Tilth offers answers to specific questions and further information. This really is a wonderful effort, and a neat example of city government working well with an alternative organization.

For gardeners with no space to spare, the big news at Tilth is worms. Worms in boxes. In your house, or basement, or garage. Actually, the earthworm composting system is very effective, if relatively complicated. It takes some planning to keep it totally odor free, but it can be done, and the resulting mixture of compost and worm castings is superlative. Tilth has plans for earthworm boxes and a book called *Worms Eat My Garbage*, by biologist Mary Appelhof, which makes a surprisingly convincing case for inviting worms into one's home.

If the thought fails to fascinate, another small-scale method is the blender special. This involves grinding appropriate food scraps in the blender and storing the slurry in large, tightly closed tubs. The idea is that the contents of one achieve parity while you are working on the next. One friend of mine alternates three 2-gallon containers and swears that the results are rich, crumbly, and smell good (her apartment never stinks, so perhaps she speaks the truth). She uses the stuff for repotting numerous house plants and maintaining a good-sized container garden during the warmer months.

There are some fetching composting containers on the market now, a far cry from the earnest but frumpy offerings of the past. The catalog of Smith & Hawken of Mill Valley, California (see Appendix C), offers the most desirable collection of gardening tools in America.

Among many treasures, they carry a particularly useful and handsome Canadian composter, the Soilsaver. Neat and practical, it is ideal for small yards and was clearly designed by users. I get two or three big batches of compost a year using mine, and others less lazy could do even better. Rotating composters really do speed up the process, and S & H has one of the best-built of those as well, but it does require a bit more room.

Tilth has produced a number of inventive build-it-yourself plans for those who enjoy such projects. If you can swing a visit, the Sunnyside site is well worth a tour just to see the variety of composting styles they have assembled. Quite a good bit of information on mulching is presented as well, with demonstrations of various sorts and uses. It's a great place to get ideas and energy, because the whole project is buzzing with it.

Once you get started with composting, you will wonder how you ever gardened without it. There is no better soil builder, and many plants like tree peonies and bulbs which resent animal manures benefit visibly from this "plant manure." Intensively planted flower beds perform far better with generous additions of compost; the plants grow and bloom well, yet require less fertilizer than usual. Ongoing applications of compost result in an open, humusy soil that promotes extensive root development. In such conditions, plants establish and reach blooming size faster. It is remarkably encouraging to compare the rich, crumbly soil in the beds that have been given compost and mulch for a couple of years with the slimy, cold, heavy clay of the unimproved local dirt in our small Seattle garden. In the oldest beds, mostly given over to vegetables, you can plunge your arm into the dirt up to your elbow with little effort. Most of the flower beds are too full to allow this stunt, but the newer ones betray their callow youth every time we set new plants in place. As we continue to build and feed the soil, it improves visibly with every year.

When you start out, you don't have tons of compost. In situations like this, it will help enormously to prepare each plant's home thoroughly, giving it the bene-

171

fit of the best you have. Don't worry if you can't apply thick blankets of compost to every inch of the beds right away. Just concentrate on getting it where it will do the most good; use your precious compost when you transplant, when you set out seedlings, and when you mulch in the fall. As your supply builds, you can become correspondingly more generous with the stuff.

Some gardeners swear by peat moss, using it for soil building, seed starting, even mulch, but peat alone has many problems. Once dry, it sheds water and is very difficult to rewet. Since it is an invaluable addition to potting soil, this can be a serious problem; adding an equal amount of compost to the peat before incorporating it will alleviate this tendency a great deal. Clearly, peat moss has drawbacks as a mulch for this reason as well, since few of us have the dedication or vigilance needed to maintain a yardful of wet peat. I grant you this: it makes a very effective background for any and all plants (except dark-leaved cultivars, which blend invisibly into it). Still, who needs the extra work? Furthermore, frequent contact with peat moss can cause viral diseases in nursery workers who have long-term exposure to the dust. Finally, peat is expensive and has virtually no nutrients. Compost is not especially high in nutrients either, but what nutrients there are are "predigested" by the microbes in the soil, well balanced, and available on a slow and sustained basis. With the addition of further amendments such as lime, dried kelp, bone meal, cottonseed and soy meals, even nasty dirt can become fine, productive soil, a pleasure to handle.

You may never get your blender involved in the composting process, and you may never invite worms into your home. Worms or no worms, when you consider all the benefits, and top them with the significant reduction of expensive garbage, city composting becomes interesting indeed.

NERINES

Glittering stars of the autumn garden bloom long and hard

Nerine bowdenii

N. sarniensis
Guernsey lily

I t is always a surprise to find the fat pink buds of the nerines shooting up in the late fall border. They appear, buxom and strapping, on thick stalks, very like the buds of their cousin, the amaryllis, that we grow indoors all winter. When the plump buds finally pop, the flowers emerge in hot pink starbursts, little curly lilies arranged in wide umbels, like those of agapanthus or flowering onion, but far jazzier. The narrow curling petals are attractively crinkled, diamond-dusted and glittering where they catch the light. Each petal has a stripe of darker pink down the center, the dark and silvery coloring reminding me of wavy, silky bands of old-fashioned ribbon candy.

On crisp fall mornings when the garden is veiled in light mist, the sight of these loose globes ashimmer with such rich pinkness is sheer pleasure. The flowers are well placed among dwarf shrubs, where they can appear amid a leafy setting—their own glossy, straplike leaves are clustered at their feet. The stems stand about two feet tall, making nerines lovely companions for dwarf rhododendrons, azaleas, and other small spring bloomers. When the shrubs have warmly colored autumn leaves, as many of them do, the effect is sumptuous indeed.

Nerines belong to the amaryllis family, and, like most South Africans, will flourish in a dry, warm year, though amazingly tolerant of ambiguous summers. The most garden-hardy is *Nerine bowdenii*, sometimes (wrongly) known as the Guernsey lily. Strictly speaking, that name applies only to *N. sarniensis*, bulbs of which were washed ashore and found blooming in the sands of Guernsey after a Dutch ship was wrecked in 1659. Whatever you call it, it is a lovely thing that makes an extraordinary addition to the late fall garden. *N. bowdenii* has a number of hybrid forms, some of which

N. bowdenii
'Blush Beauty'

'Pink Triumph'

'Garnet'
Penstemmon

'Alice'
Japanese anemone

'September Charm'

bloom well into October. 'Blush Beauty' is baby pink, soft and delicate with late-sown white cosmos, pastel phlox, or asters. The slightly taller 'Pink Triumph' is a stronger, glistening pink; this one has bloomed in Seattle as late as mid-November. It is well paired with that prolific penstemon, 'Garnet', which is usually carrying its last crop of tubular horn flowers about then. The pink and rose red combination is a little strong, but the company of Japanese anemones, either the silky pink 'Alice' or the silvery rose 'September Charm', makes it work.

Nerine bulbs are increasingly available at regional nurseries and from many mail-order sources. Van Bourgondien of Babylon, New York (see Appendix A for this and subsequent addresses) will send large bulbs of *N. bowdenii* at a reasonable price. Good sources of named varieties for the collector are both McClure & Zimmerman in Chicago, and Bio-Quest International in Santa Barbara.

These South Africans can get chilly in the Northwest, and will appreciate all the sun you can give them. Since, as usual, they want a decent soil with excellent drainage, the simple addition of some coarse sand, well-aged manure, compost, and/or peat moss to the soil at planting time will more than repay the effort. Dry bulbs (sold in bags) may be planted in early spring, but potted specimens from nurseries can be transplanted from late fall through early winter without trauma, at least to the bulbs (your hands may get pretty cold). Nerines aren't finicky, but heavy clay soils must be well amended as outlined above for best long-term results; the one thing they won't tolerate is cold, wet soil. Even if you can't offer them full sun, they are still worth a try; nerines can do quite well with five or six hours of sun if the drainage and soil are good. Feed the bulbs when they leaf out in the spring and again at bloom time (commercial bulb food is fine) to keep the show going.

These ebullient plants multiply quickly, so allow them plenty of room to spread. If you notice a slacking-off of bloom a few years down the road, it may be time to dig them up and divide the clumps. The best time for that is during the early summer when the bulbs are in their resting stage. Mark their site well, as there may be no trace of them above ground when you get around to this fun project. Don't even attempt division unless the plant is dormant; the broad leaves should be well-withered or gone with the breeze by excavation time. When you locate the bulbs, use the garden fork and try to lever out the entire crowded clump en masse; avoid spiking any through their little hearts, since that is generally fatal. Most books will tell you to replant the bulbs and the numerous offsets at several times their height, perhaps six or eight inches down, but however deep you set them, they will pull themselves up to near the surface where they seem to be more comfortable. Why fight it? Give them the well-prepared soil they need, set them in rather shallowly, and add a light mulch of chopped ferns, bark, evergreen clippings, or what not. This may not be strictly necessary, but it will make you feel better when chilly winds blow over the frozen ground.

One great advantage to growing your own nerines is that you have something unusual to cut for the house. Nerines make superlative cut flowers, lasting unnervingly well in water—they look improbable enough out of doors, and strike a distinctly exotic note in a tall vase. Even after a month in water, they retain their sparkle and curvy elegance of form, causing your friends to murmur things about how good these new artificial flowers are. If you can bring yourself to cut them, try combining your nerines with the copper, bronze, and streaky red leaves of vine maples and sweet gum (*Liquidambar*) or sprays of mountain ash (*Sorbus aucuparia*), which not only colors well but carries tomato-colored berries as well. If all this warmth is too much for your color scheme, try some cooler, lighter companions; the above-mentioned phlox in gentle pastels, airy cosmos, with its feathery foliage, tall grey artemisias, variegated or tricolor sage—any of the perennial herbs will make a calming partner for our glittering

Liquidambar
Sweet gum

Sorbus aucuparia
Mountain ash

starlet. To tone nerines down, intermix plenty of grey, white, and silver foliage plants. To play them up, try the company of glossy black-leaved dahlias, set them among the late roses or daylilies, or against a background of dark, large-leaved shrubs.

Most American gardening literature is based on advice suited to the Northeastern states. Perhaps it's not surprising that so few Northwestern gardeners realize how much more is possible here; there are hundreds of undeservedly ignored plants eager to bring their splendors to our fall gardens. Nerines may be a bit hard to find locally, but the endlessly obliging Japanese anemones, of which there are many forms to discover, languish unappreciated in many nurseries. Knowledgeable nursery people stubbornly carry these perennial anemones because they know them to be rewarding and easy plants. When people see them bloom, they want them; the problem is that so few of us visit the nurseries after Memorial Day.

In the East, such a habit is understandable, but in the maritime Northwest, we would do better to learn a trick or two from the English, whose climate more closely resembles our own. Autumn in England is lush and splendid, gardens are still full and much visited, and fall is considered one of the busiest horticultural seasons. Instead of putting away their tools, avid gardeners are dividing perennials, transplanting new plants and preparing new beds. We Northwesterners could have fall gardens full of color, and could be equally busy about the borders if we liked. All we need to do is encourage our nursery people by seeking out plant material in fall, and making our interests known. This is most convincingly done with dollars—let's all go out this weekend and cruise the nurseries. Couldn't you use a new shrub, or some Japanese anemones, or at least a few packets of bright annuals? (Sown now, they will germinate in early spring, giving you a jump on early spring bloom.) With so much potential delight out there, who can bear to hang up the trowel?

FALL CLEMATIS

Hard-blooming climbers that don't know when to quit

Out of bloom, the lilac is an unprepossessing shrub, dumpy and shapeless with nothing remarkable about the leaves or seedheads to redeem it. One of the best ways to compensate for such defects of character is to introduce some action in the form of vines, preferably bloomers, and the various clematis fill the bill nicely. One old bush in my yard carries four separate kinds of clematis that bloom in turn from June through November and add immeasurably to the stature of the lilac. In the spring when the host is at its best, the guests are barely observable among the lilac leaves. As the lilac's grand gesture fades, the clematis are waiting in the wings, ready to take over and peacock through the seasons. The lilac is a good host, untroubled at being outshone and very willing to bear the burden of four scrambling vines. If your garden has a good-sized shrub that doesn't carry its weight after spring, fall is a fine time to start such a project.

In order to get the most out of our tiny urban yard, every possible area has been planted, and that includes spots like the deep skirts of the lilac. Originally a tubby shrub, it has been ruthlessly pruned into a low, spreading tree. All the suckers and side branches are removed to about three feet above ground level and lots of violets, primroses, ferns, and small bulbs share the reclaimed turf below. To get the various clematis up into the ozone where they could best be seen, a swath of black plastic netting (sold as pea trellising) was generously draped and tied in about the base of the lilac, giving the clematis tendrils something to hoick themselves up on. An unexpected benefit of the netting (which is practically invisible) was that as cats bombed through on their seek-and-destroy missions, they would get horribly tangled in the net. At first this was a little hard on the young clematis, but the overall result was that the cats aban-

'Duchess of Edinburgh'

'Mrs. P.B. Traux'

Clematis tangutica

C. dioscoreifolia
(paniculata)
Sweet autumn clematis

doned the entire area. For years now there have been no snooze-nests under the lilac, no well-worn track running through the prize primulas, no fur among the fern fronds. Even if the clematis vines hadn't made it, the netting would have been worth installing.

Happily, the clematis did make it and now the fading lilac gives way to the goffered pleats of the 'Duchess of Edinburgh'. In May, this double-flowered beauty is covered with the lime green pompoms of the incipient blossoms. As they mature, they flatten into large rosettes of purest white, sweetly scented and long lasting. By late summer, the flowers are replaced by curling feathers as the seedheads ripen. In four years, the Duchess has scrambled all through the lilac—she takes her half out of the middle—and weaves herself over and through a white picket fence. In maturity, she makes a very pretty picture from May all through June, needing only a late-winter trimming to keep her tidy.

The next to kick in is 'Mrs. P.B. Traux', a famous old hybrid of great distinction. Like the Duchess, she blooms on old wood, needing very little pruning, and blooms mightily, unfolding enormous and furry white fans into flowers of deep periwinkle blue. Brightened with whiskery yellow stamens, these very large blossoms appear from late June through August, spangling the dull lilac in a most surprising way.

The dog days of August bring the swinging golden lanterns of a species vine, *Clematis tangutica*, one of the easiest clematis to grow. It is a bit variable; the flower color ranges from clear lemon to orange-yellow in different plants, though it may be simply that there are several varieties all being sold as the same thing, which is regrettable but not unusual. It hardly matters in practical terms; all are hardy, beautiful, and easy to please. The dangling flowers are smaller than those of the massive hybrids, yet so numerous and charming that this is no drawback.

Fall does not see the end of the show; *C. dioscoreifolia (paniculata)*, the sweet autumn clematis, is one of the nicest things about September. As the leaves of the lilac color and drop, the waved, oval leaves of this species clematis stand out in freshest green. Evergreen in the mildest years, they cheerfully persist until deep, killing frosts take them down. The small white flowers smell of hawthorn, and the lilac is simply smothered with them through October, a bush of fragrant stars. Whole sprays can be cut for the house, the pretty, whiskery little flowers mixing well with the wider stars of kaffir lilies and late roses.

Pruning is the drawback of clematis for most people, and the best way to get around it is to choose types like the Duchess and Mrs. T, who just need to have the dead wood removed, or the vigorous, late-blooming species like sweet autumn, which can be whacked off a foot or so above the ground, just over the first couple of buds, a simple and satisfying activity for a raw February day. If you are trimming, rather than hacking, wait until buds show (in late winter), then carefully cut away the dead or less vigorous branches. It is fairly easy to snip the dead wood to smithereens right on the bush, which eliminates the need to pull out long strands, rubbing all the leaves and blossoms off the neighbors in the process. The only thing to watch out for is that in tearing out the old, you can damage the buds of the new.

When planting clematis, it is crucial to add some lime to acid soil. They don't mind clay, if properly neutralized, though a generous addition of compost, peat moss, manure, and bone meal is also in order. Since clematis can last for years, it's worth giving them some long-term supplies to go on. They like to have their roots in the shade and their tops in full sun, and training them to grow up a tree or through a shrub or hedge will create their ideal conditions. Fall-planted clematis should not be pruned as you would in spring, but pot-cramped roots may need to be gently untangled. Spread them carefully in the fluffy soil and pat them in firmly, taking care that the central crown is not covered. Water well, and add a good mulch of compost and rotted manure. Again, leave the crown uncovered or it may be smothered.

From now on, an annual top dressing of compost and manure in spring and a handful of bone meal mixed with a smidge of lime and kelp meal in fall will pretty much take care of it. Dry summers will call for thorough supplemental watering, at least monthly, but established plants are really quite doughty.

Right now, the old lilac shimmers with ten thousand fragrant blossoms. The late bees cluster around it, their droning a pleasantly drowsy sound. The slanting sunshine of Indian summer picks out the glossy, twirling seedheads that glisten where the sun lies on them. The softer light of fall shows up the thick texture, like raw silk, of the ivory flowers and illuminates the last of the Chinese lanterns on *C. tangutica*. Could you use a scene like this in your yard? If you lack lilac, perhaps you have a spring-blooming cherry or plum that looks lackluster all summer. Isn't there a fence or garage wall that needs decoration? Look around with fresh eyes, there's bound to be room for a Duchess somewhere. . . .

DAHLIA DERRING-DO

These underused tubers flood fall gardens with color

'Kelvin Floodlight'

'Grand Prix'

'Eveline'

'Autumn Fairy'

L ate summer can be pretty grim around the home-front. Rows of deadheaded stubble waiting for the autumn rains to bring on that second flush of bloom look less than prepossessing. Browning lily stalks and aging annuals add the melancholy of fall to the sere scene. More than ever, the textures and tints of evergreen foliage show their worth. Is there no color in the garden? Oh, there is, there is. This is dahlia season, and the show is about to begin.

Dahlias aren't used as much as they should be. Busy people are put off by the necessity of lifting and storing the tubers and of remembering to revive them come spring. Since they are relatively inexpensive, it's worth taking a chance and leaving them in the ground with a good mulch for insurance. Some will reappear each spring for years, others vanish with the snow, but you certainly get your money's worth in even one season.

Readers of catalogs (and attenders of Seattle's Dahlia Show, fast becoming a good general garden exhibit) know that dahlias are strong and eager bloomers. Names like 'Kelvin Floodlight' and 'Grand Prix' give the hint to the discerning; these are not subtle treasures for the effete, these are flowers for the people. Crowd pleasers. If, however, you are still thinking of dahlias as flagrant, obstreperous plants unworthy of placement in the tastefully pastel border, take another look. Dahlias come in a bewilderment of colors, shapes, and sizes, and not all are strident. New colors may be soft and subtle, as in the cream and lavender 'Eveline', or quietly cheerful, like that of 'Autumn Fairy', with rippled, twisting petals of muted orange.

The smaller height and flower size of border dahlias make these plants more attractive and practical for those who must garden in restricted space; even window boxes can comfortably hold the miniature forms, of

181

'Japanese Bishop'

'Silver King'
Artemisia

'Jescot Julie'
Dahlia

'Lisa'

which there are several. Any garden could use an infusion of these newer dahlias that flower in generous quantities during that difficult period between the trailing off of July splendor and the last brave display of fall.

Since dahlias are now so varied, it is well to view them in a garden setting before you buy. Several local specialty nurseries have display areas where you can select your order for spring shipment as you stroll among the blooming plants. This allows you to assess the overall size and growth habit of the plant, and, best of all, you can take home samples as cut flowers. Amble through your own garden with an armful, poking them among existing plants to find pleasing contrasts and combinations.

Travelers to western Washington's Puyallup Fair can stop in nearby Sumner to cruise Phil Traff's garden (see Appendix A). The dog and cats are friendly, everything is marked, and you see exactly what is meant by the "pink" or "lavender" of the usual catalog description. These are very fetching plants, some with powerful garden presence. What could convey the glamour of the extraordinary 'Japanese Bishop'? Satin black leaves are lined with pewter, a smouldering setting for flowers of hot, clear red with a gold central boss. Placed amid a cloud of tall smoky grey artemisia 'Silver King' or fluttery white Japanese anemones, this plant commands attention. It simply must be seen. Another smasher is 'Jescot Julie', a huge ball of whirling, incurved petals in warm rusty copper red with a deeper reverse, very like the related chrysanthemums.

Connell's of Tacoma has a garden as well. Dahlias come in nine basic shapes and fifteen colors, and here are some of each, something for every garden. 'Lisa' is a fetching waterlily type, creamiest ivory gently tipped with lavender, utterly at home in an English border. Formal, neat, and daintily made, it carries well despite its small stature. Container gardeners will appreciate the stocky and floriferous butterfly or collarette dahlias. These diminutive plants are covered with flowers, each with a tufty ruff of contrasting inner petals at the throat.

'Choh' blooms in vivid fuchsia, its white collar making it eligible for office duty, if a suitable windowsill is available. Upper echelon, of course. 'Moonglow' is softer, a pinky lavender touched with cream, and 'Alstergruss' has deep coppery red flowers with a yellow and gold ruff.

Nearest to Seattle, Sea-Tac Gardens has some fascinating dahlias with variegated blossoms. The loveliest is 'Hulin's Carnival', its large flowers a smooth white stippled with dark, glowing red. A complementary beauty is 'Zakuro Hime', sort of a reverse Hulin, of similar velvety deep red tipped with cream. 'Vernon Rose' has tubular petals of lavender pink heavily flecked with violet, very attractive with deep pink forms of Japanese anemones, spidery chrysanthemums, or starry daisies of *Aster x frikartii* in lavender blue.

If you love the outrageous look of the biggies, but regretfully decline them because they don't fit into your overall garden scheme, put some in the cutting garden. The more splendiferous dahlias are terrific with fall foliage in arrangements, a distinct plus when garden pickings are few. Be aware of the eventual size of the plants, however, as super-huge varieties will certainly need staking, and we are not talking quarter-inch bamboo. We are talking heavy metal, or at least one-by-ones; a plant that can carry flowers ten inches across can easily stand five feet tall and weigh as much as forty pounds when wet. Add a little wind or a cat fight and you have one sorry mess on your hands. If you are looking at just such a mess right now, don't swear off dahlias forever, but do invest in some hefty stakes for next time. If staking is not your style, choose large-flowered dahlias of smaller stature; border decoratives, collarettes, butterflies, window box—the choices are many. You needn't forgo fall splendor in a fit of pique, just choose a less statuesque variety next time.

Garden snobs label big dahlias crass or ludicrous. Some indeed look strikingly similar to lap dogs, but others, more moderate in size and shape, can be a beacon of light in the late summer garden, joyous in

'Choh'
Butterfly dahlia

'Moonglow'

'Alstergruss'

'Hulin's Carnival'
Dahlia

'Zakuro Hime'

'Vernon Rose'

Aster x frikartii

the long, slanting sunlight of fall. Four feet of sunshine yellow blossoms glowing amid the tired leaves of spent summer glories is nothing to sneer at, and plenty to be grateful for.

FERNS AS GROUND COVERS
A fluffy understory

'Fluffy Ruffles'

B ack when our garden was in our apartment, one of my favorite house plants was an obese fern absurdly named 'Fluffy Ruffles' by its whimsical but talented hybridizer. Despite this grave fault, Fluffy was a great little plant, always healthy and loaded with lacy, feathery fronds, the perfect foil for pots of cyclamen, African violets, whatever was in bloom. When we moved, Fluffy was just one of nearly four hundred houseplants, but as the outdoor garden gained ground the indoor plants mostly went on their merry way. Fluffy was a survivor, and I decided to reward her with a season in the fresh air. That was a good idea, and she looked so fat and jolly under some shrubs with violets poking up nearby and tiny narcissus nodding delicate pale bells into her fronds that I wanted to let her stay. Alas, Fluff is not a hardy fern, and her own feathery down is insufficient protection from winter's chills. However, the combination of ruffled little ferns with the small bulbs was so attractive it had to be perpetuated.

So many of the commonly used landscaping ferns are large and vigorous, excellent for a woodland setting but too enthusiastic for tiny beds in small gardens. Fortunate Seattleites have a local source for all sorts of unusual ferns and fern allies. Many of them will carpet small spaces with all the restrained exuberance of Fluff yet without her frail constitution.

At Barfods Nursery (see Appendix A), Torben Barfod raises a splendid variety of ferns. Enormous or tiny, frilly, pleated, crested, ruffled, whirling, or glossy-smooth, these ferns are the connoisseur's ground cover nonpareil for shade. Call first (206-483-0205) and ring the bell when you get there; this is a family business, mostly for wholesale trade, though retail customers are welcome. Out-of-town folk may order the same plants through Fancy Fronds (see Appendix A).

185

**Polystichum setiferum
'Congestum cristatum'
Crested soft shield fern**

**Adiantum pedatum
Maidenhair fern**

Once back home, stick the plants in their pots here and there to try various effects. Hard to know where to put what? Pick a difficult, dark area, tuck in some clumps of *Polystichum setiferum* 'Congestum cristatum' (say that three times and it's yours) along the edge of the dim borders and stand back. This is the dwarf crested soft shield fern, compact (less than a foot tall) and especially rich-looking in deep, crisp sea green. Evergreen, it brings fresh color and snap to dull corners all year long. For a lush, multi-textured ground cover, mix in some selaginella, a plump club moss that happily doesn't object when you plunge your fingers into it. It's a most gratifying sensation, like stroking an enormously fat and furry cat.

Advocates of theme gardens will not be able to resist tossing in some lance-leaved sword ferns at this point and calling it medieval pageantry. There is really no good reason why one shouldn't, as sword ferns have an architectural strength that complements the less-defined little rufflers. Such a theme will appeal to laissez-faire gardeners; throw those plants together and let them battle it out, clubs and lances, swords and shields. Whether it's a struggle for turf or a united front against the slugs, the results are sure to be interesting to the observing gardener.

The sword ferns do run a bit large, and those who wish to maintain scale may prefer to use the maidenhair fern, *Adiantum pedatum*, in combination with their shields and clubs. The maidenhair has the feel of a ginkgo tree, light and airy, arching fronds fluttering with small, triangular "leaves" (pinnules to the proper). This graceful plant may reach two feet in height and spread as much or more, its refined elegance a wonderful counterpoint to the vigor of the shield ferns.

Whatever the fern, I am a sucker for the most fantastic, ornate, crested forms. Although they can certainly be overused, and will lose considerable impact if closely massed, a few well-spaced specimens will perk up a group of simple-leaved plants no end. Give these elaborate ferns plenty of room to spread their fine feathers, for each frond is worthy of careful examination. They have all the appeal of the baroque and wouldn't be out of place fluttering from a knight's helmet, the perfect decoration for the helm of a Royal Borderer. To play Lancelot, I choose the male fern; *Dryopteris felix-mas* 'Multicristata' is tall and handsome, well shaped and properly virile. Guinevere will be portrayed by the lady fern, *Athyrium felix-femina*, the frilly, tasseled form 'Cristatum' being especially appropriate.

For moderate height, the bold, structural shape of *Dryopteris erythrosora*, the autumn fern, is just the ticket. Tall and leathery, it has a satisfying firmness which gives effective support to the feathery fluff at its feet. The autumn fern is a fresh, golden green color in spring which deepens until by fall it is Christmas green, spangled on the reverse side with bright red dots (*sori*). Since this is rather an upright plant, the back side of the leaves shows up nicely and stays handsome well into the winter. The fronds start life as fat copper pink spirals, really spectacular with groups of the tiny species tulips *Tulipa batalinii* 'Bronze Charm' or *T. hageri* in copper red.

A site that is open to light in winter and spring but shaded by deciduous shrubs or trees in summer allows small bulbs to be mixed in plentifully. The textures of unfolding fern foliage suit the delicacy of crocus, tiny tulips, and miniature daffodils better than coarser large-leafed companions do. If your shady place gets too little direct light for small bulbs, pink or coppery primroses will help draw the eye to the emerging fronds. Such details add immeasurably to the overall quality of a garden. The Big Picture is important, but a varied, well-textured underplanting can make even a simple shrub group first-class. Fall is a terrific time to plant ferns, among other things. As I bring in the house plants and replace them with gentle warriors better able to withstand the rigors of winter, I can't help but feel sorry for poor Fluffy, back on the shelf. Not as hardy as Guinevere, she didn't make it to a seat at the Round Table. We still cherish her anyway; wimp or not, old Fluff will always get respect around our house.

Dryopteris felix-mas 'Multicristata'

Athyrium felix-femina 'Cristatum'

Dryopteris erythrosora Autumn fern

Tulipa batalinii 'Bronze Charm' Tulip

T. hageri

187

OCTOBER

Dirt Work

A Blaze of Chrysanthemums

Fuchsias in the Fall

Kaffir Lilies

DIRT WORK

Amendments make the support system for border beauties, long- and short-term

Making a new garden, or a new bed in an existing garden, is one of the most exciting processes there is. Doing this work in the fall is like making new wine; new soil also needs time to meld and mellow. Come spring, the various ingredients will have become one, ready for planting. For now, all is pure potential; there lies the grass or dirt, virgin territory to be marked out straight with stakes and twine or laid out in artistic curves with the hose. The sod is cut and rolled up (this is a two-person job), to be used elsewhere or composted into remarkably loamy earth. Now the ground lies bare, bursting with possibilities, open to any interpretation you choose to impose upon it. The key to carrying this excitement to maturity is in excellent, thorough soil preparation. Done now, before a single plant has been introduced, a good prep job can literally last for years. It seems like a lot of work, and it goes directly against the grain of our instant gratification age, but the payoff is tremendous and long-term. Furthermore, failure to do homework now can guarantee disappointment and expensive flops up the road. If you really hate digging, call the equivalents in your area of Seattle's Millionair Club, Gospel Mission, or Manpower, and ask for an experienced garden helper or two. For very little money and a sandwich, these guys do splendid work; they appreciate the jobs, and you can feel good about giving them something useful to do.

What needs to be done to this tempting patch of open ground? Before a single root is introduced, the entire area needs to be deeply dug up and all previous tenants peremptorily evicted. Many weeds are perennials which would love to share the fat life with your border beauties, and this is the time to get the jump on them. Bindweed and creeping buttercup are a dreadful legacy, and if you even suspect their presence, remove every strand of root that appears in the upheaval. Don't stint the job, because these characters don't fool around.

Here is where your lovely English border fork comes into play, proving that the right tool can alter the work experience dramatically. If you are unsatisfied with the local tool selection, or have ever envied woodworkers their beautiful and functional tools, you will find the catalog from Smith & Hawken of Mill Valley, California, (see Appendix C) deeply satisfying. I personally love digging, raising each clod and dropping it to shatter, giving recalcitrant chunks a whack to split them up. Most therapeutic. Part of this intense pleasure comes from using well-constructed tools that are perfectly balanced. Best of all, they are scaled for small people, not only for large men. (S & H may be unique in offering a full range of English gardening tools in several sizes. They also carry top quality tools for the wheelchair-bound and for children.) Anyway, the Bulldog border fork I favor is lighter than most, yet extremely sturdy. The square tines are short, and slice through my clay soil as if it were butter. Take that, you clod!

Now you have a sea of lumpy, root-free dirt, or so we hope. For simplicity's sake, let's pretend that it is 5' x 20,' exactly 100 square feet; all amendment quantities to follow will be appropriate for that volume. Turning dirt into soil takes time, money, and effort, but the more you do now, the less you will need to do later, and the better your return on expensive plants will be. Most basic garden books give you the rap on the mineral needs of plants (nitrogen, potassium, phosphorus, and to a lesser degree, calcium, magnesium, and a bunch of trace elements). What few of them can tell you, however, is what *your* particular garden needs.

Dirt in the maritime Northwest usually has plenty of potassium (thanks in part to all that volcanic activity) but needs more help in the nitrogen and phosphorus departments. Bone meal, my favorite additive, would provide both, but for this initial shot, and for the longest return, a beginning application of rock phosphate is in order, as much as 4-5 pounds. Rock phosphate is cheaper and has a longer, slower release-life than bone meal. In an established garden and for placing individual plants, bone meal will be the plant food of choice; it is essentially a faster-acting fertilizer, one that the plants can tap into as they need it (unlike liquid preparations). Spread the rock phosphate, and all subsequent additions, on to your dirt in an ever-thickening blanket, layer upon layer. It's far less work to mix it all up at once than to try and incorporate each addition individually.

Nitrogen is a necessity and can come from many sources; among the very best for home gardeners are compost and animal manures, which bring humus as well as moderate yet balanced and readily available (to the plants) forms of nitrogen. Higher in absolute nitrogen value are urea, horn/hoof meal, blood meal, and bone, cotton, and soy meals. The various meals can be applied freely, a couple of pounds of any or a mixture of several. Variety, after all, adds spice to any situation. Since many of us mix herbs, fruit trees, and other edibles in the borders with our flowers, I don't like to use Milorganite, or other treated sewer sludges, good as they are for strictly ornamental plantings that will never end up in your kitchen.

All animal manures are excellent, though low, sources of nitrogen; chicken rates the highest, followed by rabbit, goat, and steer. In the fall, it is fine to use "hot" manures, those which are still fresh and strong, since the stuff is going to go on composting right in the garden. By spring, the heat is off and the newly placed plants won't get burned. Composted or rotted manures are safe to use even around established plants, and can be added to new beds as generously as you like. Rough or unfinished compost can be dug into a new bed in fall in copious amounts, and it too will be ready to give by spring. Go ahead and empty the compost bin; in spring you can start all over again with the remains of last year's stuff mixed generously with grass clippings.

West of the Cascades, the soil tends to be acid

(having a low pH). This condition can be corrected by adding lime, and if you want lime-loving plants, like clematis, or if you plan to grow vegetables and fruits, you will do well to add a significant quantity of lime, 5-7 pounds. To be really accurate, invest in an inexpensive soil test kit for pH (the testing materials are usable for years). If your pH tests between 5.5 and 6, use a little less lime, (4 or 5 pounds); if it is as low as 5, use more (6 or 7 pounds). Lime needs to be well incorporated to be effective; dug in deeply now, by spring its effects will be substantial. An annual addition of a lesser amount (indicated by your handy soil test) can be mixed with compost and manure and added as mulch for ongoing effect. Gardeners who want to grow rhododendrons, azaleas, or native plants don't need to add lime, and will do better to make a small patch or two of limey soil for those plants that enjoy it, or to range lime-lovers along the foundations of the house, where the rain leaches lime from the cement into the soil anyway. In either case, look for agricultural lime, not the stuff used in outhouses (hydrated lime).

An excellent supplemental source for potassium is wood ashes from the fireplace, or the remains of your garden bonfire. Once or twice a year, after the major garden overhauls, all detritus unsuited to the compost pile is burned. Persistent weeds, pest-ridden or diseased plants, large woody roots, and other garden junk are given over to the fire, the ashes of which are returned to the source in unthreatening form. Ashes from woodstoves are O.K. as long as the wood burned did not have paint on it—lead poisoning is no fun—and as long as the stove is not used for coal as well as wood. For those near the sea, kelp and other seaweeds can be added to the compost pile. Use a pickup truck for the hauling, rather than the family car, or you will never lose the smell of the sea. If you get ambitious and gather large quantities of seaweed, hose it off before introducing it to the compost pile. This will reduce saline buildup, since too much salt in any form can burn plants and stunt growth. Commercial kelp meal is fine too, and small amounts added to the annual mulch mix will help to maintain a good supply of trace elements often missing from conventional fertilizers.

What if you have no compost pile? Start one, by all means, whether in a fancy box or a homely heap. Nothing you can add to the dirt will be of greater benefit to your plants than compost (with the possible exception of water). Composting can be as difficult or as simple as you like. The truly lazy might do best with two sizable boxes or containers, filling one each year, and letting the material rot at its own slow pace. A good turning session with your border fork, once a month or so, will speed decomposition, but the stuff will break down on its own eventually, no matter what you do or don't do. To accelerate this interesting process, shred, slice, hack or grind the material you are composting, reducing it to the smallest possible pieces. Alternate a heap of grass clippings with a bag of chopped leaves, a bucket of kitchen scraps (bury them in the heart of the pile) with pureed perennials. Stir the stuff around to let air in. If you like to add lime, or compost starter, you certainly may, though decomposition buffers the pH all by itself (most compost is roughly neutral). Compost needs to be moist enough to rot, yet not so wet that air can't circulate; a handful, squeezed, ought to feel damp, but should not be dripping wet.

It is not enough to improve the nutritional quality of the soil, however, so don't get your hopes up too soon; we aren't finished yet. No matter what the soil is like now, add all the humus you can muster in the way of compost, manure, peat moss, and so forth. This gives a great start toward building real soil, but an annual renewal mixture of all of the above made into a mulch is a necessity. For thick, sticky clay, humus alone is not enough; the addition of an inch or two of coarse builder's sand will do wonders to loosen and lighten the soil, improving both texture and drainage. Once is usually enough, but if the clay proves intractable, adding sand or fine gravel to every hole you dig, when you place new plants, will help even further. Fine, sandy soil, such as is found here and there in the Northwest, has the opposite sort of drainage problem; it doesn't know where to stop. Here, all you can do is add humus, humus, and more humus, along with the rest of the list, and be vigilant with both water and fertilizers, since this kind of soil is basically a sieve.

Persistence pays, and those who go way overboard with the peat, compost, manures, and amendments will eventually have something very good indeed. Sawdust can be a wonderful soil improver if you prepare the garden in the fall. It is cheap and plentiful, and can be a swell mulch, giving good frost protection to tender plants during the winter. There is one major drawback, however; it has a nasty habit of depleting nitrogen and phosphorus in the surrounding soil as it breaks down. To balance a two-inch cover of sawdust, we must add about 5 pounds of hoof/horn or blood meal to our dirt. For a sawdust mulch on individual plants, add a handful of bone meal first.

O.K., back to our new garden; we are ready for some action. Having added our amendments, with such creative additions as suggest themselves to our fertile imaginations (ground peanut hulls, wine lees, zoo doo...) we will make the final mix, a meal fit for the worms. I like to use the fork for the mixing, but there are many proponents of the shovel, and you will just have to experiment. The only essential is to combine everything with the dirt as evenly as possible, removing rocks, broken bottles, old shingles, and so forth as they occur. When you have done your best, get out the short-tined rake and smooth it all out. Isn't that inviting? You aren't the only one to think so, so read on.

Now the bed needs a coverlet of mulch, something loose to let the winter rains do the final mixing and mellowing for you, but piled deep enough to prevent those same rains from washing everything away; rotted or chopped straw (not hay, as it is full of seeds), medium-ground bark, or more sawdust (mixed with additions as described above) are all fine. Top that with a large, loose piece of plastic netting (the kind which keeps birds out of fruit trees will do). Propped here and there with twigs, it makes a springy, irregular surface that cats hate, and saves you some nasty surprises come spring. Dogs need more of a barrier than that—like six or eight feet of chain link fencing. Kids generally respect those little barriers of twine and sticks with white rags at uncertain intervals, especially if they get to help set the fences up.

As winter rolls on, make some sketches, draw plans, scribble lists, and study the catalogs. While the rain pours down, mail off those plant and seed orders and head back to the fireside to take your ease. Come spring, the resulting flood of packages will be a treat rather than a panic-producing event. You can stay relaxed, because your work is practically all done. Hit the local nurseries with gay abandon and smile when you get home. Each plant can go right into its assigned spot, and the new garden will take shape faster than you would think possible. Watch with increasing pleasure as little twigs become shrubs, small tufts of leaves turn into regal border queens. Your plants will go quickly from strength to strength and you can hit the hammock, the reward of a good job well done.

'Spinning Wheel'

A BLAZE OF CHRYSANTHEMUMS
Late season splendors
that bloom for months

As the air gets that crispy edge to it and fresh cider floods the market, the pungent, spicy scent of chrysanthemums pervades the garden. There are thousands of them now, from simple daisy shapes to the bizarre Fujis, ornate, quilled spiders and spoons, huge football types with padded shoulders or the boudoir cushion, plump pillows solid with pompoms. Although many newer colors have appeared, thanks to extensive hybridizing efforts, the classic autumn tones of copper and gold, rusty red and bronze still predominate.

Chrysanthemums are easily found and easily grown; the fatal problem is that there are too many of them. Hundreds of irresistible varieties exist, and it is impossible to fit them all into a small garden. Vigorous hybrids need division nearly every year to avoid deterioration of the quality and size of the flowers. It becomes most practical to grow most as annuals and only keep a special few as perennials. Surplus plants can pass from our yards to a useful life of service, beautifying traffic circles, nursing homes, churches, the local health clinic, or other public spots that don't get much attention. The public gain is my gain too, since such thinning of the ranks makes room for the many new kinds I simply must try out. Certain family members have suggested that such strength of appreciation borders on the acquisitive, but I think my fellow gardeners understand the collector's passion all too well.

A handful of varieties qualify for permanent placement through a combination of tolerance to wind and rain, late and long blooming season, good performance as cut flowers, or sheer gorgeousness. I never tire of 'Spinning Wheel', a semi-double spoon with warm white quills eyed in creamy pink. The rays have a distinct tilt, wheeling merrily around a central boss of greenish stamens. If picked in the bud, each will open into whiskery, fringed blossoms far whiter than those out of doors, only lightly brushed with pink. On the plant, the flowers are strongly pink and deepen to a rosy old age. Interplanted with clumps of tall white Japanese anemones, the flowers overlap for several months, the silky poppy-flowered anemones a delicate contrast to the spinning chrysanthemums.

'Bold Adventure', cinnamon rust with a butterscotch reverse, is handsome and huge. Like all the exhibition types, it is best as a cut flower unless the weather is unusually clement; rain and wind do not improve its style. It is splendid if grown on a sheltered porch or deck, one of those "oh, wow" plants we all love to grow. It combines wonderfully in arrangements with autumn leaves, the bright tomato-red berries of *Iris foetidissima* and the bronzed seedpods of crocosmias, or the silvery round moons of honesty (*Lunaria annua*).

'Autumn Bride' is an eager bloomer that carries on from early till late fall. The dainty vanilla blossoms are formed of long tubular petals that flare out into rounded spoons. Citrus yellow stamens with a texture like finely grated lemon peel make a fluffy central boss. These charming flowers are extremely long-lasting when cut as well as in the garden. The pinwheel effect of the narrow rays contrasts well with heavier, more solid chrysanthemums, late roses, and ferny foliage. Simple and pretty, these open, airy flowers darken with age to old rose.

For a weatherproof display, try 'Fine Feathers'. It carries large, ruffled heads which open molten bronze rinsed with auburn, and cool with time to the color of dry sherry or tawny port with highlights of peachy gold. Planted beneath a pendant, lace-leafed Japanese maple and spangled with the delicate red and gold maple leaves, they make a most attractive group. The metallic tones of 'Fine Feathers' complement baroquely beaded seedheads of crocosmias and montbretias colored in rich shades of tobacco and leather. If brought into the house for arrangements, the seedpods split open

'Bold Adventure'

Iris foetidissima

Crocosmia

Lunaria annua Honesty

'Autumn Bride' Chrysanthemum

'Fine Feathers'

'Amazing'

'Sun Spider'

'Pink Pagoda'

'Alice'
Japanese anemone

Artemisia ludoviciana
albula
'Silver King'

when ripe to display fat crinkled seeds nestled in small cups. The seed germinates well, and can lead to hundreds of plants, should you wish for them.

Sunny yellow is especially welcome on grey days, and 'Amazing' is beautiful as well as sunny. It has very flat, double-quilled spoon flowers on a large plant that definitely needs staking to keep its bright face out of the mud. It doesn't take heavy weather well, but in a protected place will bring the warmth of sunshine to the yard. 'Sun Spider' is less formal, almost raggedy, its narrow tubular rays arranged with pleasing irregularity around gold button centers. This one weathers well, but burns out quite quickly; if you have room to indulge in brief pyrotechnical displays, keep 'Sun Spider' in mind.

I love spiky, punky spider chrysanthemums, and 'Pink Pagoda' is a wild one in flaming pink. It makes a lovely counterpoint to the silky broad petals of 'Alice', a silver pink double Japanese anemone. These plants both want all the room, and the two duke it out for space every year. Intermingled plumy grey feathers of *Artemisia ludoviciana albula* 'Silver King' lift this planting out of the ordinary, and the good color and strong shape of Alice's leaves keep it interesting even without flowers. It's appalling to realize that the chrysanthemum list could continue—not quite indefinitely, but far too long. But why not? Think of the snap and dazzle brought to our gardens by the stalwart chrysanthemums, and thumb your nose at those who caution restraint. Restraint has its place, but surely not in the fall, when most of our gardens need all the oomph we can muster. No, no, forget restraint; let's go for the gold. And the silver. And the bronze. And the copper. . . .

FUCHSIAS IN THE FALL
For best results, do nothing

'White Friendship'
Gladiola

I do not wish to hear complaints about the rain; gentle, moist maritime weather allows gardeners too many rewards (or compensations, if you prefer) for that. True, the Pacific Northwest west of the Cascades is not tanning territory, but if you would rather have extra color in your garden than on your face, this is the place. The region is blessed with perhaps the most cooperative climate on earth, at least to those thinking in terms of making world-class gardens. The unconvinced need only tour Seattle's Washington Park Arboretum, Vancouver's VanDusen Botanical Garden, Portland's Berry Botanic Garden; clearly, plants from all over the world thrive in this region.

One result of this mild and merciful climate is that lazy gardeners reap a rich and wholly undeserved reward. A number of plants thought to be tender will in fact winter over in the maritime Northwest; dahlias, acidantheras, gladiolas, and callas are among them, and will often reappear in spring despite the gardener's negligence. Standard reference books urge us to dig up a great many things each year, but such accidental rewards lead Northwest gardeners to wonder whether so much work was really necessary. After all, the English are divided on this point, and we are better off taking our cultural lead from them. It seemed appropriate to take a more scientific approach, and deliberately leave a variety of these questionable plants in the ground with and without protection. I had some dahlias I was willing to risk, and any number of volunteer gladiolas which I didn't like much.

The results were mixed; most of the gladiolas died out, except for the sturdy 'White Friendship', which consistently recurs about every third year as the mother bulb is replaced by seedlings that need a year or two to reach blooming size. Luckily it is a very attractive

Cymbalaria muralis
Kenilworth ivy

Acidanthera

gladiola, especially where it emerges with stiff pride through tangles of Kenilworth ivy (*Cymbalaria muralis*). Results with the dahlias were also variable, but it seems that the smaller border decoratives and window box types persist best, and that excellent drainage is crucial to success. Also surviving were acidantheras, those sultry Abyssinian gladiolas in soft white, dramatically splashed with burgundy. Tall, willowy, and elegantly drooping, they are a welcome addition to the late summer garden, fragrant and mysterious-looking. They survive and bloom after winter lows of perhaps fifteen degrees. The tough little bulblets come through best of all, though needing several years to reach blooming size; you think you have lost them, then they reappear in glory.

Those were my first intentional subjects, but there have been others; an entire colony of fuchsias became established in our yard through a combination of sloth and distraction. For years I had carefully induced dormancy, pruned lightly, and stored all the fuchsias for the winter. They were lined up in rows, hanging from hooks on the ceiling beams, in the basement workshop. One fall, life got complicated and the fuchsias were simply forgotten. The resurgence of the fuchsias was a complete surprise, and at least one family member was quite pleased. What an I-told-you-so! What a triumph for the irate home hobbyists, who so bitterly resent cold, damp soil dripping down their necks as they labor with their wood-working tools. They knew it was unnecessary, and said so, early and often. Each year when their winter fastness is rudely breached by anxious gardeners who commit hostile takeovers of precious basement space for what any fool can see are dead plants, each year these long-suffering and noble hobbyists make the same ineffectual protests. No more! No more bumping heads on those stupid baskets! No more tripping over bags of tubers! No more boxes of sand to stub toes on! As I say, the rejoicing was general.

Since then, several dozen varieties of fuchsia have survived the assorted temperatures and conditions of our capricious winters. Older gardens often boast a shrub

Fuchsia magellanica 'Tom Thumb'

'Pumila'

'Maiden's Blush'

Molinae 'Alba'

or two of the old-fashioned hardy fuchsias, shapeless bushes with tiny flowers in harsh shades of red or magenta. Though most gardeners are aware of them, they are seldom planted now, being too large and sloppy for most yards. Fewer gardeners know that many of the so-called "upright" fuchsias sold in regional nurseries will take our winters in stride as well as these tough old shrubs, and bring their considerable charms to the garden year after year. There is a minor trick involved, however, one tidy gardeners would never stumble on by themselves; fuchsias must NOT be pruned or cut back at all until spring. Fall cleanup is almost invariably fatal. Wait for strong shoots to sprout from the base, usually in April, before cutting away the sorry mess of last year's top growth. There now, isn't it nice to be told to leave something alone for a change?

Some of the trailing fuchsias are winter hardy also, but the upright fuchsias (named for their vertical growth habit) are generally the most effective as garden plants anyway. The trailing kinds used in baskets belong there, since in the garden they need significant staking to display their beauties to other than ants and slugs. There are literally thousands of cultivars, something for every taste and color scheme. One of the most generous bloomers is tiny, just right for the front of the border, pots, or window boxes. *Fuchsia magellanica* 'Tom Thumb' is a vigorous, deep green dwarf, only about a foot tall. Most years he will be heavily covered with his pink and purple lanterns from midspring till severe frosts cut him down. 'Pumila' is similar, the flowers glistening scarlet.

'Maiden's Blush' is a small billowing shrub almost three feet tall and about as wide. A late bloomer, it can take a year to settle in, but once established it is tireless. By midsummer it is spangled with delicate ballerina-blossoms of palest pink. Cut branches last wonderfully indoors and the flowers are so charming that they really deserve closer scrutiny. *Molinae* 'Alba' is quite similar, the flowers a light shell pink, and comes into bloom a few weeks earlier.

A sleek and unusual variety brings light to a shady

203

Fuchsia magellanica
folia variegata

'Madame Cornelissen'

Gypsophila paniculata
Baby's breath

'Golden Marinka'
Fuchsia

'Marinka'

'Gumpo'
Azalea

Tricyrtis hirta
'White Tower'
Toad lily

'Madame Dacheau'
Fuchsia

Carex buchanani
Leatherleaf sedge

corner with its slim, graceful variegated leaves. Carried on wine red stems, the leaves are an ashy, creamy olive grey touched with pink and butter yellow. Sprays of this are gorgeous in cut arrangements even without flowers. Hung with glowing ruby blossoms, each with a tightly furled skirt of inky midnight purple, it is mysterious and suggestive as the curious illustrations of Edmund Dulac or Arthur Rackham. This is *Fuchsia magellanica folia variegata*. Easy to grow as daylilies, it is nonetheless a connoisseur's plant. A bolder contrast is provided by the famous 'Madame Cornelissen', belle of many an English border. Her distinctive sprays of red and white bells swing in the breeze, especially appealing through a haze of white cosmos or baby's breath (*Gypsophila paniculata*).

'Golden Marinka' is a variegated sprawler, sister to the more common 'Marinka' with similar garnet red blossoms. Goldie has large leaves marked with bright yellow, warm gold, cream, and white on a medium green background, and in my yard she sends her arms in loving embrace through the small shrubby 'Gumpo' azaleas in her vicinity. In October her sunny arms are divided by arching swoops of toad lilies, *Tricyrtis hirta* 'White Tower', their freckled flowers set like little orchids along the leafy stems. Another hardy trailer is the dainty 'Madame Dacheau' with flowers of muted pink and ivory. Mme. D. is surrounded by swirling tufts of the leatherleaf sedge, *Carex buchanani*, a caramel-and-copper-colored ornamental grass under two feet tall; this is a harmonious combination even when the fuchsia isn't blooming.

All these plants will have a better chance if left strictly unpruned till late spring. A generous mulch of sawdust dumped about the base of each plant is further insurance, and takes very little effort. Lazy gardeners should take heart from this advice; when those near and dear to you comment on the unkempt garden, you may scornfully reply that the twiggy superstructure protects those plants. Furthermore, if the critic persists in objecting, he or she may pay for the replacements that a tidy cleanup session might necessitate. And remind those hobbyists of the many indirect advantages of this laissez-faire approach. . . .

Schizostylis species

Schizostylis coccinea

Crocosmia masoniorum
'Lucifer'

KAFFIR LILIES
Ladies of the night invade your beds

Planted amid the homely chrysanthemums and dahlias, plants known and loved since childhood, the silky cupped stars of the Kaffir lily or *Schizostylis* species introduce a rich and rare element, a satiny surprise, to the autumn border. Pink or salmon or red, these bloom spikes blend beautifully with the reds and purples, the russets and browns of the fall foliage around them. Four or five varieties of *Schizostylis* are available from regional nurseries; between them, Kaffir lilies will bloom from August through late fall. In mild years, certain types will persist in bloom through the new year, sometimes overlapping the earliest of spring bulbs. The slender sheaves of iris-like foliage look delightfully fresh just now, especially when back lit by slanting fall sunshine. The slim stalks emerge from the leaves, each tightly packed with plump buds in a herringbone pattern. The buds expand into lustrous blossoms like rounded stars, shimmering and delicate. The overall effect is frail and exotic, like an ethereal gladiola, yet these are among the toughest plants in the border.

The Kaffir lily is an herbaceous perennial from South Africa. Its root is a rhizome like that of the iris, though it is often sold as a bulb or even as a lily. In fact it wants quite a different treatment from what most lilies would demand, preferring fullest sun and not picky as to soil. Drainage, of course, is a consideration, but any open sunny site can easily be amended to suit these vigorous plants with the addition of sand or gravel, humus, and some compost. Kaffir lilies are so showy, so easy to please, it is odd that they are so seldom grown. They make terrific plants for gardeners who want RESULTS.

The species plant, *Schizostylis coccinea*, is a splendid thing, tomato red and brilliant amid sheaves of *Crocosmia masoniorum* 'Lucifer', unmatchable in arrangements with autumn-colored chrysanthemums. It blooms rather early in the fall, sometimes in August. Next comes 'Mrs. Hegarty' in soft rose, a September treat among the dusty blue leaves and cobalt flowers of small shrubs of *Caryopteris* 'Heavenly Blue' and interplanted with silver grey dusty miller, the kind with broad, flat, undivided leaves (*Senecio maritima* 'Cirrhus').

All of the Kaffir lilies look very nice with grey-leaved things, and the lacier kinds of dusty miller or the filigree foliage of the low-growing artemisia 'Silver Mound' make very suitable and attractive companion plants. A newer Kaffir lily hybrid, 'Sunrise', is salmon pink; intermingled with grey, fuzzy lamb's ears and a creeping round-leaved sedum in muted pink and grey (*Sedum canticola*) it makes a satisfying picture. 'Sunrise' blooms in midfall, and once established, a clump may stay in bloom for two months.

The endlessly prolific 'Vicountess Byng' is a silvery shell pink variety named after a famous English gardener. Lady Byng is quite a vigorous gal, often still in flower at Christmastime. She has almost too much energy; some gardeners go so far as to call her the lady of the night, not because she flowers then (Kaffir lilies close up at night, which makes them so long-lasting), but because she gets into every bed in the garden, and in record time. (This is in no way a reflection on the character of the original vicountess).

All the Kaffir lilies will spread, but none quite so shamelessly as Lady Byng. To keep them out of trouble, plant them in tubs or containers, or in isolated beds. The roots and seedlings are perfectly easy to dig out if they do encroach more than you intended, and the extras make swell gifts for your friends. Garden snobs generally call anything this enthusiastic a weed, but I don't know anyone who would label these bright stars that way. Such willingness on the part of such a lovely thing is to be treasured. Having said all this, I must add that Kaffir lilies do require ordinary care and culture. It is a sad fact that we tend to skimp on things that we feel are "easy." When they put on a mediocre

'Mrs. Hegarty'

Caryopteris
'Heavenly Blue'

Senecio maritima
'Cirrhus'
Dusty miller

'Silver Mound'
Artemisia

'Sunrise'
Kaffir lily

Sedum canticola

'Vicountess Byng'
Kaffir lily

performance, we are puzzled and disappointed. To give their best, Kaffir lilies must be fed and watered like anything else.

Feed them when the leaves emerge in spring, once in summer and again as the flowers begin, for best long-term results. Aged manure mixed with compost and bone meal, soy or cottonseed meal, a little kelp meal, and a bit of lime will do wonders. Commercial fertilizers will work perfectly well, especially those developed for feeding bulbs. Use commercial preparations half-strength to avoid burning or shocking the plants, and soak the ground well beforehand, especially in hot, dry weather. Organic materials are taken up more slowly by the roots, so it is much harder to harm a plant when feeding with soil amendments or supplements.

If you plant Kaffir lilies in the fall, try a winter mulch of compost and aged manure zipped up by the addition of handfuls of bone, blood, and cottonseed meals. When all signs of growth have stopped (late fall or early winter) heap a good shovelful around each clump. The winter rains will carry the nutrients to the active roots, where they will be much appreciated.

Do not despair if you don't get tremendous results the very first year. Many vigorous plants take time to settle in. Ivy, for instance, will sulk for a year or two until you have forgotten all about it. Then it will suddenly take off, covering everything in sight as you gape in amazement. Such plants establish an extensive root system before much top growth is produced; once this base of operations is in place, you can almost watch these plants grow. Kaffir lilies are not in the same class as ivy, yet once established, they are yours for life. As each returning autumn spangles your borders with their silky stars, you will be grateful indeed for these strong-minded ladies in your garden.

NOVEMBER

209

Ampelopsis
This sociable climber has clinging ways

Pollarding: Kindest Cuts
Hard pruning can yield the showiest plants

Plugging In the Bulbs
Plant them till the garden freezes over

A Remnant Shall Remain
The last gasp from the tattered border

AMPELOPSIS
This sociable climber has clinging ways

**Parthenocissus
tricuspidata
'Veitchii'
Boston ivy**

**Parthenocissus
quinquefolia
Virginia creeper**

I n a cutting and memorable one-liner, Lord Peter
Wimsey deftly depresses the pretensions of a social
climber: "Bit of an ampelopsis, what?" Since the
golden thirties, the complicated intertwinings of the
many plants called ampelopsis have been unscrambled.
What Lord Peter was thinking of is now called *Parthenocissus tricuspidata* 'Veitchii', rather a mouthful even
for that silver-tongued peer. If you would rather call it
Boston ivy, I would not blame you. It is a marvelously
quick-growing vine, often used to cover large expanses
of brick or stone. With leaves very like those of
grapevines, with which family it is closely allied, it makes
a very handsome jacket for a stately home or institu-
tion. The large, solid leaves color to clear and startling
crimson in the fall, appearing to better advantage against
grey stone or concrete than against brick of any description. A close relative, *Parthenocissus quinquefolia* is
equally renowned; this is Virginia creeper, a five-fingered
version which also colors sumptuously in fall, though
in deeper, subtler tones of claret, hock, and sherry.

Both are splendid plants, but not especially suitable
for the average garden or house. Such vitality requires
a good deal of scope, and would soon smother a modest
home under a thicket of lusty leaves. Fortunately, these
Tarzans do have a few less dramatic relatives of a far
more manageable scale. Some are suited to window box
culture, others need a fence or wall to scramble over,
and one could be safely introduced to a youthful tree
in the smallest of gardens.

These moderate ampelopsises (ampelopsces?) first
came to my attention a few years ago when I tried to
use reference books to key out a plant recalled from
childhood. I knew it had berries in unusual shades of
blue, but had no idea of the leaf shape, which made

211

Ampelopsis
brevipedunculata
Porcelainberry

identification slightly difficult. Finally I wrote to friends who still live near my childhood home and asked for a better description.

In New England, things can change very slowly, and sure enough, the plant was still there. One faithful correspondent provided not only a description but a piece of the action. "I hope this is right," she wrote. "It was quite hard to untangle it from a grapevine nearby." The sample arrived, carefully packaged, and was put in a vase where it slowly opened leaves and flower buds and proved to be—mock orange. Hmm. But the bit about the grapevine provided an important clue, so I wrote again to ask for a piece of that.

A second trip to Dr. Johnson's fence yielded gold; the plant in question was *Ampelopsis brevipedunculata*, the porcelainberry, or blueberry climber. Stuck hastily into a glass with a handful of late flowers, my sample piece soon rooted, so we planted it out in the yard. In a single season, it took off and busily began covering a chain-link fence with three-fingered leaves the size of my palm. In the fall, they redden, the color of ripe currants. Perhaps this vine would be evergreen in a warmer climate, since here in Seattle, small and rosy new leaves open sporadically and tentatively through a warm winter, tumbling off to deck the ground below with brilliant color. In spring, the leaves turn verdigris and bronze, deepening, as the weather warms, to a rich smooth green. The vine can reach ten or twelve feet, even more, and is best content to stretch out along a fence or climb a tree. Unlike its bigger relatives, which are armed with suction cups, this one climbs by twining its tendrils around other things. It is not self-clinging on a wall, though it can be used to good effect dangling down over a retaining wall or rocky slope, scrambling over an arbor or up a trellis.

The leaves are handsome, but the berries are the main beauty, and are well displayed on a low fence or arbor where they are easily admired. They grow in loose, open panicles, and in extreme youth are tiny, like acid green beads. As they swell, they pale to porcelain

212

white with a faint green cast, then begin a prolonged series of color changes; at any one time, there may be berries of opalescent white and china blue, turquoise and slate, French blue and a pearly blue-grey.

This acquisition was so thrilling and satisfactory that soon several other small ampelopsis joined the family. *Ampelopsis brevipedunculata* 'Elegans' is a refined version of the regular porcelainberry. The variegated leaves are a mere few inches across, and beautifully marked with pink, rose, and creamy yellow on a background of gentle green, almost celadon. In the fall, they turn to palest gold, the berries glowing in this lustrous setting like handfuls of sapphires and moonstones, turquoises and tourmalines. Dainty and neat in every part, this diminutive vine is justly named, for a more elegant plant does not exist. It rarely exceeds six feet in height, and will grace the canes of a climbing rose, insinuate itself delightfully into clambering ivy, or weave through to cover the bare lower legs of a rowdy clematis. It is very well suited to pot culture, a lovely companion for a Japanese maple in a half barrel, or pouring in a sumptuous cascade from a standing urn.

Tinier still is the miniature Boston ivy *Parthenocissus lowii*, with minute splay-fingered leaves barely an inch across. This one will embroider itself in a delicate tracery over a wall, ornamental as a tapestry. The new leaves are lacquered in fresh parsley green like little enameled badges. By autumn, they are richly tinted with a whole wide palate of gold, copper, bronze, and rust, with flaring flames of scarlet as fall deepens. A miniature version of the ultravigorous Boston ivy, its tendrils carry the same tiny sucker disks, making this vine as self-clinging as ivy. It looks charming indeed hoisting itself into a small tree, or dangling long colorful strands from a window box.

Any of these vines will bring you a great deal of pleasure in return for the routine care that you would offer any plant. It is well worth the effort to prepare a decent bed for them, since these vines will be around for many years. Dig in generous quantities of the usual:

Ampelopsis brevipedunculata 'Elegans'

Parthenocissus lowii

compost, aged manure, bone meal, a tad of kelp. Barring this, use a helping of commercial slow-release fertilizer designed to be incorporated with the dirt at planting time, but in any case, add as much humus in the way of peat moss or compost and manure as you can work in. If the ground is at all boggy, humus and some sand or gravel will open and loosen the texture and improve the drainage.

These willing workers take many difficulties of the urban setting in stride: pollution, crowding, heavy clay soil, and the constant depredations of cats. All perform well in full sun or partial shade, though the leaves will not color as splendidly without some direct sun. The smaller, more delicate sorts can take a year or two to settle in, appreciating extra water and a compost mulch, but once established, all will become sociable little climbers you can count on.

POLLARDING: KINDEST CUTS

Hard pruning can yield the showiest plants

When we moved into this house, there was a perky maple sapling growing through a tangle of large rocks by the alley. We each gave it a half-hearted tug and muttered, "later." That was one of the many mistakes we made here; with maple trees, there is no second chance. If you miss the opportunity to pull them up as seedlings, you are in for a full-scale removal operation. Our little gift from the birds is a Norway maple, a tree which I dislike intensely. An overbearing thug of a tree, it spreads huge and horribly durable leaves far and wide, dripping sticky honeydew from its aphid colonies. It creates pools of dry shade as its extensive, greedy roots suck up moisture, and when the big leaves drop, they refuse to rot like normal happy leaves but remain in a dusty, smothering mat for several years.

The only thing the Norway maple has going for it is good leaf color in the spring—if you like copper red, which I don't especially. The second or third year that I was trying to cut this Hydra down, I did grudgingly admit that the unpleating new leaves had a certain charm. Veined and traced with blackish red, where they catch the sun they shimmer in brooding tints of flame and bronze, like banked embers or smoked glass.

That in itself could not win me over, but it became increasingly obvious that the removal of a young maple woven through large rocks was not the work of but a moment. Fortunately, like all good gardeners, I know when to admit defeat. After all, tradition demands "consulting the genius of the place," leaving a few striking features or plants gathered to the site by natural processes. Horace Walpole, no mean gardener himself, coined the word "serendipity" for just such an occasion. The maple could stay (since blasting might damage the house, a mere four feet away), but on my terms. Since

215

Ailanthus altissima
Tree of heaven

its best feature was the juvenile foliage, I would take a tip from the Europeans and pollard the brute.

Pollarding is essentially decapitation, which suited my mood to the ground. You choose the height you want the small tree to be, and cut off everything above that. Generally, one clean cut is made the first year, removing all top growth, and unwanted side branches are trimmed off as well. In subsequent falls, each year's new growth will be cut back to the desired height or whacked off entirely. This is a lot of fun, especially if you don't mind the risk of killing the plant through repeated stress. If you do mind, and are just adapting the technique to encourage the more attractive young leaves, you must exercise more ruth and leave a few good shoots to winter over. The next year, those shoots will go, while some of the new growth will remain. This spares the plant the necessity of total reconstruction each spring, and the likelihood of sudden death is greatly lessened. The proper time for such a ceremonial cutting is late fall or early winter, after the leaves have departed and the shape or shapelessness of the plant is revealed.

Many trees and big shrubs can be kept to an appropriate scale for small gardens by such repeated pruning. It is especially attractive with plants that have their most pleasing color or form when young, such as several species of eucalyptus, the juvenile foliage of which is round as little buttons and colored a metallic, dusky blue-grey. Most of these make gangly trees, and in maturity their leaves are less interestingly formed and colored, so the perpetually young look suits them. The ubiquitous city tree *Ailanthus altissima*, or tree of heaven, with its long double-edged rows of leaves, is another good candidate; pollarded, it yields fewer but enormous and shapely leaves and will cause your friends to scratch their heads and wonder if you have been to Hawaii recently, so exotic does it appear.

After a few years, your tree or shrub will develop an unsightly bulbous head at the point where all this hard pruning is going on. When it gets too ugly, make a fresh start by cutting the whole thing off. If you begin the decapitation very low, six or eight inches from the ground, as is sometimes recommended, there isn't much scope for this, but a swollen blob at ground level is less offensive than one three or four feet off the ground. This excrescence isn't as likely when the pruning consists of cutting half the stems to the ground, as with dogwoods and willows, where you want to encourage the brightest stem and bark color which appear on the youngest growth. If you are nervous about the long-term health of your plant, you can reduce your pruning to about a third of the total shoots and still get improved color without the risk of losing the plant through overzealous attentions. If you aren't especially fond of it, this is a great way to make it shape up or ship off to plant heaven.

In the case of the maple, I would be only too glad if it shipped out, yet this spring, when it showed no sign of life till well into the season, I was conscious of a certain pang of loss. Could it be that the horrid lump of a tree had won me over? The rubicund fans unfolded at last and the spreading bush was glorious through June, but as soon as high summer brought the dull matte green back to those ruby leaves, my allegiance was lost once again. No stay of execution; off with its head!

PLUGGING IN THE BULBS
Plant them till the garden freezes over

The temperature dipped below freezing last night and has hovered in the thirties all week. Despite this, the days continue fairly mild and we are still setting out bulbs. In the benign climate west of the Cascades, one can do this from September until mid-spring, whenever the ground is diggable. A general rule of thumb is to put bulbs in the ground on arrival or purchase, but in practice there is considerable leeway. The point of prompt and early planting is that bulbs need time to make root growth in order to produce the best flowers. Since our cool, wet winters promote such root growth, halted only by occasional and rather short-term freezes, there is less pressure on coastal Northwesterners to get their bulbs in the ground than on New Englanders, for instance, who have but one brief chance at it before the ground freezes solid for months on end.

Feeding your established bulbs contributes more toward good performance and permanence than anything one can do at blossom time. As you tidy the garden, scatter commercial bulb food or a homemade mix of raw bone meal (which releases nitrogen more slowly than the steamed kind), aged manure, soy or cottonseed meal, and compost over your bulb areas to encourage strong, healthy growth. Fall is the ideal time to feed bulbs, but anytime from now through early winter will do.

Life can be complicated, and if your spring bulbs don't get planted right away, it isn't a disaster. As long as they are stored in a cool, dry place, they will stay viable for months. It is true, however, that daffodils planted in February will bloom in May and June, their simple charms dimmed by the lusher splendors of early summer. Such late flowers will rarely be well formed and will lack their usual finish, but such treatment won't damage the bulbs. In the following year, the flowers will appear at the proper time and look as crisp and polished as they should. If you want to see your daffodils blooming in the spring but just aren't able to get them in the ground, you may be more successful if you plant them indoors in pots. Give the bulbs the outdoor chilling period they need, then enjoy the flowers inside or out. Set yourself a modest goal, one or two pots a week, use bagged potting soil, and go for it. For variety, combine flowers with similar bloom times; plant the largest bulbs the deepest, add more soil, then set smaller ones in an overlapping circle. Cover the whole with more soil, water well, and spring will bring a mixed bouquet. For a very pretty effect, use miniature, narcissuslike 'Tete-a-tete' with its fragrant lemon trumpets, or the pale yellow, flat-faced 'Baby Moon' intermixed with *Anemone blanda*, the Grecian windflower. Both 'White Splendor' and the mixed blue shades combine pleasantly with these tiny daffodils. A white dwarf trumpet, 'Jenny', is charmingly framed by a ruffle of pink anemones, soft pink primroses, and white pansies. Any smaller bulbs (minor bulbs) can be used; check the packages to match bloom times for early- or midspring flowers. To really get the timing right, it helps to keep garden notes as the flowers open. Which blossoms coincide? Which overlap? What blooms first, and when does it usually start? Which colors complement, which clash or fail to please? It doesn't need to be a major undertaking; even quite sketchy information and dates can still be useful when you are ordering bulbs and planning additions to the borders in the fall. Dates of bloom can be rough: "In '84, the first King Alfreds opened during the second week of April." If this date recurs over and over, it tells you when to expect the old fellow, and what to plant next to him (something else that was open then). After a few seasons you have a little notebook with invaluable material, specific to your particular setting and conditions. Since bloom time can vary considerably, this is the most reliable way to get good results from intended flower combinations. Whether you want to enjoy the flowers inside or out, the preparation is the same. Forcing bulbs

'Tete-a-tete'
Daffodil

'Baby Moon'

Anemone blanda
Windflower

'White Splendor'

'Jenny'
Daffodil

in water alone is poor practice; spent bulbs are fit only for the compost heap. Furthermore, they never perform as well as when their basic requirements are met, and soil is one of them. It is a good idea to add some peat moss and steamed bone meal to any potting mix, but it is not strictly necessary. Properly treated throughout the process, most forced bulbs can go back to the garden after the display bloom is over. Heeled in to a nursery bed until the foliage ripens and withers, when dormant they can be placed where you want them in the garden proper. They generally skip the next year, putting up foliage but no flowers, but quite often they will get back on track and flower in subsequent years.

A long, cold session in the dark is another basic requirement; four to six weeks for tulips and ten to fifteen weeks for narcissus is what it takes to get good flowers. Cold can mean icy, but not freezing. Hopefully your closets do not provide such conditions; many older reference books suggest forcing bulbs in dark closets, but that dates back to unheated houses. If your house qualifies, great. If not, a cool cellar, storage area, or garage, a box on the deck, or a trench in the ground are all possibilities. If the kids' sandbox isn't used in winter, it makes a handy shelter for tender plants or bulbs. (Any box will do, really; pack the pots in and fill the spaces between them with sand or dirt.) The pots can be dug in a bit or just set side by side if the sandbox is fairly deep. Cover the box with plywood and leave it alone. That last is the operative phrase; if the pots are removed too soon, the foliage will be weak and floppy, it may yellow prematurely, and, worst of all, there won't be any flowers. Check the pots periodically, since they must be kept moist if not soggy, but otherwise they should be undisturbed until signs of growth are obvious. When the new shoots are several inches long, the pots can have the plywood cover off, or can come inside. Indoors, keep forced bulbs in a low-light situation for a week or so; this adjustment period makes the transition to full light and warmth less shocking. From here on, water is their greatest need, and the supply must be steady and generous. Once moved into strong light, the plants will take off, moving as quickly from shoot to blossom as they would in a warm spring. When the buds plump out, the pots can be moved anywhere. The cooler and dimmer the setting at this stage (within reason) the longer the flowers will last. In a sunny window the flowers will be more fleeting, while on a coffee table in the living room they may persist for weeks. Out of doors, the bright blossoms will brighten a window box or the porch steps for longer still.

Cut off spent flowers as they occur, to prevent seedhead formation. Reduce watering gradually as the ripening foliage yellows, until both bulb and soil are bone-dry. Bulbs in this dormant condition can be stored in their pots or removed from the soil, cleaned up, and tucked into labeled paper bags. Store them in a cool, dry place—basements are usually good, as is the back of the garage—until fall rolls around again. Eventually (this is next year we are talking about) you find the time to plant them where you really wanted them, and with any luck, they will settle down and stay awhile.

'Will Goodwin'
Clematis

Laurus nobilis
Sweet bay

Aster x frikartii

'Jackman's Blue'
Rue

'Garnet'
Penstemon

'Purity'
Cosmos

'The Fairy'
Rose

A REMNANT SHALL REMAIN
The last gasp from the tattered border

Look at this little jug full of flowers: purple and lavender, pink and white, palest yellow and clear orange, rosy red and scarlet. Like arrangements seen in old tapestries, this one is charmingly informal and varied. Even after weeks of light freezes, wind, and chilly rains, the garden still offers enough to make up such delightful little posies, largely because the borders are not pruned to the ground in September. Most of the plants are left to fend for themselves and the protection of their own upper growth brings even quite tender things through very cold weather—if not unscathed, at least alive.

The biggest blossom here is nearly four inches across, a clematis hybrid called 'Will Goodwin'. Icy lavender in the cold, when the performance begins in August the flowers are purest sky blue. The whiskery stamens are lemon-juice yellow richly tipped with purple, and the back of each petal bears a thick stripe of creamy white. At Thanksgiving, a vine of 'Will Goodwin' which has made its way into the upper reaches of the sweet bay (*Laurus nobilis*) was still abundantly covered with upturned saucer flowers. This is in a sheltered, north-facing part of the yard where a number of late bloomers persist, unconcerned by frost. A clump of lavender blue *Aster x frikartii* has been carrying plentiful sprays of bright-eyed fringed daisies since July and is still going strong. Where it mingles with some silvery 'Jackman's Blue' rue, the effect is sparkling, even at this late date. Next to them, the deep red tubular blossoms of the garden penstemon, 'Garnet', are still to be found through a mist of white cosmos, 'Purity', sown in late July.

Here are roses as well; tiny clusters of vibrant pink ones from 'The Fairy' have the delicacy and opulence of a Redoute. This low-spreading rose is a workhorse, in good and steady bloom from May till Christmas. Buds may be brought inside to open even in the coldest weather. Paler shell pink with a hint of cream, the full flowers of a China rose, 'Old Blush', open semidouble and sweetly perfumed. In the cold months, the buds are glazed with rosy lacquer, and when the small flowers unfold, each petal is lined with creamy parchment, veined with raspberry markings. They too may be found in all seasons, giving this antique its common name of "the monthly rose." A miniature regrettably called 'Rise 'N' Shine' is another stalwart. Broken to the ground by dogs in April, it came stoutly back, fought off powdery mildew (a problem it never suffered before the dog day) and bloomed all summer. Its tight buds of soft apricot open to light sunshine yellow. When they coincide with the flowers of a neighboring (and related) plant, *Geum x borisii*, the buds of both are seen to be the same saturated orange. These roses never seem especially fragrant in summer, but now their mild sweetness is well received.

A double form of matricaria, featherfew or feverfew (*Chrysanthemum* or *Tanacetum parthenium*), adds pungency to the nosegay. Small flowers perhaps an inch across are attractively tufted, the fluffy yellow stamens a showy button amid white fringed petals. This ancient plant has many folk medicinal uses; in England it is used even now to treat migraine headaches. A single leaf, eaten daily, is supposed eventually to have the effect of reducing the constriction of blood vessels and therefore the pain of these devastating headaches. (Ask your doctor before trying it; it has been written up in *Lancet* more than once.)

The last of the lingering fuchsias are represented; airy, wide ballet skirts of the puffy double 'Pink Galore', the elegant Chanel tailoring of the red and white 'Mme. Cornelissen', and the narrow hummingbird blossoms of 'Senorita' are so glad to be rid of their aphids that they have all taken on renewed vigor and glow, a second spring in the tail end of autumn. On several mornings, fuchsia flowers have been encased in a thin coat of ice,

'Old Blush'
China rose

'Rise 'N' Shine'
Miniature rose

Geum x borisii

Tanacetum parthenium
Chrysanthemum

'Pink Galore'
Fuchsia

'Mme. Cornelissen'

'Senorita'

Meconopsis cambrica
Welsh poppy

Alchemilla mollis

Alchemilla alpina

yet in the protected north beds, they thaw so slowly that they are unharmed. A nearby sprig of self-sown mallow also has stronger color now than in mid-summer; streaked with sumptuous royal purple, it strikes sparks with a scattering of ruffled late-sown cosmos in vivid tones of rose, lavender, and pink.

Northwest gardens are full of that most willing of the generally difficult meconopsis family, the Welsh poppy (*Meconopsis cambrica*) in yellow and orange. They are lovely things, practically everblooming, with their attractive divided leaves and frail petals of crushed silk thickly centered with clustered greenish yellow stamens. The orange form seems the strongest and is well represented in our tussie-mussie. Welsh poppies are often sold as alpine poppies or even as the rare blue poppies (quite different meconopsis), in which case disappointment is inevitable. However, Welsh poppy is a very good plant in itself, and doesn't need to be blue to please.

For leaves we have twigs of glossy, spruce green rosemary, and the dusky green pleated fans of *Alchemilla mollis*, the lady's mantle of herb gardens. The diminutive *Alchemilla alpina* contributes the same form in tiny trailing sprays, each leaf holding a drop of water like a diamond chip. Fuzzy grey velveteen leaves of scented geraniums release wafts of mint and roses when handled. Geraniums root easily if potted into a sandy soil mix and left on the windowsill. Rooting a few cuttings in this way is a good safeguard, since a harsh winter may remove the mother plant from your borders. Well mulched, however, scented geraniums are apt to survive the average maritime Northwest winter. The plants are always killed to the ground, but more often than not, new growth appears with the robins each spring.

There are more flowers outside for observing eyes to find: sweet scented primroses, calendulas, violets, a snapdragon or two. Even in the heart of a coastal Northwest winter, a little sunshine, distilled into these rag-tag remnants of summer, remain to cheer us on to the real spring ahead.

DECEMBER

225

Along the Primrose Path
Act now for spring benefits

Fleas and the Killer Oranges
Indoor fun for one and all

Pollarding II
The return of the secateurs

Everyday Magic
In praise of the unkempt garden

ALONG THE PRIMROSE PATH
Act now for spring benefits

Once brilliant clusters of color, gay as an old-fashioned nosegay with a deep green ruff for a doily, by autumn the primroses are reduced to a few weatherbeaten leaves with a ragged flower or two. The drought and heat of summer can leave the gems of spring in pretty sad shape. Those dark, wrinkled rosettes are seedy now, slug-tattered and sunburnt, and definitely in need of help. To rejuvenate our long-season performers, a few simple chores are in order.

The first thing to do is uproot each entire clump. Often the rootball will be considerably larger than one would suppose, so a stout garden fork is a big help. If you leave a few roots in the ground, so much the better; they frequently sprout and produce tiny new plants. Shake the dirt off the old clump and take a good look at it. There will be several crowns visible, the round central place from which the pinky purple stems emerge. Notice a woody, gnarled mass pimpled with reddish points? This attractive object is what's left of the original plant you got at the grocery store in March.

Tease the crowns apart—there may be two or twenty, so it can take some time. If the tangle is just too much, it's O.K. to grab a knive and slice off sections. Each crown of leaves requires some roots, but leafless pieces of root will make new plants nicely. Take inch-long bits of the finger thick root, with some attendant strands of finer feeder roots attached, and make a slanting cut on the lower end and a straight cut on the top end to avoid directional confusion (upside-down roots can have orientation problems). Bury them upright, and shallowly, in a nursery bed where they can peacefully grow on to full size. If you get a large crown but few roots, pull off most of the leaves. Practically every piece will grow, but if the root/shoot ratio is really disproportionate, the results are less satisfactory.

Before replanting your primroses, spade up the area you plan to use and amend it generously with the usual: peat moss, sand, or gravel if the soil is claylike, manure, lots of compost, a good handful of bone, blood, or horn/hoof meal. For good measure, throw in the whole cow (vegetarians must content themselves with soy meal). Fishmeal is not a good choice for urban areas, since it is fatally attractive to the many, many city cats. Equal parts of sand, peat, and compost or garden loam make an excellent medium for filling window boxes, planters, or pots, and the same meal additions are suitable. Mix up nicely whatever combination you prefer, breaking up any large chunks, and you are ready to go.

If you haven't finished setting out your spring bulbs yet, this is the perfect time and place to do it. Alternate clusters of five or ten bulbs with your new primrose plants for a wonderful pathside trimming, border edge, or potfuls of pleasure in springtime. When you place the primroses, allow for their natural exuberance, since what you tuck in now as a six-inch baby can easily be two or three times larger come April.

It may help to keep each plant's offspring in a separate bag if you want to make certain color arrangements. Naturally enough, the divisions will be exactly like the parent plants, but unless a few flowers are showing or you have charted your garden very well indeed, it can be tough to say just which primrose is that nifty pink one, or the apricot, or the moonlight yellow. . . . With the bag method, you may not be totally sure what color they are, but you can be sure that you are creating pools of the same color, which generally gives the strongest visual effect.

Once you have the area planted and everything is firmly patted into place, what do you think is going to happen next? That's right, the cats are going to treat it like kitty litter. This unforeseen but inevitable stage is usually forgotten, and great is the gnashing of teeth when the site of future magnificence is revisited. There you are, strolling down the path, hugging yourself at the thought of your fine handiwork and the delightful fruit it will bear, when a dreadful sight meets your unbelieving eyes. Damned bloody cats. Instead of tender, hopeful shoots, bulbs and plants are scattered everywhere and large piles of internally processed cat chow cover the carefully raked ground.

Relax. If your blood pressure shot up just reading this, take heart. There is a way to avoid the preceding scene, and it isn't even hard. It took me years to figure it out, though, so I hope you are suitably grateful for the hint. What you need is a great big piece of black plastic pea netting, the kind used for trellising in the vegetable garden. If you have some ratty old lengths of it in the basement, so much the better. Take a big chunk and stretch it loosely over your treasures, shoving the edges into the dirt here and there with your trowel. Not too tight, now; part of the trick is remembering that cats detest walking on things that feel insecure. Keep the mesh baggy and they won't mess with it at all. For larger areas, a number of twiggy sticks can be used to keep the netting propped up and springy. Even if you mulch the bed well, which I highly recommend that you do, the net trick is still a good ancillary precaution. The netting can be removed in late winter when the ground is frozen, or kept in place until the planting shows obvious signs of settling down. Blood pressure better now? Damn the cats, full speed ahead, up the Primrose Path!

FLEAS AND THE KILLER ORANGES
Indoor fun for one and all

One of my early musical memories involves a brother tunelessly crooning, "My dog has fleas, and so do I" to the plunking accompaniment of a new ukulele. No ukulele now, friends, but this is the time for the invasion of the fleas. They arrive unseen, sneaking past the door guards on loads of holiday greenery, on fire wood, on houseplants brought back indoors for the winter. Many of us who time-share houses with animals are finding evidence of the little bloodsuckers on our pets, our furniture, and even, horrors! on our children. People with small kids are often correctly reluctant to launch massive chemical spray campaigns in the house. Who wants to saturate the rug upon which the next generation is at play, or expose their children and themselves to unsympathetic and even dangerous substances?

We can ignore the annual onslaught for a while, but sooner or later the situation has to be faced. Our reluctance to cope with the fleas stems in part from a distaste for chemical warfare. For years, we half-heartedly fiddled around with herbal remedies that employ garden herbs; our poor cats have been rubbed down with ground-up rosemary and wormwood, bathed in tinctures of walnut leaves, pyrethrum (*Chrysanthemum cinerariifolium*), tansy, and various other ill-smelling concoctions which we were loath to put on the furniture as suggested by the eager herbalists. (Perhaps they are also dealers in the new furniture trade.) To nobody's surprise, none of them really worked. Good things from the garden only go so far in this particular struggle. Rather than submit to chemical saturation, we vacuumed a lot (some cats really enjoy being vacuumed), and hoped that guests wouldn't notice the balletomane antics of the splendid jumpers among our resident colony.

A few years ago, we read a short article in *Science News*, a weekly newsmagazine sponsored by the American Association for the Advancement of Science, and reputable in a way that most herbals, however well meaning, are not. The gist of the article was that there had recently been extracted from the peel of citrus fruits a pesticide so potent that it killed fleas (among other things) on contact. The research company was frustrated by its inability to market this wonderful substance since it is an extremely volatile essence that evaporates quickly and is at present impossible to package commercially. Working on behalf of the citrus industry, the scientists experimented with a number of extraction methods and found to their dismay that at this point, the consumer could make just as effective a preparation at home. This was bad news for them, and great news for us.

One of our children is very tasty to fleas. He has often had multiple bites: hard, red little knobs, sometimes in scattered patterns, sometimes in line-of-march stripes. We took him to the family doctor, thinking they were spider bites and possibly harmful. Assured that spiders rarely if ever bite more than once, and that these markings were typical of flea bites, we were given a list of commercial preparations and told to call a professional fumigation service which would let off flea bombs for us. Flea Bombs! No way; this is a Quaker household, bombless at all times. We won't nuke even the fleas around here.

Unwilling to rub the kids down with powdered pyrethrum, we were very willing to try something as user-friendly as orange peel. We went home, got out the grater, and went to work. The article suggested that even small amounts would do the trick, so we started with two oranges. We sprinkled freshly grated peel all over the children's beds, under and over the mattresses, into the rug and even on some highly suspicious stuffed animals. That night at bedtime, we vacuumed it all up, and repeated the whole sequence in the morning, including the cats in the action.

To everyone's surprise, it really worked. Evidence

in the form of dead fleas was revoltingly abundant. After doing the peel trick all over the house for a couple of days, we stopped and gave the fleas a few days to regroup. Nothing. It was over a year later before we had to repeat the process, to the intense disappointment of the kids. They enjoyed it enormously, and would have been glad to scatter orange peel around indefinitely.

I know of only one caution associated with this neat trick; most citrus oils will stain cloth, especially light-colored materials. We have a white furry monkey who will never be the same, and some champagne-colored flannel sheets have an oil slick that could use some EPA intervention. Eventually, experimentation showed that lemon or grapefruit peels were less likely to leave marks, and orange peel most likely—though again, only on light or white things. For us, this was more than balanced by the non-toxic (to people) nature of the substance.

I haven't tried it in the garden yet, but am wondering if a daily dose of fresh peel scattered around tender seedlings and transplants might keep the cutworms at bay. What could it do to aphids? We are always on the lookout for pest repellents which are safe to use on edible plants. Killer oranges seem more attractive then even friendly bacilli or parasitic wasps—the citrus are right up there with marigolds and ladybugs, those beloved garden problem-solvers with high cute quotients.

Inside the house, the tried and true citrus offensive is now considered an unqualified success; cheap, readily available, easy to prepare, perform, and clean up. One of the many unpleasant aspects of the chemical bomb technique is the lingering and terrible odor. Citrus warfare leaves a wonderful fragrance; even the cats smell good for a change. After several years of great results, we are committed to the citrus peel approach. As far as I know, oranges are one of the few substances left on earth that aren't addictive, don't cause cancer, are nutritionally sound, and taste good. I'm not ordinarily an Anita Bryant fan, but I have to agree that oranges belong in every household. You may not like her ideology, but one thing's for sure; there are no fleas on Anita.

POLLARDING II
The return of the secateurs

A gentle reader who reports success with the decapitation of maples wishes to know whether the same technique is appropriate with other trees as well. It certainly is, and with a few modifications, it can work on nearly anything. You can get a little carried away, however, and I would like to put in a word for the trees. Trees are our friends, let's remember that.

On the other hand, if your small lot is choked with trees, however beautiful, you do well to remove many, if not all. The sentimental school would have us treasure each trunk, wherever it is—that's why there is still a tree growing through part of Seattle's Swedish Hospital —but that's another story. It is not a horticultural crime to cut down crowded, misshapen trees, or poorly placed ones which have outgrown their positions. A mature specimen tree is another thing, possibly worth more than the house it shades. Such a tree is a figure in a far-reaching landscape, valuable to the whole neighborhood, to the greater community which admires it, and to the community it houses.

It is possible to own a lot full of trees without having much worth saving. In wooded areas, take advantage of the neighbors' trees, using them as "borrowed landscape" features, a technique seen in traditional Japanese gardens. You can largely clear your own property, using shrubs and smaller trees to frame views which include trees beyond the property lines as a focal point. Perfectly legal, and you don't have to rake up the leaves. Further, you may then plant a few small trees appropriate in scale to your site.

Large, well-grown trees ought to get at least passing consideration as keepers—if they are shapely, if you like the variety, if they are not growing through the sewer line. Try to envision each tree separately, seeing

how it might look on its own. Where thickets of saplings crowd nuzzling round the trunks of their elders,
go ahead and remove all the seedy-looking late com-
ers you like, but don't clear-cut right away. Choose a
few candidates for permanency, and watch them through
the winter. Do the branches make an attractive tracery?
Some do, some don't. Which is the handsomest? Are
there views you would rather block than expose? Could
selective branch pruning open up the yard to more light
without removing the tree entirely? Light-dappled shade
can be very attractive, and it suits an enormous variety
of plants down to the ground.

Once the decisions are made, you may be faced
with the removal of some large trees. A general rule
of thumb is never to try and cut down a tree significantly
bigger than you are. Don't get carried away by Northwest tree-machismo; call a qualified contractor. The services of a good tree surgeon or removal service will cost
you less than a new roof or a broken neck; this is no
time for bargain hunting. It is true, however, that you
can pay the earth for a lousy job, so don't just grab the
yellow pages. There are some better ways to go about
it. First, check out the neighborhood. Ask around, find
out which services have been used by the neighbors,
and be sure to view the results yourself. If you don't
like what you see, call your favorite nursery and ask
for names of people they like to work with, always good
leads.

If you decide to pick on something your own size,
you have a real treat in store. Even a smallish tree is
going to surprise you by how much it weighs, where
it is going to fall, what happens when it does, and more.
Take a hint from the Boy Scouts on this one and be
prepared. You should have stout work gloves that fit
you well, a pair of protective goggles and a pair of good
secateurs (pruning clippers), a wood saw, and lots of time.
Additional helpful items include a chipper-shredder
(rented for the occasion), large and sturdy trash bags,
the forced removal of all uninvited relatives and friends.
A mattock, a wheelbarrow, and a hand-ax are also useful.

To begin, prune off all the whippy little side branches you can reach. Do the same with any suckers, and remember P.T. Barnum's admonition about the birth rate of these objects. If it suckers now, it is most certainly going to sucker after this little operation. This goes double for hawthorns, the object of one sap-thirsty gardener's enquiry. If you heeded the word of experience, the tree we are working on will not squash you flat if and when you succeed in wrestling it to the ground. Review this requirement periodically, and if you get nervous, back down. Do try to assess where the upper portion is going to land, and remember that small trees are generally bigger than they look. If they have an abundance of smallish branches, that will cushion the impact a good deal. Even so, a crash landing won't do the perennial beds any good at all, ditto the plate glass window of your sun porch. Keep your eye on the ball, folks.

For the second stage, the presence of a second person, preferably non-related, is a good idea (actually, my brother is a dab at this, and we work together very well, but this is unusual). If the upper part of your tree is tall but small, it may be enough to have your assistant reach up and support the trunk as you make the cut. A rope, or several ropes, secured to fence, house, or another tree, can help too. You of course all know the old trick of cutting a Brie-like wedge out of the trunk on the side toward which you wish the tree to fall. It's a good trick, so do that, and then begin your felling cut. As you do, keep in mind that when the tree is sliced through, it jumps off its stump with great energy. In order that it does not take your jaw or stomach with it, leave a flap or hinge intact between the Brie cut and the business cut; this gives you control over where the tree will fall. For very short trees, where you are making a classic ground-level Christmas cut, it is still a consideration, but more in terms of kneecaps and ankles. The saw bites deeper, the tree tumbles or more likely sails through the air—Timber! Oh, well done.

Once the thing is on the ground, the side branches

235

come off. Don't on any account remove your goggles, since these small branches can do a lot of damage as they spring loose. The trunk may be burned in the fireplace and provide a focal point for a good deal of bragging. The branches can be cut up and bagged or run through the chipper for a wonderful supply of homemade mulch. Stout twigs make excellent pea-vine supports, and are also useful in the border for propping up recalcitrant perennials. Leaves and small twigs go on the compost heap. All done, right? No indeed, the hardest part of all remains to be experienced.

The stump must be cut nearly to the ground, and then the work begins. Getting the roots out can require ingenuity, but persistence is dramatically repaid. If the roots are large and deep, use the mattock to loosen the soil, removing as much as you can. Pass a chain around and through, attach it to your friend's jeep, and haul away. Otherwise, you must grub out what you can with pick and ax, taking care that the springy, tough roots don't bounce you over the fence. You may be amazed—and dismayed—at the extent of the root system. Just replant everything that got uprooted in the struggle, firmly patting it into place. It will recover, and so will you, and an enormous amount of reclaimed garden space with root-free soil will be your rich reward.

EVERYDAY MAGIC
In praise of the unkempt garden

For some years now I have been putting off the great garden cleanup until late winter or earliest spring. There are several reasons for this, of which acute laziness is only one. Small, full gardens like ours require constant grooming throughout the growing season. Luxuriant growth and great variety have their price; from earliest spring, control is a daily issue. Autumn in the Northwest sees gardeners busier than ever, planting out bulbs, shifting perennials, transplanting things that have outgrown the nursery, and dividing the overdeveloped. By November I'm tired of chores, ready to appreciate arching sprays of toad lilies (*Tricyrtis* species), mottled purple or lilac or white, their curious curving stamens like snail's horns. The persimmon-colored fruits of the stinking iris, *Iris foetidissima*, are cupped in their split tan sheaths, the carmine berries cluster thickly in little club-heads on the stout stems of Italian arums, *Arum italicum* 'Pictum'. The dappled, lance-shaped leaves are marked with swirling tortoiseshell patterns, cream, soft gold, or ivory on deepest green. The caramel curves of the leatherleaf sedge, *Carex buchanani*, have glints of pink and gold, each grassy leaf edged with threadlike strands in wispy curlicues. The garden is full of subtle treasures, and effects unknown to the incurably neat.

To the horror of such tidy-minded gardeners, we leave the tobacco brown stalks of phlox and asters to ripen their seeds, sparkling with a million sequins where they catch the frost. Palest of the yarrows, *Achillea taygetea* has fernlike leaves of sea green powdered with silver. The broad, flat seedheads turn silver black like cut-steel buttons, when rimed with hoarfrost. The sweeping foliage of Siberian iris turns a toasty color, and lies in elegant swales over the paths, inconvenient but lovely. Large sedums like 'Autumn Joy', 'Carmen', and 'Indian

Tricyrtis
Toad lily

Iris foetidissima
Stinking iris

Arum italicum
'Pictum'

Carex buchanani
Leatherleaf sedge

Achillea taygetea
Yarrow

Siberian iris

'Autumn Joy'
Sedum

'Carmen'

'Indian Chief'

237

Euphorbia characias
wulfenii

'Silver Mound'
Artemisia

Senecio greyi

Lychnis coronaria
Rose campion

'Black Dragon'
Lily

'Regale'

Chief' retain faint tints of their autumn rosiness through the winter. The warm hues and sturdy lines of the sedums are pleasant accents among the careful neutrals of the season. All these seedheads become favorite gathering places for finches and chickadees, and the companionable chirping commentaries of the small birds bring life to the quiescent garden.

Stately, architectural stalks of *Euphorbia characias wulfenii* swath their lower leaves in scarves of purple-mauve, violet and scarlet, coral and buff. Old stalks that have already bloomed are trimmed to the ground in the fall, if not in early summer, leaving a clear field for the next generation; this is practically all the care these magnificent creatures need. Now stems of flowering size curve their necks gracefully early in December, like Christmas candy canes, and dangle awhile before rising, freshly garbed in lime green as winter falters.

Most of the grey and silver foliage plants are left strictly to their own devices for the winter. Artemisia 'Silver Mound' is a fragile froth of silver that turns in cold weather to a haze of the mildest shades of pink and lavender. Aglitter with ice crystals, the grey senecios and santolinas are like metallic sculptures in the browning borders. The fuzzy leaves of *Senecio greyi* look as dapper as ever, unfazed by frost, and the dusty millers rally whenever the sun comes out, their splotched fur regaining silvery good looks as it dries.

However reluctantly, a certain amount of fall pruning and grooming must be done. Flopping wands of climbing roses need tying in to their supports, or, if extraneous to your design, they must be cut to the ground. Otherwise, winter winds can whip them around briskly enough to rock the roots loose, which is frequently fatal. The lank stalks of rose campion, *Lychnis coronaria*, look ratty, but trimming reveals the rippled rosettes of grey plush, presentable all winter. Spikes of delphiniums and hollyhocks, lamb's ears, and campanulas, and those of most lilies are better for a close cropping. The stalks of certain lilies, notably purple-flowered ones and white trumpet lilies of the 'Black Dragon' and 'Regale' strains, assume purple-black tints in fall. These stark onyx rods rise majestic among the lowly mats of creeping ground covers till at last they tumble in late winter. It doesn't seem to harm the bulbs one whit to leave the stalks to ripen this way, though lily specialists recommend cutting all lily stalks quite short in late fall.

**Perovskia atriplicifolia
Russian sage**

**Caryopteris
Bluebeard**

Top-heavy plants can't be left to shatter in wind and ice, so such things as spent chrysanthemums get chopped into mulch, to be scattered about their own crowns, which then winter over unscathed. A pair of somewhat frost-tender small shrubs, Russian sage (*Perovskia atriplicifolia*) and bluebeard (*Caryopteris* hybrids), bleach to powdery white or silver brown skeletons, rattling eerily in the wind. They are ordinarily perfectly hardy here in the maritime, but both are far likelier to survive the occasional severe winter when left with the protection of their own twiggy superstructure. Amid the fluttering rags and tatters of the hydrangea, many of the big, blowsy flower heads persist in stormy cloud colors; these, too, know not the knife.

Not everything looks interesting or attractive in winter; the hardy fuchsias are certainly a sorry sight, yet even in the coldest years, the unpruned bushes resurge in spring. If you have lost beloved plants from the recent rash of hard winters, the simple non-chore of NOT cutting everything to the ground in the fall might prevent such losses from recurring. For any plant considered borderline-hardy, an extra thick blanket of mulch, compost, or sawdust mixed with bone meal, laid on with a generous hand in late fall, can persuade frost-sensitive roots to hibernate—the Little Death, rather than the Big Sleep.

Besides an extra degree of frost protection, the unkempt garden offers some positive pleasures. Dozens of birds enjoy the great variety of seeds, and their bickering and scraps of song sound cheerful on still, chilly mornings. Naked bushes shiver, ashimmer with silver floss where seedheads of intertwined clematis persist. Streams of thin winter sunshine reveal frost traceries along the veins of fallen leaves which lie in richly

Hellebore
Christmas rose

Erica carnea
Heath

Schizostylis
Kaffir lily

Lithodora rosmarinifolia

Alstroemeria
Peruvian lily

Calendula

colored piles of mahogany, ebony, chestnut, and oak. These provide some protection for small and tender bulbs, or the half-hardy among the perennials. Berries and twigs of black or purple, red or blue, punctuate the softer colors of winter shrubs. The multihued greys, silvers, browns, and creams of the sleeping garden have subtle, woodland beauties impossible to appreciate in the bleak stubble of sternly leveled borders.

Another fitful pleasure lost to the efficient is that of stray flowers. Each Christmas morning, our breakfast table is graced with a small bouquet. What began one balmy year as a celebration of the mildness of maritime Northwestern winters has become a tradition; since we can't reasonably expect blankets of snow and jingling sleighbells in our part of the world, we make do with the beauties at hand. The bouquet is rarely an impressive display, but the thrill of the hunt is a major part of the fun. The whole family enjoys searching the frosty borders for a few rimed buds, the whooping delight of a good find in an open year. In a harsh year we find primroses, pansies, and a calendula or two, as well as true winter bloomers like Christmas roses (*Hellebore* species and hybrids), heaths and heathers (*Erica carnea* and others), witch hazel, and winter jasmine. In a mild year, we triumph in roses, violets, cyclamen, anemones, Kaffir lilies (*Schizostylis* species). Intense indigo florets of *Lithodora rosmarinifolia*, snapdragons, Welsh poppies, Peruvian lilies (*Alstroemeria* species), chrysanthemums, valerian, wallflowers, clematis—twenty things and more bring an intimation of renewal and the coming of spring, an appropriate seasonal message.

Like our colder neighbors, we have armloads of greens, the sticky pitch of noble fir and the pungent incense cedar smelling like the very essence of the holidays. The unexpected addition of humble summer strays adds a piquant note to arrangements of holly and ivy, junipers and apples, teasel and pineboughs. Shaggy calendulas whirl like little orange suns, cheerful in winter's chill. In Italy, vegetable stalls display bucketsful of these sunny flowers at Christmas time and the very name (derived from the same word as calendar) suggests their long season. These little toughs bloom off and on all year, though naturally the generosity of their output is greatly affected by the season. They self-seed, and it is usually the youngest plants which are still trying to prove their point at Christmas.

Primroses are always on the holiday table. The very hardy and obliging polyanthus hybrids are represented by enormous blossoms of the 'Barnwells' or 'Pacific Giants', some nearly three inches across. Primula hybrids are smaller but just as willing. Some of the smallest have petals banded in gold or silver, each plant a prim nosegay. They splashed the sleeping borders with gay patches of velvety red or blue, pink or coral, salmon or lemon, gold or snowy white, each surrounded by a ruff of fresh green leaves. Many of the primroses smell delightful, and last well enough in water to merit a place on the table, small and short of stem as they are.

Precocious violets spill their sweetness throughout the house. *Viola odorata* 'Semperflorens' really is nearly ever-blooming, and it is rare that a few buds or blossoms can't be found among the heart-shaped leaves of their spreading clumps. Snowdrops make frequent December appearances, each drooping bell closed tight against the cold. On sunny days they open wider, and you can see that each inner petal is marked with a tiny green fish. Portly yellow buds and Irish green stems of winter jasmine (*Jasminum nudiflorum*) lighten winter gloom in golden sunny sprays, a faint wild scent unfolding sporadically in a warm room. (Scent in many plants has this on-again, off-again quality, causing no end of indignant argument and dissension among gardeners.) The chunky windmill flowers of periwinkle (*Vinca minor* 'Bowles' Variety') are French blue with a perky white eye like a cloud in a summer sky. The trailing stems of neat, shining leaves enhance any winter arrangement, and the golden variegated kind (*V. minor* 'Aurea Variegata') glitter sumptuously by candlelight.

Winter pansies are all very well, but the preference must go to a hybrid of the redoubtable *Viola cornuta*,

'Barnwell'
Primrose

'Pacific Giant'

Viola odorata
'Semperflorens'

Jasminum nudiflorum
Winter jasmine

Vinca minor
'Bowles' Variety'
Periwinkle

V. minor
'Aurea Variegata'

241

Viola cornuta
'Clear Crystals'

Lobularia maritima
Sweet alyssum

'Old Blush'
China rose

'Vicountess Byng'
Kaffir lily

Cyclamen orbiculatum

C. coum

Iris unguicularis (stylosa)

the 'Clear Crystals' series. These carry hundreds of velvety, unmarked (faceless) flowers unremittingly from
earliest spring through fall, tapering to a scattering of
smaller flowers during winter cold spells. The plants have
the climbing tendencies of their species parent and will
twine themselves into nearby shrubs to a height of
several feet. Their great vigor is diminished in winter,
but a flat flower or two will open at the first hint of
sun. In cold weather some colors change, sky blue
deepening to cobalt, apricot becoming warm peach,
lemon warming to gold.

Sweet alyssum (now *Lobularia maritima*) is margin-
ally perennial in the Northwest, a restrained self-seeder
that never wears out its welcome. The youngest plants
bloom through most of our moderate winters; in a few
memorable years, honey-scented tufts of white alyssum
kept Christmas company with the last buds of a China
rose, 'Old Blush', the "last rose of summer" of the old
song. The plump buds echo the satin pink of a persistent Kaffir lily, 'Vicountess Byng'. This last gets rather
tattered outside, but its frail starry stalks open gracefully in water to the last tight bud.

We can generally count on some flowers from the
hardy *Cyclamen orbiculatum*, its dark, rounded leaves
zoned with silver, its fat buds and butterfly flowers wine
red. It may well be joined by *C. coum*, with spruce green
leaves stained red underneath and flowers of rose or
white. The deep, jewel-toned reds and rich greens gleam
richly among twining sprigs of miniature ivies and
clustered low candles on the holiday table.

In a banner year, the wide flowers of *Iris unguicularis (stylosa)* consent to bloom, gold dust at my feet.
There are several species and a number of hybrids, all
with large flowers of mauve or lavender, purple or sky
blue or white with moth-wing markings. Big as they
are, the flowers are on such short, tubular stems that
they are often half-hidden by the vigorous grassy leaves.
If you want some for the house, the flowers must be
pulled, not cut, from the plant, in order not to destroy
the younger buds nestled beneath the open blossom.

242

'Walter Butt'
Iris

Narcissus minimus
Reticulated iris

N. cyclamineus

Crocus ancyrensis

Since slugs have an unholy passion for these iris, pulling the buds to open indoors may be the best way to enjoy the flowers without competition.

At close range, the warm, fruity scent is apparent, and all the detail of the markings can be appreciated. Each translucent petal bears a narrow stripe of gold and a halo of white at the throat, and each is distinctly veined and pencil-marked with deeper blue or purple. The feathery styles are prominent, looking like tiny pairs of arms longing to embrace. Encircled by the petals, the styles glitter with pale powdered gold dust, drawing the eye to the heart of these winter beauties.

Native to Algiers and scattered Mediterranean locations, winter iris want all the sun they can get. They revel in a gravelly soil with sharp drainage, and will appreciate a position by a south-facing wall, where the reflected heat will give them a good summer baking. The maritime Northwest, while not exactly hot and dry, can nevertheless offer adequate conditions for these late bloomers if care is taken in their placement. They are worth a little care; a raised bed of loose soil with sand or gravel mixed in generously, as sunny a site as you can offer, a bit of bone meal scratched in the soil each fall and spring—that's all it takes. Some years, these creatures begin to flower in November (especially the pale lilac blue hybrid, 'Walter Butt') and continue until March, but even a scanty flowering is greeted with jubilation. No matter what treats lie under the tree, no presents are more treasured than these garden gifts.

The garden does get spruced up eventually, usually during the January thaws. It is remarkable how quickly great armloads of stalk and leaf, now light and brittle, can be cleared and composted. One job, freeing the bulbs, is most pressing, since the small flowers of spring are not displayed to best advantage amid a tangle of has-beens. But what better chore, weather permitting, between the old year and the new? And how Secret Garden–ish, clearing little circles of mulch away from emerging shoots. Reticulated iris, the tiny *Narcissus minimus* and *N. cyclamineus*, *Crocus ancyrensis* and

243

Crocus tomasinianus

C. tomasinianus, all are on their way. Such work brings its own epiphany, the electric, familiar shock of recognition; the gardener's year is endless, and the magic of Christmas is everyday stuff, especially in the unkempt garden.

APPENDIX A
Northwestern nurseries with mail-order catalogs or lists

Only a few regional nurseries are listed here; all are places that I have actually visited and/or ordered from. I included only places that seemed of general interest, or that are mentioned in the text of this book. The Pacific Northwest is full of fine nurseries, with new ones appearing all the time, so lack of mention here does not mean that a nursery isn't wonderful. If I have skipped any that you think ought to be better known, please write to Ann Lovejoy c/o Sasquatch Publishing, 1931 Second Avenue, Seattle, Washington 98101.

BRITISH COLUMBIA

Alpenflora Gardens
17985 40th Avenue
Surrey, B.C. Canada V3S 4N8

Alpines, dwarf, and miniature plants. Good selection, some unusual. Catalog $5, credited to order of $100 or more.

Clay's Nursery
3666 224th Street
P.O. Box 3040
Langley, B.C. Canada V3A 4R3

Specialties are rhododendrons, kalmias, azaleas, junipers, cedars. Catalog free—wholesale to trade only. Nursery open to all.

CALIFORNIA

Alpine Valley Gardens
2627 Calistoga Road
Santa Rosa, California 95404

Splendid collection of modern daylilies, good size and quality, reasonable prices. Send SASE for catalog.

Bio-Quest International
P.O. Box 5752
Santa Barbara, California 93150

Bulbs and seeds of South African natives. Nerines, homeria, lots more. Catalog $2.

Canyon Creek Nursery
3527 Dry Creek Road
Oroville, California 95965

Exceptional collection of border perennials, many unavailable elsewhere. Catalog $1—excellent quality.

Cordon Bleu Farms
P.O. Box 2033
San Marcos, California 92079

Daylilies galore—great selection. Spuria and Louisiana iris too. Catalog $1.

Las Pilitas Nursery
Las Pilitas Road
Star Route, Box 23X
Santa Margarita, California 93453

California native plants; wide and great selection. Price list free; catalog $4.

Roses of Yesterday & Today
802 Brown's Valley Road
Watsonville, California 95076-0398

A splendid collection of roses, old and new. A must. Catalog $4.

APPENDIX A

Yerba Buena Nursery
19500 Skyline Boulevard
Woodside, California 94062

California native plants, good selection
and quality. Catalog $1.

OREGON

Angelwood Nursery
12839 McKee School Road NE
Woodburn, Oregon 97071

Ivy by the score, many fine types unavailable
elsewhere.

Bateman's Dahlias
6911 SE Drew Street
Portland, Oregon 97222

Good selection. Send SASE for catalog.

The Bovees Nursery
1737 SW Coronado
Portland, Oregon 97219

A Pacific NW heaven of a nursery: shrubs,
shade plants, natives, everything. . . .Catalog
$2, credited to first order.

Caprice Farm Nursery
15425 SW Pleasant Hill Road
Sherwood, Oregon 97140

Daylilies galore, lots of iris and hostas also, tree
peonies, other perennials. Catalog $1, credited
to first order.

Chehalem Gardens
Chehalem Drive
P.O. Box 693
Newberg, Oregon 97132

Iris, Siberian tetraploids, and newer hybrids.
Spurias and others of interest. Price list free.

Forestfarm
990 Tetheral Road
Williams, Oregon 97544

NW natives, many perennials and shrubs.
Excellent quality and selection. Catalog $3.

Russell Graham, Purveyor of Plants
4030 Eagle Crest Road NW
Salem, Oregon 97304

Most unusual selection, some wonderful
bulbs, native plants, great quality. Catalog $2,
credited to first order.

Grant Mitsch Daffodils
P.O. Box 218
Hubbard, Oregon 97032

Top American hybridizer offers exceptional
bulbs, very different! Catalog $3, credited to
first order.

Schreiner's Gardens
3625 Quinaby Road NE
Salem, Oregon 97303

Iris, tall and dwarf. Visit if you can. Wonderful
color. Catalog $3, credited to first order.

Siskiyou Rare Plant Nursery
Dept. 72
2825 Cummings Road
Medford, Oregon 97501

Extensive selection of alpines and dwarf
plants; shrubs, trees, perennials. Catalog $2,
credited to first order.

WASHINGTON

A & D Peony and Perennial Nursery
6808 180th SE
Snohomish, Washington 98290

Many modern hybrids, some Saunders
seedlings. Fine plants, good prices. Price
list $1.

246

Aitken's Salmon Creek Garden
608 NW 119th Street
Vancouver, Washington 98685

All sorts of iris, NW natives, hybrids. Catalog $1, credited to first order.

B & D Lilies
330 P Street
Port Townsend, Washington 98368

Good selection of lilies, also alstroemeria; helpful staff. Catalog $1, credited to first order.

Barford's Hardy Ferns
23622 Bothell Way SE
Bothell, Washington 98021

Ferns and fern's allies—wonderful stuff. Call first (206) 483-0205. For mail order, see Fancy Fronds.

Connell's Dahlias
10216 40th Avenue East
Tacoma, Washington 98446

Great selection, display garden. Catalog $2, credited to first order.

Dahlias by Phil Traff
State Rte. 162
Sumner, Washington 98374

Great selection, nice display garden. Size of tubers and prices both right. Catalog $1.

Donna's Lilies of the Valley
1221 Highway 7 North
Tonasket, Washington 98855

Wonderful list of modern daylilies, true lilies, and hostas. Quality and prices tops. Send SASE for catalog.

Dunford Farms
P.O. Box 238
Sumner, Washington 98390

Agapanthus and alstroemerias. Excellent quality. Price list free.

Fancy Fronds
1911 Fourth Avenue W
Seattle, Washington 98119

Many, many ferns; wonderful selection, excellent quality and prices. Catalog $1, credited to first order.

Foliage Gardens
2003 128th Avenue SE
Bellevue, Washington 98005

Ferns for the gardener and the connoisseur—many unusual things. Prices very fair. Catalog $1.

Heaths & Heathers
62 Elma-Monte Road
P.O. Box 850
Elma, Washington 98541

Large selection, great plants. Selections to bloom in all seasons. Send long SASE for catalog.

Lamb Nurseries
East 101 Sharp Avenue
Spokane, Washington 99202

Excellent selection of border perennials, shrubs, unusual stuff. Catalog $1—quality exceptional.

Pacific Berry Works
963 Thomas Road
Bow, Washington 98232

Specializes in varieties of berries for the Pacific NW. Catalog free.

Raintree Nursery
391 Butts Road
Morton, Washington 98356

Trees, shrubs, vines, all with edible fruit. Great selection for the NW. Catalog free.

Rex Bulb Farms
4310 Highway 20
P.O. Box 774
Port Townsend, Washington 98368

Lilies of all sorts. Species and hybirds. Also dahlias, iris. Catalog $1, credited to first order.

Sea-Tac Gardens
20020 Des Moines Memorial Drive
Seattle, Washington 98198

Dahlias, display garden, cut flowers, helpful staff. Send long SASE for price list.

West Shore Acres
956 Downey Road
Mount Vernon, Washington 98273

Good selection of bulbs, top quality, nice display garden. Catalog free.

OTHER NURSERIES OF INTEREST

Bluestone Perennials
7211 Middle Ridge Road
Madison, Ohio 44057

Wonderful selection, great prices. Rooted cuttings only. Catalog free—excellent.

Busse Gardens
635 East Seventh Street
Route 2, Box 238
Cokato, Minnesota 55321

Fine perennial collection; lots of daylilies, iris, and hostas, species and hybrids. Catalog $2, credited to first order.

Carroll Gardens
444 East Main Street
P.O. Box 310
Westminster, Maryland 21157

Iris, daylilies, other perennials, shrubs, trees, roses; unusual stuff. Catalog $2, credited to first order over $25—for connoisseurs.

The Daffodil Mart
Route 3, Box 794
Gloucester, Virginia 23061

Family-run bulb farm, wide selection, many unusual, including botanical bulbs. Catalog free.

Dutch Gardens
P.O. Box 200
Adelphia, New Jersey 07710-0200

Exceptional stock of bulbs from Holland. Minimum order of $20. Catalog free.

Gurney's Seed & Nursery Co.
110 Capital
Yankton, South Dakota 57079

Perennials, shrubs, roses, trees. Catalog free—fun, too.

McClure & Zimmerman
P.O. Box 368
Friesland, Wisconsin 53935

Bulbs of all sorts, many unusual. Pricey but quality is good. Catalog free.

Van Bourgondien Brothers
P.O. Box A
245 Farmingdale Road, Route 109
Babylon, New York 11702

Solid selections of bulbs and perennials. Quality is tops, very consistent. Some true bargains. Catalog free.

Wayside Gardens
1 Garden Lane
Hodges, South Carolina 29695

Splendid selections, many rare and unavailable elsewhere. Color. Catalog free.

White Flower Farm
P.O. Box 50
Litchfield, Connecticut 06759

Some choice plants, unavailable elsewhere. Lovely catalog, $5, credited to first order over $25.

Gilbert H. Wild & Son, Inc.
P.O. Box 338
Sarcoxie, Missouri 64862

Daylilies in full and accurate color—excellent quality, true bargains. Catalog $3, credited to first order.

APPENDIX B
Seed Companies

S ome catalogs cost a bit initially, but once you get on mailing lists, the succeeding catalogs are free.

Abundant Life Seed Foundation
P.O. Box 772
Port Townsend, Washington 98368

NW natives, flowers, herbs, vegetables. Catalog $1.

Butchart Gardens
Box 4010, Station A
Victoria, B.C. Canada V8X 3X4

Flowers; collections from the Gardens. Old-fashioned favorites. Catalog $1, credited to first order.

Chehalis Rare Plant Nursery
2568 Jackson Highway
Chehalis, Washington 98532

Seeds of primula only by mail. Visit for many small plants, alpines, daylilies, hostas, primroses. Long SASE for seed list.

Gardenimport
P.O. Box 760
Thornhill, Ontario Canada L3T 4A5

Canadian source for Sutton's Seeds. Many flowers, excellent vegetables. Catalog $4.

Good Seed Company
Star Route Box 73A
Oroville, Washington 98844

Interesting collection of unusual and old-fashioned vegetables. Catalog $1.

Gurney's Seed & Nursery Co.
110 Capital
Yankton, South Dakota 57079

Flower, vegetable and herb seeds, for the NW; Catalog free.

Ed Hume Seeds
P.O. Box 1450
Kent, Washington 98035

Flowers, vegetables for the NW. Catalog free.

Moon Mountain Wildflowers
P.O. Box 34, Dept. YB
Morro Bay, California 93443

Wildflowers, mixes, and blends for wet or dry areas, sun or shade. Catalog $1.50.

Northwest Fuchsia Society
P.O. Box 33071
Seattle, Washington 98133-0071

Regional coordinating umbrella organization for fuchsia clubs specializing in growing techniques for maritime Northwest. Spring plant sale, summer flower show. Publishes Fuchsia Flash periodical ten issues a year; subscription $10.

Nichols Garden Nursery, Inc.
1190 N. Pacific Highway
Albany, Oregon 97321

Many herbs, also vegetables and flowers. Catalog free—a classic.

Park Seed Company, Inc.
Cokesbury Road
Greenwood, South Carolina 29647-0001

Flowers, herbs, and vegetables, some unusual.
Catalog free.

Peace Seeds
2385 SE Thompson Street
Corvallis, Oregon 97333

Herbs and vegetables, many rare. Seed list $1;
catalog $3.50; '91-92 research journal $15.

Sanctuary Seeds/Folklore Herb Company, Ltd.
2388 West Fourth Avenue
Vancouver, B.C. Canada V6K 1P1

Herbs, vegetables, and flowers, some unusual.
Catalog $1.

Shepherd's Garden Seeds
30 Irene Street
Torrington, Connecticut 06790

Vegetable, herb, and flower seeds. Catalog $1.
Lifetime charge.

Territorial Seed Company
P.O. Box 157
Cottage Grove, Oregon 97424

Thompson & Morgan
P.O. Box 1308
Jackson, New Jersey 08527

Vegetables, herbs, and flowers. A Pacific NW
classic. Catalog free.

Thompson & Morgan
Dept. 7
Jackson, New Jersey 08527

Possibly the largest seedhouse in the world;
flowers, herbs, and vegetables, shrubs,
trees...Catalog free.

A.E. McKenzie Company, Ltd.
3 Ninth Street
Box 1060
Brandon, MB, Canada R78 6E1

Canadian source for Thompson & Morgan
seeds. Catalog free.

APPENDIX C
Tool and supply sources

Throughout this book, the importance of improving and maintaining garden soil is stressed repeatedly. Where local outlets for suggested materials are scarce, here are some reputable and efficient suppliers of soil amendments, garden tools, and other supplies, sources for those gardeners who must buy through the mail. Many of these items are very heavy and costly to ship, especially the soil amendments, so it is worth a few trips—or telephone calls—to local feed stores, co-ops and rural hardware stores to try to locate sources for some of these things closer to home. Certain items, like Bulldog tools, are simply not available except by mail. If you know of good regional sources which are not included below, please write about them to Ann Lovejoy, c/o Sasquatch Books, 1931 Second Avenue, Seattle, Washington 98101.

Ernst Home Centers
Throughout our region

Sale prices on manure excellent. Many soil amendments in spring.

Green Earth Organics
12310 Highway 99 South
Unit 119
Everett, Washington 98204

Numerous amendments and fertilizers. Some safe pesticides, more. Catalog free.

Puget Consumers' Co-op
Ravenna & Kirkland stores
(in Seattle area)

Has bulk soil amendments in 5-, 10-, or 25-lb. bags. Discount for co-op members. Good selection. No mail order.

Raintree Nursery
391 Butts Road
Morton, Washington 98356

Some soil amendments in bulk, good tools, netting, woven mulches, "ecological" pesticides. Catalog free.

Smith & Hawken
25 Corte Madera
Mill Valley, California 94941

For excellent garden tools, there is no finer source than this. The quality and service are exceptional. Catalog free.

Territorial Seed Company
P.O. Box 157
Cottage Grove, Oregon 97424

Offers row covers, knives and tools, heavy-duty sprinklers, books, more. Catalog free.

APPENDIX D
Plant societies

O ne of the great pleasures of gardening is the company of other gardeners. Sooner or later, most of us meet up with like-minded friends, but joining a garden club or plant society can hasten the process and increase the pleasure enormously. Most of these groups meet monthly, and hold plant sales, lectures, slide talks, garden tours, plant-seeking hikes, and similar activities throughout the year. Many have newsletters or magazines as well, and welcome articles from gardeners at every level. You don't have to go to any meetings at all; some people join plant societies just to get in on the seed exchanges. Attending even an occasional meeting can be refreshing, and you are certain to go home with new ideas, and possibly new plants.

For local garden clubs, check the yellow pages of your phone directory. Regional addresses are given below; a letter of inquiry will put you in touch with any local activity in your area.

BRITISH COLUMBIA

Alpine Garden Club of British Columbia
Box 5161 MPO
Vancouver, B.C. Canada V6B 4B2

Monthly meetings, plant sales, talks. Has bi-monthly newsletter. Friendly with several NW (U.S.A.) groups. Dues $13/year (Canadian).

Canadian Rose Society
Ann Graber
10 Fairfax Crescent
Scarborough, Ontario
Canada M1L 1Z8

Chapters throughout Canada. Quarterly publications, meetings, Dues $18/year (Canadian).

The Canadian Wildflower Society
1848 Liverpool Road
Box 110
Pickering, Ontario
Canada L1V 6M3

Groups forming throughout Canada. Seed exchange, meetings. Dues $25/year, U.S. funds for U.S. dwellers. $25/year Canadian for Canadians.

Vancouver Island Rock and Alpine Garden Society
P.O. Box 6507, Station C
Victoria, B.C. Canada V8P 5M4

Active group, open to islanders only. Some co-meetings with U.S. groups. Monthly newsletters, plant sales, trips. Dues $8/year (Canadian).

PACIFIC NW—USA

American Fuchsia Society
Dept. P–County Fair Building
Ninth Avenue & Lincoln Way
San Francisco, California 94122

Very active group in the Pacific NW. Monthly meetings, talks, plant sales. Most local units have newsletters, plus national bi-monthly bulletin. Dues $12.50/year.

American Hemerocallis Society
Elly Launius
1454 Rebel Drive
Jackson, MS 39211

Daylily fans are few but avid in the NW, with frequent round-robin letter flights and annual meetings. Great group. Journal, newsletters. Dues $18/year.

American Horticultural Society
7931 East Boulevard Drive
Alexandria, Virginia 22308

Bimonthly magazine with newsletters in
alternate months. Dues $35/year.

American Iris Society
Jeane Stayer
7414 East 60th Street
Tulsa, Oklahoma 74145

Active NW chapters abound. Special group
for NW native iris fans. Meetings, seed exchange.
Quarterly bulletin. Dues $9.50/year.

American Primrose Society
Jay G. Lunn
6620 NW 271st Avenue
Hillsboro, Oregon 97124

Local interest runs high, thanks to natural
affinity of these plants to NW conditions.
Quarterly journal. Dues $15/year.

American Rhododendron Society
Barbara Hall
P.O. Box 1380
Gloucester, Virginia 23061

Again, local conditions make this one a
natural. Much local activity. Quarterly journal.
Dues $25/year.

American Rock Garden Society
Jacques Mommens
P.O. Box 67
Millwood, New York 10546

Splendid source of information, attracts the
best gardeners in any area. Meetings, sales,
seed exchange, tours, trips, more. Quarterly
bulletin excellent. Dues $25/year.

American Rose Society
Kris McKnight
P.O. Box 30,000
Shreveport, Louisiana 71130

Active NW chapters. Seattle group hosted
National Rose Show in 1986. Monthly
magazine, meetings. Dues $25/year.

Bellevue Botanical Garden Society
P.O. Box 7081
Bellevue, Washington 98008

Recently formed support group for the
development of a botanical garden near
downtown Bellevue. A great group, and a
rare chance to participate in such a major
project. Quarterly newsletter, meetings, talks.
Dues $20/year.

Hardy Plant Society
Margaret Willoughby
4228 SE Steele
Portland, Oregon 97206

First U.S. chapter was in Washington, the second
in Oregon. Regional interest and activity high.
Annual study weekends exceptional. Same
seed exchange and biannual journal as English
HPS. Dues $15/year.

Heritage Rose Group
Miriam Wilkins
925 Galvin Drive
El Cerrito, Califonia 94530

Local interest considerable. Meetings, plant
sales. Quarterly newsletter. Dues $5/year.

Native Plant Society of Oregon
1930 Engel Avenue NW
Salem, Oregon 97304

Just like it sounds. Dues $12/year.

253

APPENDIX D

Northwest Horticultural Society
Isaacson Hall
University of Washington, GF 15
Seattle, Washington 98195

An estimable lecture series, unmatched in the region, makes this group stand out. Meetings, plant sales, and quarterly magazine. Dues $20/year.

Pacific Northwest Lily Society
19766 S Impala Lane
Oregon City, Oregon 97045

Another natural for our region. Seed exchange, bulb sales. Dues $5/year.

Puget Sound Dahlia Association
Roger Walker
P.O. Box 5602
Bellevue, Washington 98006

Strong local group, new members welcome. Annual Dahlia Show in Seattle a classic. Meetings, shows, monthly newsletter, annual bulletin. Dues $10/year.

Rhododendron Species Foundation
Pamela A. Elms
P.O. Box 3798
Federal Way, Washington 98063

Excellent display garden (Federal Way). Talks, walks (for spring flowers and fall foliage), slide shows, seed exchange. Quarterly newsletters, Dues $30/year.

Tilth Association
4649 Sunnyside Avenue N
Seattle, Washington 98103

Pacific NW network of groups interested in composting, soil building, urban gardening, and more. Monthly newsletter. Dues $15/year.

Washington Native Plant Society
836 NE 58th Street
Seattle, Washington 98105

Field trips and lectures are a draw for this local group. Great speakers. Quarterly magazine. Dues $12/year.

Washington Park Arboretum
Arboretum Foundation
University of Washington XD-10
Seattle, Washington 98195

A group dedicated to the support and development of the Washington Park Arboretum. Has fine quarterly bulletin, monthly newsletter, many lectures, sales and activities. Dues $15/year.

APPENDIX E
Magazines, books, and garden writers

Public libraries in the Pacific Northwest tend to have very good collections of older gardening books. This reflects the historically strong local interest that, sadly, waned after the war. As gardening regains popularity, public collections are becoming stronger, with recent works better represented. Libraries will often track down requested books through the inter-library loan system. Some bookstores will seek books for you as well, both modern and out-of-print. With any expensive books (and garden books can be very expensive indeed without being correspondingly useful), it is a good idea to borrow a copy from the library before making a major investment. Exploring the garden books section (appropriately placed within the arts) is a fine way to discover unfamiliar garden writers. As you develop favorites, it becomes a pleasant game to track down ALL their books. British Columbia has been a hotbed of gardeners for many years, and used bookstores in that area are particularly rich in garden treasures. Plant society book sales nearly always yield gold.

The GARDEN BOOK CLUB is an excellent source of books that may be hard to find elsewhere. The selections are varied and reasonably priced, often listing at substantial discounts. Some very attractive bonuses are offered to new members; currently either a set of four Gertrude Jekyll books or a copy of HORTUS THIRD for $19.95 (HORTUS in a bookstore will run you $125). The initial obligation is to buy three more books during the first year; this is not a chore. Each fourth book bought thereafter brings a choice of free bonus books as well. Many imported books and gardening classics are offered.

MAGAZINES

Harrowsmith
Ferry Road
Charlotte, Vermont 05445
Bimontly issues
$15.97/year

Celebrates country life, regular garden articles (this is the U.S. version of the well-known Canadian magazine of the same name).

Horticulture
The Magazine of American Gardening
P.O. Box 51455
Boulder, Colorado 80323
10 issues/year
$24/year, $42/2 years, $56/3 years

The best general gardening magazine around.

Pacific Horticulture
P.O. Box 485
Berkeley, California 94701
Quarterly issues
$15/year

Joint publication of five horticultural or arboretum societies. Has a California bias, yet most articles are of value for the entire maritime Northwest. This magazine has improved markedly over the years; now is of consistently excellent quality.

Rodale's Organic Gardening
33 East Minor Street
Emmaus, Pennsylvania 18098
Monthly issues
$25/year

Originally an organic farming journal;
gardening has taken over. Recent years have
seen many changes, and in its present form,
OG will be of interest to many gardeners who
do not necessarily embrace the entire organic
doctrine. This newest version has lightened
up considerably. If you were turned off in the
past, take another look.

Sunset Magazine
80 Willow Road
Menlo Park, California 94025
Monthly issues
$18/year

Needs no introduction; has regular garden
section, monthly activity calendar.

BOOKS AND WRITERS

A few books stand out as indispensable;
Sunset's NEW WESTERN GARDEN BOOK, for
instance, belongs on every Northwestern
gardener's shelf. The carefully charted zone
maps make this book unique and exceptionally
useful for experimental gardeners as well as
beginners. For the most part, however, maritime
gardeners will find that English garden books
better serve their needs than those written for
the eastern U.S.A. Since our climates are so
similar, English cultural and hardiness tips are
far more valuable than any from Massachusetts
or Ohio.

It used to be a common complaint that English
books were frustratingly full of wonderful plants
unavailable locally. Thanks to the efforts of keen
regional gardeners and far-sighted nurseries,
this is no longer the case. Perhaps the bulk of
English imports are still found chiefly in mail-
order catalogs, but we are fortunate in having
innumerable and reputable small nurseries
throughout the Northwest. The majority sell
plants of top quality, ship with care, and stand
behind their offerings. Barbara Barton's splendid
compendium, GARDENING BY MAIL, will give
you hundreds of addresses for regional nurseries.

It is dull to read long lists of any kind, so the
following will be a short sampler of recommended books and writers. Further pursuit, and
the joys of discovery, are left up to you.

The Garden Book Club
250 West 57th Street
New York, New York 10107

An excellent source for garden books; good
selections, great prices.

Gardening by Mail
Barbara J. Barton
Houghton Mifflin

A remarkable, fascinating reference book for
everything and anything a gardener might
want. Highly recommended.

Sunset New Western Garden Book
Lane Publishing Co.

Arguably the single most important book for
Northwest gardeners.

Right Plant, Right Place
Nicola Ferguson
Summit Books

One of the most useful books for the home
library. Plants are listed and described according to the conditions they tolerate: urban
pollution, boggy ground, etc.; to appearance:
variegated leaves, silver or grey, winter beauty;
or to the use they serve: ground cover, shrub,
etc. A must.

The Complete Shade Gardener
George Schenk
Houghton Mifflin Co.

Mr. Schenk is an experienced Northwest
gardener who presents a lot of material in a
most readable form. A useful and delightful
book.

256

Color in Your Garden
Penelope Hobhouse
Little, Brown and Co., Inc.

One of the few oversized, beautiful coffee-table garden books worth its price—or its weight in gold. An excellent resource.

Making a Cottage Garden
Faith & Geoff Whiten
Salem House

A practical handbook. Strong on design, rather basic as to plants, but an excellent and accurate guide and a lovely book.

Principles of Gardening
Hugh Johnson
Simon & Schuster

Practical and fascinating overview, recommended.

Hillier's Colour Dictionary of Trees and Shrubs
H.G. Hillier
David & Charles

The Complete Handbook of Garden Plants
Michael Wright
Facts on File

The Color Dictionary of Flowers and Plants for Home and Garden
Roy Hay & Patrick Synge
Crown Publishers, Inc.

Pretty picture books abound, but few are of much use. These three heavily-illustrated plant dictionaries are all very useful.

Dictionary of Plant Names
Allen J. Coombs
Lubrecht & Cramer

Another dictionary that is accurate and thorough, yet small enough to be in constant use.

Any discussion of garden writers must include Vita Sackville-West, who for many years wrote a weekly newspaper column beloved throughout England. Some of her columns are reprinted in her GARDEN BOOK, still widely available. The late Margery Fish wrote a number of fascinating gardening books; she grew thousands of plants, and passes on invaluable experience to her readers in a pleasantly informal style. At least five of these have been recently reprinted; all are well worth reading and re-reading. Christopher Lloyd is a contemporary writer with enormous experience and a playful, relaxed style; all of his many books are both useful and delightful. Graham Stuart Thomas is a much-respected horticulturist and writer of great depth; try his THREE GARDENS for a start.

Across the water, we should all be thankful to several university presses for reprinting the wonderful garden books by Elizabeth Lawrence. Although some of her titles might suggest that the books are strictly for Southern gardeners, Mrs. Lawrence had numerous correspondents throughout the Pacific Northwest. She refers often to the similarity of climate in the Southeast and the Northwest, and notes the many plants that do well in either area. Both Henry Mitchell and Allen Lacy have books of gardening essays in print, and both are frequent contributors to national magazines.

Nearly all of the above writers focus on ornamental plants. Those interested in raising food as well will enjoy THE COMPLETE BOOK OF EDIBLE LANDSCAPING by Rosalind Creasy (Sierra Club), as well as Ms. Creasy's other books. Steve Solomon's GROWING VEGETABLES WEST OF THE CASCADES (Sasquatch Books) is unmatched for solid cultural advice for the maritime Northwest. Even those who are not especially interested in organic gardening will find practical information of tremendous value here.

Pacific Northwest native plants are many and varied, and there are quite a few guides to their identification. Some of the very nicest come from the British Columbia Provincial Museum, and the booklets are well represented at bookstores and museum shops all over the province. The series is underwritten by the province's Department of Recreation and Conservation, and numbers in the dozens. All are amply and clearly illustrated, and all are intelligently presented.

257

INDEX

259

261

263

264

Did you enjoy this book?

Sasquatch Books publishes books and guides related to the Pacific Northwest. Our books are available at bookstores and other retail outlets throughout the region. Here is a selection of our current titles:

GARDENING

The Border in Bloom
A Northwest Garden
Through the Seasons
Ann Lovejoy

Gardening Under Cover
A Northwest Guide to Solar
Greenhouses, Cold Frames,
and Cloches
William Head

**Growing Vegetables West
of the Cascades**
Steve Solomon's Complete
Guide to Natural Gardening
3rd edition

Three Years in Bloom
A Garden-Keeper's Journal
Introduction by Ann Lovejoy

Trees of Seattle
The Complete Tree-finder's
Guide to 740 Varieties
Arthur Lee Jacobson

**Winter Gardening in the
Maritime Northwest**
Cool Season Crops for the
Year-Round Gardener
Binda Colebrook, 3rd edition

The Year in Bloom
Gardening for All Seasons
in the Pacific Northwest
Ann Lovejoy

COOKBOOKS

Breakfast in Bed
The Best B&B Recipes from
Northern California, Oregon,
Washington, and British
Columbia
Carol Frieberg

Eight Items or Less Cookbook
Fine Food in a Hurry
Ann Lovejoy

**The Territorial Seed Company
Garden Cookbook**
Homegrown Recipes
for Every Season
Edited by Lane Morgan

Winter Harvest Cookbook
How to Select and Prepare
Fresh Seasonal Produce
All Winter Long
Lane Morgan

To receive a Sasquatch Books catalog or to inquire about ordering our books by phone or mail, please contact us at the address below.

SASQUATCH BOOKS
1931 Second Avenue
Seattle, WA 98101
(206) 441-5555